PEMBROKESHIRE TRILOGY

Vols: 1

TALES OF THE SEA

James Hedley Phillips

[signature: James Hedley Phillips]

2014

DEDICATED TO:
Mam: Vera Phillips
Dad: Graham Phillips
Nana: Evelyn Birt

Copyright © James Hedley Phillips 2014.

First Printed 2014.

Published by James Hedley Phillips Associates, Haverfordwest, Pembrokeshire, Wales.

ISBN 978 0 9930454 0 0
British Library Cataloguing in Publishing Data.

Also by Shipwreck Researcher & Author: James Hedley Phillips:

> Swansea Bay & Gower Shipwreck Chart 1998.
> Pembrokeshire Shipwreck Chart 1999.
> Reprinted with updates 2009.

[2014] Diver, Shipwreck Researcher & Author: James Hedley Phillips has done his honest best with the accuracy of dates, places and names etc., etc., and I would be ever so pleased to hear from you if any part needs correcting or updating.
E-mail me at: info@pembrokeshiretrilogy.co.uk

Have a look at youtube videos:
http://www.youtube.com/channel/UC7Hu9g0zs03PbP_oUCHA0Iw

Introduction to the Author of the Pembrokeshire Trilogy books PEMBROKESHIRE TRILOGY – VOLS: 1 – TALES OF THE SEA Diver, Shipwreck Researcher and Author: James Hedley Phillips

James Hedley Phillips who lives in Haverfordwest, Pembrokeshire has been researching Pembrokeshire Maritime History since 1968.

Thankfully, at last Jim has put together this long awaited book; PEMBROKESHIRE TRILOGY – Vols: 1. - TALES OF THE SEA

Jim was born at Stout Hall, Gower, Swansea in 1948. At the age of 10, Jim was the only boy in his school that could read nautical charts. He learnt this skill from his father, a Master Mariner. Six generations of Jim's family were Master Mariners. Jim's family history can be traced back to the 17th Century. The family has strong maritime and family links with Pembrokeshire, Gower, Devon and Cornwall. Jim is a well-known Pembrokeshire Shipwreck Researcher and Diver with over 3,000 dives under his belt and has over 45 years of knowledge of the local seas. Off the Pembrokeshire coast Jim has searched and located over 30 undiscovered shipwrecks. In his first year of diving (1968) Jim discovered two shipwrecks.

Pembrokeshire Trilogy Vols: 1 – Tales of the Sea.
Jim is a skilled story teller; he will give the reader a wonderful insight into Pembrokeshire maritime history, from smugglers, shipwrecks, press gangs, people who lived on Skomer Island, the building of the Smalls light-house by Mr. Whiteside, plus many other maritime stories, in fact over 60 unpublished stories.
This amazing collection of untold stories which will absolutely capture your imagination. If you think you know Pembrokeshire's maritime history, then you're going to be shocked, and thrilled.

Shipwreck Researcher

When I first started researching shipwrecks [1968], and other stories of the people who lived and made a living from the seas off the Pembrokeshire coast, I use to write the information on bits of paper. Afterwards, I went over to cards, indexed, year, sea area, you can imagine how much room all that took up, and I was in a right 'shipwreck researcher records mess.' Then in the early 1980's computers come along. [It's now hard to believe of a life before computers] By 1987 my nephew Michael Phillips had moved to Brighton, England, and started up his own computer company. He did a shipwreck program for me and it made life, so much easier. At the touch of a button I could call up material by year, or area, or type of vessel or cargo or a name could be found, and that really made life of a Shipwreck Researcher much easier and so much faster. It took me months to put everything on the computer -- then I had an empty spare bedroom come office "so that's what my spare bedroom come office floor looks like!"

After years and years of being hounded, and nagged to do something with all this accumulated research information on shipwrecks and sea related stories by my diving colleges, "You must produce a shipwreck chart or even a book" they kept saying. I produced my first Gower Coast Shipwreck Chart in 1999. A year later, I did another chart this time on the Pembrokeshire Coast. I've learned a lot from these two shipwreck charts. I call it [SRPLC] "Shipwreck Researcher's Publishing Learning Curve." So, here I am publishing my first book: - "Pembrokeshire Trilogy'- Vols: 1 - Tales of the Sea. Author James Hedley Phillips." It's only taken 46 years 1968 – 2014 to get the 1st book published, if I keep this speed up then it's going to be the year 2060, for the 2nd book in the Trilogy is published. Seriously, I'm working on Vols. 2 now.

I just have too much material for one book, so I came up with a planned Trilogy; for three books. To give the book a title took months. My team of expert advisers: Carl Richards with his theater and marketing background; Peter Northcott, with his design and book marketing background, even my brother Peter Phillips was roped in with his common sense approach; my nephew Michael Phillips with his computer expertise; and myself, I did the hard bit and came up with the word "Trilogy," just because I like the word. To be fair it has been over 40 years of research, and at last a book comes forth, and we have a title!

Pembrokeshire Trilogy - Tales of the Sea. Vols: 1. James Hedley Phillips.

AUTHORS ACKNOWLEDGEMENTS

I would like to take this opportunity in expressing my thanks to the following, for their help along the long road which eventually lead to producing the first of the Pembrokeshire Trilogy Books. Vols: 1.Tales of the Sea. 2014.

Peter Phillips. [My brother] for his encouragement and advice.
David Evans. Diver, Swansea Sub Aqua Club.
Mr. Morgan, Porth Clais Farm. His kindness, help and advice to me over many years.
Alan Jeffery. Diver.
Dai the Mill. St. David's. Local shipwreck knowledge and a really good story teller.
Michael Phillips. [My nephew] for his computer IT work, writing the computer shipwreck
.   programme (1986) computer, youtube, website and book advice.
John Lewis. Diver, Neath Sub Aqua Club.
Bruce Jones. Diver, Use of his photographs, and research material.
Tom Bennett. Diver, Shipwreck Researcher, use of drawings and his research material.
Greg Evans. Diver, Shipwreck author, and cameraman above and underwater filming. My
.   thanks for your GPS wreck positions web site and book advice.
Howell Lewis. Diver, photographer Cumtawe Sub Aqua Club.
Margaret Senior. Diver from Wakefield England, thank you Margaret.
Clive Llewellyn. Diver.
Bob Arthur. Editing text, planning, writing press releases, book and web adviser.
Clive Harris. Diver with his 'local knowledge' of the seas around St. David's.
Jen Jones. Diver, 'Deep Sea Marine Biologist' photographic help with the book Trilogy 1.
Andy Jack. Diver, Shipwreck Salvage Supervisor.
Richard Powys. Diver.
Eric Valerio. Diver, underwater film cameraman.
David Chant. Diver, with 'local knowledge' of shipwrecks and salvage expert.
Jane Phillips. My IT computer genius, thank you Jane.
Phil Landeg. Diver, Film director, cameraman above and underwater filming. Who made two
.   classic films: "LOST WITHOUT TRACE" and "DIVERSE ADVENTURES"
Clive Hayes. Diver.
Cindy Pearce. Diver, IT computer fixer, thank you Cindy.
Peter Northcott. For the book and website advice.
Carl Richards. Film director, Theatre stage manager, website and book advice.
Lanara Mitchell. Project Manager - Toolkit Websites Ltd. Design of website.
Castle Photography, Haverfordwest. David and Edward. For the photo shoot at Porth Gain.
Sonic, Adam Evans. Editing Technician of DVD'S, used on youtube.
Helen Harding. Proof reader. Thank you Helen.

CONTENTS

Privateers and Pirates around the Pembrokeshire coast:

NAPOLEON BONAPARTE, PRIVATEERS & PEMBROKESHIRE

During the war against Napoleon Bonaparte, the 'Monster' or 'Old Boney,' as he was also known as, France licensed French and American merchant ships to take any British ship, or any ship of her colonies; they would then sell the ship and cargo, making a tidy profit. Most Privateers never fired their guns, just threats and shouting were enough, and most vessels just gave in.

They were known as Privateers and were granted 'Letter of Marque' which meant they were not Pirates but Privateers.

Well, would you believe this was accepted as quite legal, by all parties. Actually, the British were very good at it; after all they had been doing this for hundreds of years. Let me put it another way, if you were onboard a Privateer and captured, you were treated as a prisoner of war, given a cup of tea and a cucumber sandwich. The captain of the Privateer would have to dine with the Royal Navy Captain and his officers; they were like the pop stars of the day. On the other hand if you if you were caught on a Pirate ship, Pirates were a disgusting bunch of low life, murdering, scum who could be hanged when caught. Now you know the difference. [The good old days when things were simple and not so 'complicated']

Whilst merchant vessels were normally armed to defend themselves against pirates, but, when at war, merchant ship owners would take out those so called 'Letters of Marque' issued by the government. It was a license to seize any enemy merchant ship and sell the cargo and vessel. If the ship's crew fought back, and some of the crew was killed whilst in this very honourable act of seizure, it was not a problem. Privateering was seen as a patriotic and honourable thing to do for 'gentlemen', and a 'gentleman' might even make some money while doing his duty, well, a 'gentleman' has expenses.

Reports have reached Cork, on March 23 1805 that the PERSEVERANCE, under Captain Donovan, a Bristol trader bound for Cork, fell in with a French schooner privateer, a little to the westward of the Smalls, and was unfortunately captured. A number of passengers were on board, and they with the PERSEVERANCE, were sent to France, as a prize ship.

The PRESEVERANCE had been captured by the Privateer ship called the CONFIANCE, a schooner from St. Malo, France she carried 14 cannons. This privateer was causing a lot of trouble with the British Merchant fleet off Pembrokeshire, and in the Bristol Channel, there were a number of Royal Navy frigates after her. She had been chased once by one Royal Navy frigate and, to escape the Privateer Captain, threw over the side 12 of his 14 cannons, then being lighter, he got away.

Captain Donovan of the PERSEVERANCE who had been captured by the French Privateers, they put him onboard another vessel that had had just been captured, and let him and the vessel go, the reason was, the French Privateer ship was already full of prisoners. "As I said earlier, it was all very honourable," Captain Donovan once landed ashore, he immediately informed the authorities and they dispatched a fast sailing cutter, the RESOLUTION, to go in pursuit of the privateer and her prize ship.

April 1st: The RESOLUTION cutter returned after falling in with the French privateer brig CONFIANCE and had commenced battle for three hours. The French vessel was a vastly superior ship, and the RESOLUTION was obliged to give up the contest. The French Privateer did not run, she actually took on the RESOLUTION cutter, and sent her packing.

Captains Donavon's ship, PERSEVERANCE, was later retaken by the Royal Navy frigate DECADE and both made for Plymouth. But, there was no sight of the French Privateer Captain.

Now even more frigates were sent to capture this Privateer CONFIANCE, including HMS DRYAD and HMS BRILLIANT. There was good reason to believe she would shortly visit the Bristol Channel or Pembrokeshire.
The Cambrian Newspaper in 1805 reports that two French privateers, one of which is commanded by one of the French Officers, who was on parole in Swansea town in the last war. [On parole in Swansea town, the French Officer, would give his word as an Officer and Gentleman that he would not try to escape, on giving his word, he was free to go anywhere, as long as he kept in the Town's Boundaries. But he was locked up at night]
These French privateers cruise continually from the Smalls, off Lundy, and to Land's End. It is rumored that one of the French privateers has a St. Ives man on board; I think this is our French Privateer ship CONFIANCE. If they did have a St. Ives man on board, then his knowledge of the local seas was invaluable to the French Captain. If this St. Ives man, 'the bounder' was ever caught he would be hanged.

By 1807, off the Pembrokeshire coast and in the Bristol Channel, we had Privateers coming from France, America, and Spain; even the Dutch had got involved. They were looking for easy pickings. In one day alone, over twenty small coastal traders had been taken by Privateers. They were sunk, or only the rich parts of the cargos taken or the Captain's paid them off with Bank of England notes or in gold coin, strange how they did not bother with coal or salt cargoes, they were after general cargos, which they could get a high price for back in France, because the Royal Navy blockaded the ports of Europe; there was a shortage of general goods. Anyone would think the privateers were just in it for the money, not for victory for France and Napoleon Bonaparte, 'the Monster'.

The problem with the Royal Navy was they were just too busy blockading the ports of Europe, and had nothing spare to guard the coastal ships sailing around Pembrokeshire's coast. To make it worst, the Privateers had change tactics, the 'dirty rotters,' the British Privateers would never do such a thing, never, well, really, all they were doing was following the idea from the British Privateers; who were doing very nicely with this trick. [Here is example of another brilliant British idea stolen by those foreigners.]

This is the notice that went around the ports of Pembrokeshire and the ports in the Bristol Channel: -

Bewared of Privateers off our coast: the following description of a French Privateer, seen on the 20th December 1807, off North Pembrokeshire coast, this may be useful to Masters of vessels trading between South Wales and Ireland. Keep a lookout for a three masted schooner, with three square top-sails, mountings for 14 to 16 guns; painted black – but changes her colour and appearance occasionally, by sailing as a lugger or schooner, with two or three masts.

On 23 April 1808 an American Privateer chased a locally owned sloop for nearly the whole day, off the Pembrokeshire coast. The master of the sloop could just keep her out of cannon shot range. Fortunately, the master of the sloop was a local man and he knew the Pembrokeshire waters well. He give the Privateers a merry dance around the Bishops and Clerks Rocks, off St. David's Head, and then using the currents and tides he took his sloop into Solva, leaving a good distance between him and the Privateer.

By November 1812, the Privateers were taking merchant ships daily. This example shows how the War with France was conducted by the Privateers. All very gentlemanly.

Arrived at Milford Haven on 11 November 1812, the schooner UNITED SISTERS, Captain John Webb, from Poole, bound for Bristol, with a cargo of pipe-clay, having, on the 6th November been captured off Start Point by LA FURET a French lugger privateer, from St. Malo, France mounting 18 guns and 140 men, under the command of Captain Louis Marenwart. After plundering [stealing anything useful or they can sell or use] the ships stores, they even took the masters clothes, spying-glass, and four pounds in Bank of England notes. He was then taken on board the privateer, where he remained for two hours, having to sit with the French Captain and drink French wine. A sloop came in sight, which, after a short chase, she was also captured. Both vessels were, however, soon liberated, upon the master of the UNITED SISTERS Captain John Webb, signing this paper. [Now let me get this straight, both ships, masters and crews will be freed; and not taken to France as Prisoners of War, if the ship's Captain John Webb signed this paper, sounds okay, but, I bet there's a catch].

This is the exact wording of the legal document that Master John Webb of the UNITED SISTERS signed:

That immediately on his arrival in England 'Master John Webb' of the Schooner UNITED SISTERS; should make every application in his power to exchange against himself for the ships' company, and Master M. Joseph Gautier. Who were taken on the 15ᵗʰ February, 1810, on board the French schooner privateer CONFIANCE, now confined as a prisoner of war at Chatham; and that if he should not succeed in liberating the said French prisoner, in two months from the date of the said agreement, he is to proceed to France as a prisoner of war; and also not to bear arms against France, or her allies, before the execution of the said conditions.

It was also witnessed, and signed, all legal and above board. These French Privateers now turned into Sea Lawyers. I know this sounds strange today, but it was quite accepted and honourable in those days.

Consider how the French officers were treated after they surrender at Fishguard in February 1797. All they had to do was sign a document saying: '*As a French Officer and Gentleman I give my solemn promise not to escape'*. Once signed off they went to Carmarthen Town, to spend the rest of the war. Of course they had to be locked up at night, but, in the day time they had the freedom of Carmarthen Town to the boundaries. If they were invited to any social engagements outside Carmarthen Town, then of course a special pass was always granted.

"Here's a good example of why passes were given - a week in the country shooting on a respectable gentry's estate. These French Officers were very popular at Balls and Parties thrown by the gentry, the daughters of gentlemen may have swooned at the sound of French accents. French Officers were treated like pop stars of the day. So we can see why it was quite expectable for the ship's Captain John Webb to sign that document.

French Officers Parole 1811
In November 1811 it is reported that one-fourth of the French officers, 'prisoners of war,' have broken their parole. [But they had given their word!] And when the chance came! Whoosh! Off back to France! The perishes scarpered! It's that darn Monster! Napoleon Bonaparte, his officers and men are so loyal to him.

Their conveyance across the Channel is always facilitated by 'smugglers' who, according to the statement of the Attorney-General, in the Court of King's Bench, London are permitted to land on the French coast, on the condition to bringing over at least one native officer at each time. [Well, business is business].

In September 1813 the Cambrian newspaper reported that the brig SAMPSON, under Master Harris, from Dublin for Swansea, had arrived at Milford, and reported that on the previous Sunday morning last 12ᵗʰ September, she was chased by a large schooner, supposed to be an American Privateer. The vessel had yellow sides, but, Captain Harris being well acquainted with the coast, ran through Ramsey Sound, and escaped. The privateer schooner would not follow the brig SAMPSON through Ramsey Sound. The paper also added this:

We trust that Government will pay due attention to the safety of Milford, which, in its present defenceless state, having only two small cutters of four guns and ten or twelve men each to protect that important place, is exposed to much alarm on the appearance of an enemy in this channel. [Well, that's told the enemy their defences at Milford, the French don't need spies, all they have to do is read the Cambrian newspaper, and they will know everything].

Now with the Privateers painting their ships in bright colours, yellow, red, white, even black to show the crews of their intended victim who they were, and not to resist, but our Captain Harris was smart, he took a chance that the Privateer would not follow him through Ramsey Sound.

An American Privateer ship was working the seas south of the Pembrokeshire coast in 1814. On Sunday 14th August the BERWICKSHIRE PACKET, [Packet means a ship on regular voyage with mail] under the command of Master Crosby, while on her voyage from Cork to Bristol was boarded and taken off the Pembrokeshire coast by the America Privateer PRINCE OF NENFCHATEL. Once the American privateer had what they wanted of her cargo, especially the ships food stores, they then released the ship without any damage, but, they put on-board the crews of other ships they had captured earlier. Crew from the GENERAL DOYLE, under Captain Simpson, from Leghorn, (Livorno) Tuscany, Italy to Bristol, England which she had been captured and burnt, after taking out the most valuable part of her general cargo. The PRINCE of NENFCHATEL had also taken a brig, loaded with culm [Culm is coal dust] and several other vessels over the days before. The Privateer ship was now over flowing with captured seamen. Problem with all these seamen aboard the Privateer vessel. Short of room, feeding them, they might even turn on their captives, plus, they were moaning constantly about their conditions. The Privateer Captain had asked them if they would like to go to France as 'prisoners of war' or be put aboard this captured vessel and be allowed to "sail for home." [That's a difficult one that, home or France, nice of him to ask. Really, I bet the Captain of the Privateer was glad to get rid of them. Of course they all wanted to go home].
'Home' they all said, then the Privateer Captain asked all the prisoners, if any had been badly treated, or mishandled by him or his Privateer crew. 'None' was the reply. They all parted the best of friends after shaking hands with the Privateer Captain and his crew.

There was certain thinking behind not harming captured seamen. If the Privateer sunk the ship just captured, then they would take aboard the crew for their safety, and once they captured another vessel, then they would put aboard the crew of the captured ship, as long as they weren't going to sink it, that is. All gentlemanly and above board, so let's think about this. Say you're a seaman and you're about to be captured by a Privateer, with no chance of out running her. You know they would not harm you, if you did not resist. Then why fight? If you are injured or killed, your family would get nothing, and all you want to do is earn a living to support your family. If you wanted to fight, then you could always join the Royal Navy. Why would you fight an enemy who is so pleasant and courteous? You can see why no ship's crew fought back, it was a smart move, and most importantly, 'it worked'.

Loss of Pirate ship 1795.

Mrs. Morgan who lived near St. Gavan's Head, mentions the story in her letters in 1795. *'A silver bell was stolen from the St. Gavan's Chapel by Pirates* [Now these are pirates, you remember they are the ones who are: cads, bounders, rotters]; *but it was not out of sight of this place. A storm instantly sprang up as soon as they set sail, and the sacrilege was punished by the vessel being wrecked and all the pirates were drowned'.*

We have similar stories all around the coast. One comes to mind regarding Ramsey Sound.   Pirates had stolen the bells from St. Justinian Chapel, in the 16[th]century, as the pirates sailed away with these two bells. Suddenly a great storm blew up 'and of course' blew the Pirate ship back right under the chapel of St. Justinian's where she was wrecked. None of the pirates survived and even today when gales blow you can hear under the waters of Ramsey Sound the bells tolling for the souls of the lost pirates.

Ramsey Island Pirates Landed, this happened in 1633 when a Pirate ship entered Ramsey Sound, they were Breton pirates, landing near the Waterings on Ramsey Island. Two pirates went up on the island and killed a sheep, and brought the meat back to the ship, around the first week of Lent [April 1633].

Later in the year, the same pirate ship returned; Magistrates where told by Gilbert Williams at Haverfordwest on 19th October 1633, that he had seen pirates and St. David's men together. The St. David's men were immediately arrested and brought in chains before the magistrates. These are very serious charges, even to be seen with pirates, was a hanging offence. Pirates were a big problem around the Pembrokeshire coast and in the Bristol Channel.   Merchant ships could not get insurance, especially if they had to sail around Pembrokeshire or the Bristol Channel. The island of Lundy had become a pirate stronghold, due to its high cliffs for defence and its strategic position in the Bristol Channel.

In their defense the St. David's men said they had no idea this was a pirate ship when they boarded her in Porthlysgi Bay. Only one of them Mr. Hugh Badcock, could speak their language, and the Captain had asked if they would show him a safe passage to the Waterings, in Ramsey Sound for they were short of fresh water".

Gilbert Williams went aboard by invitation of the crew and recognized not only the Captain but also a 'gaggle' of St. David's men, including one of the local squire's men. After dropping anchor in the Waterings the St. David's men left the ship. Later, the pirate captain landed with 30 men and raided Ramsey Island farm, they came back about midnight with four cheeses from the farm house and one sheep.

Next morning about 27 men went ashore armed with pistols, swords, half-pikes and muskets and again raided Ramsey Island farm house. This time they got away with 10 stolen sheep, a lamb and all the farmers' eight cheeses. They then sailed away. Ramsey Island cheeses were worth a lot of money.

Those cheeses were worth a lot of money. Do you remember reading about the 1666 Great Fire of London? Samuel Pepys, as the fire got closer to his house, went and buried in his garden his most valuable items: gold coins, documents and his 'Dutch cheese'. Cheese was worth a great deal of money in the 16th century, so the farmer on Ramsey Island had invested all his money in the making of these chesses, now stolen. You can see why pirates were hanged.

The St. David's men did get off. They had witnesses, respectable witnesses, who give evidence saying they had left the ship once arriving at the Waterings, in Ramsey Sound. But, if one of them had been involved in any of the two pirate raids on Ramsey Island Farm, no messing, they would have been hanged.

SUSANNAH shipwrecked at Porthlysgi Bay:

[Carreg yr Esgob Island, in Porthlysgi Bay. The island in the centre of the bay, that's where John Ellis ship had been wrecked]

The SUSANNAH, a 100 ton sloop, was launched on Wednesday 9th April 1817, at Bangor, North Wales. For ten years she sailed the seas carrying her cargos around Wales, even to the ports in France. While the SUSANNAH was on voyage from

London, England to Bangor, North Wales with its general cargo, she was sailing north across St. Bride's Bay, Pembrokeshire without warning a southerly gale blew up. At 11 a.m. Wednesday 13th February, 1828, she was wrecked against the south side of Carreg yr Esgob, an island at the entrance to Porthlysgi Bay on the north side of St. Bride's Bay. [Carreg yr Esgob, Porthlysgi Bay lies west of Porth Clais, just before Ramsey Sound] Waves were breaking over the vessel as she was being smashed against the rocks. The only survivor was fifteen year old cabin boy named John Ellis, who, managed to scramble onto the island.

John was soaked to the skin, cold, bruised all over and his hands were badly cut. This was a very frightened 15 year old boy, and he was the only survivor from a crew of six, also its one of the coldest winters, you can just imagine how cold and frightened was John Ellis.

For the rest of that night he sheltered amongst the rocks from the heavy rain and gale force winds. The wrecking had been observed by the fishermen and farm workers of Porthlysgi, but the gale was blowing too strong for any fisherman to venture out.

At 10 o'clock the following morning, John Perkins, a lobsterman of Porthlyski and others who had been watching the seas 'all night' and now with the morning light, they could see that the waves had calm down, just enough to have a go. "It's now or never" said John Perkins, "I need two volunteers." Ten St. David's fishermen stepped forward. John Perkins said, "I'll take no married men." [I think you know what he means by "that"] They rowed straight out into the waves, and then suddenly, about half way, up blew the southerly gale again. "We'll just have to keep going, it too late to turn back," said John Perkins.

With mountainous waves coming straight at them, with gale force winds and heavy rain, they manage to reach the island.

His rescuers found the boy John Ellis in the middle of the island, curled up sheltering from the rain and gale force winds. They called to him, but he did not move, thinking he was dead. Then he opened his eyes, "he was still alive, just."

He could not speak or move, because of exposure, another few hours at the most, and he would have been dead. Getting John Ellis aboard was very difficult. Once onboard this small rowing boat, they headed back to Porthlysgi beach, now they headed back with following seas, really I should say following 'surf breaking behind them'. On a number of occasions they thought they were going to meet their maker, but with expert seamanship John Perkins, at the tiller, brought them safely back ashore.

John Ellis was more dead than alive, by the time he was put ashore, he could not walk, talk. He was carried to the a local Porthlyski farm, where the farmer's family took good care of him, he was so ill that it was four weeks before he was fit enough to travel back to his home in North Wales. John Ellis had no money to reward the farmer for his kindness. And anyway the Porthlysgi farmer and his family would not accept one penny for caring and feeding John Ellis and nursing him back to health. [They are Pembrokeshire's Finest].

While he was still at Porthlysgi farm John Ellis wrote home, he was still in no state to travel. The Cambrian Newspaper states on 1st March:

A letter from John Ellis, the only survivor of a crew of six men belonging to the sloop SUSANNAH, of Bangor, North Wales, which was wrecked 13th February 1828, off St. David's Head, addressed to his father and mother, resident in Bangor, states, that the misfortune happened on the rocks off the above head in a dreadful rolling sea. Ellis fortunately got on a small Island at no great distance, where he remained from eleven o'clock that night until ten o'clock the following morning.

July 1828, the newspaper Cambrian reports:

The Committee of the Shipwreck Institution in London has directed Messrs. George Paynter and Co., of Milford, to pay £3. 10s. to John Perkins, of Porthliski, near St. David's, and his boat crew, for their laudable exertions in saving the life of John Ellis, the only survivor of the SUSANNAH'S crew, wrecked at Carrog Vran,
[Carreg yr Esgob, in Porthlysgi Bay] *near St. David's Head, in the month of February last. Too much praise cannot be given to those brave fellows, who, at a period of such imminent danger, fearlessly risked their lives to deliver a fellow-creature from that devouring element which had only a few hours before hurried five of his unfortunate shipmates into eternity.*

Skerryback Farm, shipwreck and Court case:

A NICE PIECE OF 'SCRAMBLE' from Skerryback
On Thursday, the 27th November 1862 the brigantine DEFENCE of Bristol, Captain Guy, built 1862, she was not even a year old vessel, while beating out [leaving] Milford Harbour was driven on the rocks near Great Castle Head, where she became a total wreck. Crewmen all saved. Wrecked near Skerryback Farm, at Great Castle Head, St. Ishmael, in Milford Haven.

There followed a Court Cast at Haverfordwest one week later:
CHARGE OF ASSAULT
Mr. James Hodges, of Skerryback Farm, at Great Castle Head, [born at Laugharne, Carmarthenshire, in 1844 now aged 18 the second son of Farmer Isaac Hodges who farmed Skerryback Farm of 264 acres] James Hodges was charged with assaulting Martha Jenkins, of Marloes. Mr. James Hodges denied the assault.
Martha Jenkins deposed that a vessel was wrecked at Skerryback, Near Great Castle Head; and she went down there like everybody else, for the 'scramble.' [The word 'scramble' for helping yourself to the wreck, it's only to be found in Pembrokeshire] She met the defendant there Mr. James Hodges. He did not want people to come

there. Her sister took up a little board, and he told her not to take it. There were two pieces of board there, and she threw one over the cliff, and her sister the other. The defendant then knocked her down twice, and dragged her along the ground. She knew she was trespassing on the defendant's land; he had ordered her away before he struck her, but she would not go.

Elizabeth Collins deposed that she saw the defendant strike the complainant on the cheek.

James Hodges stated that he did not strike Martha Jenkins at all; he merely pushed her. Two boards were thrown over the cliff, and as Martha Jenkins was about to throw a third over the cliff, he shoved her back to prevent her doing so, says James Hodges. The wrecked vessel was opposite his land, [James father Isaac Hedges had died 6 November 1861. He is the farmers 2nd born son, not the owner of the land] and he said he had been placed in charge of it by the captain. Mr. James Hodges was fined 1s, and costs 14s. 3d.

The mystery is why did Martha Jenkins want these bits of wood in the first place? Thinking about it; she'll have one long walk back to Marloes carrying bits of wood! Then we have James Hodges, you remember he says "He was placed in charge of the wreck by the captain," well, I don't go for that at all. You could have anyone saying that, 'the captain put me in charge of this wreck.' I'd ask 'may I see a letter of authorization from the captain,' plus does the Receiver of Wrecks know you are the 'legal' person in charge of this wreck, as there will be 'legal costs' and a court case coming up? I bet our farmer's 18 year old son James Hodges would have run a mile. These are the most dreaded two words a Pembrokeshire farmer does not want to hear "LEGAL" and "COSTS."

Interestingly:

A few years after this court case, James mother Esther moved to Castle Martin with two of the children and by 1871 she was farming a small holding of 23 acres (Esther d. 1877 aged 68). James (you remember the alleged owner of the wreck) on 22nd September 1864 he married Martha Maria Thomas (b. 25 January 1846 Haverfordwest) of Hill Street, Haverfordwest, at St. Thomas Church, Haverfordwest.

They had two children in Pembrokeshire, the boy born 1866, and the girl was born 1867, then James, Martha and the two children in 1869 up sticks and immigrated to the USA where he worked as a labourer, there Martha and James had a further three children, two children were born in Mississippi, a son in 1871, a daughter in 1874 the third a daughter was born in Tennessee 1877. In 1880 they were living at Jackson, Madison, Tennessee. James Hodges died on 2 December 1881 aged 37, from pneumonia and is buried at Spring Green County Cemetery, Wisconsin, USA. North of Chicago. Martha remarried in 1884 to her cousin Robert Whittow. Martha died in 7th January 1927 aged 81. [I've got to admit it's been an interesting journey]

Honest shipwrecked seaman & Whales off Smalls:

On Monday 6th March 1815, a seafaring man presented himself to the Magistrate's at Milford Haven for relief. He stated that he had just walked from Tenby, after having been landed there a few days previous. Four days earlier in thick fog, the brig UNION, of Dartmouth, bound from London for Liverpool, laden with a general cargo, struck on the Hats and Barrels, Reef, near the Smalls, and immediately sunk. The crew of nine took to the rowing boat, but it capsized. Only him and a boy were saved, by clinging to the bottom of the upturned boat, where they remained for a considerable time, eventually being saved by the sloop FRIENDS, of Carnarvon, which landed them both, at Tenby.

Milford Magistrate's paid for a meal for this poor shipwrecked seaman, and while enjoying his meal his story started not to sound right, he kept changing things. They became suspicious and a constable on horse [at considerable expense to the court] was sent to check out his story at Tenby. And would you believe it, there had been no survivors landed at Tenby, no boy was found. Now, this honest seaman was more closely examined and after persisting for a considerable time the story of being shipwreck on the Hats and Barrels, he was at last obliged to confess that the whole of it was false, and that he had just arrived from Ireland. [Well; I'll be blowed', he sounded an honest seaman to me].

The Milford magistrates were not happy, for wasting their time, and more importantly they had incurred costs, in checking out his story at Tenby, and especially they had been made to look fools, (remember that expensive meal they paid for). They showed their displeasure by sentencing him to 5 years in the Royal Navy. It just so happened at Milford Haven was His Majesty's ship HMS SPITFIRE; [Launched 19th March 1782, with a complement of 121 men] and it just so happened, they were looking for honest seamen to join their happy crew, and moreover they would be so pleased to take our 'volunteer' aboard.

The following morning, with chains on wrists and ankles [No way was he going to escape] our reluctant 'volunteer' was taken aboard. On arrival he was taken to the Captain's Cabin, there he told the Captain of HMS SPITFIRE that he's a shipwright [ship builder, carpenter] by trade and a native of Dorset. He told the Captain all the ships he had been a carpenter on, while in the Captain's Cabin he even said the Captain needed a new cupboard door which he kept his clothes in. What's more, he would work on it straight away.

You could imagine the glee of the Captain's face, for shipwright's were very much sort after, especially a shipwright from Dorset, and this shipwright knew what he was talking about, [He sounds an honest man to me, don't you agree], so instead of being thrown in the 'ships brig' [ships cell] his chains were removed. He was shown around the ship, by an officer. This man was an 'Honest Dorset Shipwright. He was shown every curtsy, given a good meal, given plenty of grog [rum] as well as new clean clothes. The Captain was going to look after this seaman or should I say this 'Honest Dorset Shipwright Tradesman.' [What a nice carpenter man he sounds].

I know you'll be shocked when I tell you this, but, our friend the 'Honest Shipwright Carpenter from Dorset' disappeared only two days after his arrival aboard HMS SPITFIRE. I didn't want to mention this, but, coincidentally, some of the Captains clothes went missing. Have you any idea who has taken them?

EARL OF LEICESTER PACKET

The sloop SWALLOW, Master Crawford, from Waterford for Swansea, with five hogs [pigs], was met at sea off Milford Haven, Saturday 3rd June 1809 by the EARL OF LEICESTER PACKET, [PACKET, means regular voyage carrying mail]. On seeing the SWALLOW dismasted, the EARL OF LEICESTER took her in tow, but with wind and tide against her she could not reach Milford. She was anchored off Skokholm Island, and the crew taken aboard and later landed at Dale, in Milford Haven.

Next day with favourable winds the SWALLOW was towed into and anchored up at Dale, in Milford Haven, for repairs.

Nine years later its 1818; The EARL OF LEICESTER PACKET, with Wednesday's mail from Waterford, while off the Smalls, about half-past seven in the evening, Wednesday 30 July 1818; struck upon a whale, and the main stem had been so damaged by the accident that it had to be replaced. A large piece of the skin of the whale was found attached to a bolt which projected out of the bottom of her keel. Several other whales were seen sporting in the early part of the afternoon.

[This is not the first time while researching shipwrecks that I've come onto "collision between ship and whale", but, normally this happens way out at sea, not off the Smalls]

Skomer Island & Mr. Vaughan Palmer Davies:

SKOMER ISLAND STORIES

[Photograph: looking across Jack Sound to Skomer Island. Jack Sound has over 40 known wrecks in such a small stretch of water, with possibly another 80 unknowns. People have been living on this island going back 4,000 years and more]

Skomer Island; let me start off with this Court case; It will give you, an insight into minds and attitudes of local Pembrokeshire folk, about the Island of Skomer in the 1860's. Not only its remoteness and its dangerous tides, but also the best quote ever said about Skomer Island. This case was brought up in front of Roose Petty Sessions at the end of February 1865; "I laughed out loud myself when I first read this." "Now sit back and enjoy."

NON-PAYMENT OF WAGES

Background of this case: Elizabeth Warlow, from Marloes Village, is offered a position on Skomer Island Farm, but before she accepts the job, she cuts a deal with Mrs. Davies the wife of Vaughan Palmer Davies farmer of Skomer Island: It's this, "if she don't like living on Skomer Island then all she has to do is give a months' notice. One of the problems with working on the islands off Pembrokeshire coast, such as Caldey, Skokholm, Ramsey or Skomer, was the isolation, so near yet you can't just can't, get off. Winter gales can cut you off from the mainland for three or even four months and workers would miss their families, on birthdays, Christmas times, and missing their friends. Family bonds were much stronger than they are today, and the loneliness could get to them, particularly if they didn't get on with their employer, or other workers.

There was the problem of getting to and off the island, crossing the dangerous tidal race of Jack Sound. Today it takes 15 minutes by boat from Martins Haven, but then, before power boats, it was by the power of rowing, and you didn't do this lightly crossing the notorious Jack Sound. Jack Sound has over 40 known shipwrecks and many more unrecorded ones.

Now for the Court Case:

Roose Petty Sessions were held at the Shire Hall, on Saturday 25th February 1865 before O. E. Davies, Esq., S. Hartford, Esq., and Rev. P. Phelps:

Mr. Vaughan P. Davies, [b. 1826 aged 41] of Skomer Island, was charged by Elizabeth Warlow with non-payment of wages.

This is the wording from the court case:-

> **Elizabeth Warlow:** *deposed that she was an agricultural servant, and hired to enter the service of Mrs. Davies of Skomer Island, for twelve months, on the condition that the hiring should terminate at any time on her giving a month's notice. The wages were £6 a year,* [about 2s. 6d a week, with all food and board] *and she now claimed £1 16s 9d. She had given a month's notice, which terminated on the 9th.*
>
> **Vaughan Davies:** *stated that the complainant was engaged by his wife, who was now near her confinement,* [confinement was the excepted practice then, for a pregnant woman, on showing signs of pregnancy, the lady would stay indoors, thus confinement, and of course because of her confinement Mrs. Davies could not attend this court]. *Mrs. Davies told me, that the hiring was for twelve months, without any agreement as to its termination on a month's notice.*
>
> **Elizabeth Warlow:** *I wished to leave as I'm going to get married.*
>
> **The Clerk:** *When is the wedding to be?*
>
> **Elizabeth Warlow**: *In three weeks.*
>
> **The Clerk:** *Well after that, Mr. Davies, I suppose you will let the girl go. You would not like to prevent her getting married?*
>
> **Vaughan Davies**: *No, I would not, Sir, if she will stay till I get another in her place, I will let her go. I have told her that before. I may let her go in three weeks; or it may be a month, and I told her so, or I may keep her till Michaelmas* [29th September; that's another six months working on the island].
>
> **The Clerk**: *Well I think you had better let her go under the circumstances. Men are slippery beings, and I hope deterred maketh the heart sick.*" (Loud laughter in court).
>
> **Vaughan Davies**: *I will let her go only it must be understood that it is not according to law, for the hiring was for twelve months. 'Mrs. Davies states that there was nothing about a months' notice.*
>
> **Elizabeth Warlow**: *I agree to give a month's notice.*
>
> **Vaughan Davies**: *Mrs. Davies says differently; it was for twelve months, at £6, and £6 10s if she gives satisfactory. The man she is going to be married to, also works with me; his engagement finishes this week, but I will keep him long as I keep her, if she will wait till I get another.*
>
> **Elizabeth Warlow**: *I have a witness to the hiring agreement.*
>
> **Witness was sworn in; Lettice Thomas:** [b. 1843 at Marloes] *deposed that she was present when the hiring took place between Elizabeth Warlow and*

Mrs. Davies of Skomer Island. Elizabeth Warlow would not be hirer except on the condition that a month's notice should be given, as it was an island, and she Elizabeth Warlow might not like it. Mrs. Davies said she never engaged a girl on that condition before, but she would engage Elizabeth Warlow on those terms.

Vaughan Davies: *Well I knew nothing of the matter myself, but Mrs. Davies declares that there was nothing said about a month's notice.*

The Clerk: *If you were to bring Mrs. Davies here, it would hardly assist you. There are two witnesses against one, and the magistrates would be bound to give a verdict for the girl, Elizabeth Warlow.*

The Bench gives a verdict for **Elizabeth Warlow** for the amount she claimed and expenses.

[There's more, just read this and enjoy]

P.C. Thomas: *Here is a bill, sir, from the fisherman* [Martins Haven fishermen].

The Clerk: *What is this?*

P.C. Thomas: *It is there charge for conveying me to Skomer Island to issue the court summons on Mr. Vaughan Davies.*

The Clerk: *They charged you £1, and what's more, a gallon of ale?* (Laughter in court).

P.C. Thomas: *They would not carry me to the island unless I gave them a gallon of ale. I have not paid them the £1 yet.*

The Clerk: *This is an imposition; £1 is an exorbitant sum.*

Vaughan Davies: *They are my boatmen, and I will settle with them.*

P.C. Thomas: *They told me that they were not supposed to carry anyone except those belonging to Mr. Davies.*

The Clerk: *And they are supposed not to be guilty of any deception.*

P.C. Thomas: *I gave them a gallon of beer; will you please allow the amount; as I paid for it?*

Vaughan Davies: *I will pay that, and settle with the boatmen.*

The Clerk: *And bear P.C. Thomas harmless from any claim they may make upon him.*

Vaughan Davies: *Yes.*

Mr. O. E. Davies (Magistrate): *I think £6 is a very small wages to go on the island* [adding these words, what a one liner]:-

"I would as soon myself; be transported to the deserts of Siberia as go to Skomer Island". (Loud, laughter in Court).

Vaughan Davies: *She got a future husband there, sir, at all events.* (Loud, Laughter in Court).

Vaughan Davies was ordered to pay Elizabeth Warlow £2 10s, which he paid then and there, but after he left the court it was discovered that no allowance had been made to the two witnesses who were in attendance; he was brought back and was made to pay a further sum of 6s.

"I would as soon myself; be transported to the deserts of Siberia as go to Skomer Island". Thank you Magistrate Mr. O. E. Davies, for those words, they certainly made me laugh. You'll be agreeing with the Magistrate; going to or from Skomer was no light matter, before the power boat came along.

SKOMER ISLAND TO LET; an advertisement in the Cambrian Newspaper dated: Friday 19 July 1817 states that Skomer Island, being between 1,000 and 1,200 Acres of Arable and Pasture Land, with a very extensive and valuable Rabbit Warren thereon. It is a most desirable property, and will be Let or Lease of one life; -- and for further particulars apply (if by letter, post paid) to R. H. P. Laugharne, Esq. Orlandon, near Haverfordwest; or to Messrs. Evans and Son, Solicitors, Haverfordwest.

WHO IS VAUGHAN PALMER DAVIES FARMER OF SKOMER?
Who was Captain Vaughan Palmer Davies the farmer of Skomer Island? He was born in 1826 at Broomhill Farm, Dale, Pembrokeshire, one of seven children to Farmer Thomas Davies and his wife Emil Davies, he was their fourth child. He and his brother went to sea. Vaughan worked aboard the opium brigs in India; on 13th October 1852 at Swansea he got his Masters Certificate. In 1858 [aged 32], Captain Vaughan Palmer Davies, married Angelica Ellen (Nelly) Robinson, [Aged 25, born 7 May 1833, Isle of Wight] daughter of Edward Robinson, of Skomer. In 1861 Vaughan [aged 35] returned from India to farm Skomer Island, taking over the lease from his father-in-law Mr. Edward Robinson.

Vaughan and Nelly's family:
Married on 14 January 1858 at Mumbai, Maharashtra, India.

Charles Edward Davies.	Born 1859	Bombay, India.	d. 1930
Mary Alice Davies.	Born 1861	Dale, Pembrokeshire.	d. 1944
Clare Ellen Maria Davies.	Born 1863	Skomer Island.	d. 1951
Howard Davies. Twin	Born 1864	Dale, Pembrokeshire.	d. 1906
Walter John Davies. Twin	Born 1864	Dale, Pembrokeshire.	d. 1906
Annie Maud Davies.	Born 1865	Skomer Island.	d. 1944
Hugh H. Davies	Born 1869	Pater, Whitchurch, Solva.	
Augustus H. Davies.	Born 1870	Pater, Whitchurch, Solva.	

IN 1863; MR. WILLIAM GREENISH OF HERBRANDSTON HALL, is retiring from farming and auctioned off the farm and stock etc., Mr. Vaughan P. Davies [aged 37] of Skomer Island won the bidding on: Crops, 80 mows of prime red laminas seed wheat (first produce of English seed), 350 mows of superior malting barley, 150 mows of black oats (produce of seed from V. P. Davies, Esq. Skomer Island), one rick and one stack of well-saved clover hay, about 12 tons, a large quantity of wheaten thatch and straw, in lots. [As you can see, since Vaughan P. Davies took over farming Skomer, he's spending big time on everything you would need to make farming Skomer a success].

AT HAVERFORDWEST FAIR, Tuesday 12 July 1864; Captain Davies of Skomer Island bought cattle for stocking Skomer Island Farm.

[Photograph taken at North Haven, Skomer Island; showing the problems with farming any one of the islands off the Pembrokeshire coast such as Caldey, Skokholm, Skomer and Ramsey; transporting livestock or crops across the waters. When the tide is out you place the cow and calf aboard the rowing boat, tide comes in and you row to Martins Haven across north side of Jack Sound. Then you have to unload the cow at Martin's Haven.

Take the cattle to market, then what if the prices are too low, do you sell or return with the cattle, imagine when you have 10 cattle to sell. Farming anyone of the islands is not to be taken lightly]

VAUGHAN & PUFFINS
This letter was printed in a local newspaper in 1869. By Then he would have been aged 45. The top part of the letter is missing and some other parts are unreadable. I think it must have got wet. From what I can work out he says in the first part that he seen: -
"he has seen Puffins take rabbits out of their holes and the Puffins eat them. He's seen gulls catch and drop rabbits, then eat them at leisure, and he's also seen gulls kill and eat his young ducks".
The legible part of this letter reads: *"in the act of doing so. I lose also a great number of young ducks by the gulls. They have taken a brood in one day, and I have seen then take plover from the moors, and I believe (though I have not seen them) that they take young partridges and pheasants also. Should sea birds be protected by law, I hope there will be a clause permitting them to be killed on rabbit warrens.*
I desire a large number every year, but I do not see that they have decreased; indeed, some gentlemen who come to look at the birds are of the opinion that they increase every year.
Should anyone doubt this statement, I will prove it to them, if they will pay the island a visit in the month of June.
If the game laws give our magistrates trouble, a law protecting sea birds will give them more.

Should you think this worth inserting in your paper, you will oblige me by doing so.
I am, Sir, your obedient servant
VAUGHAN P. DAVIES.
Skomer Island, March 22, 1869.
P.S. We know some inland parts of England where an immigration of rabbit-killing puffins would be looked on as a great blessing.

TRESPASSING ON SKOMER
ROOSE PETTY SESSIONS
This session was held at the Shire Hall on Saturday 10th September 1869; before S. Harford, Esq., J. M. Jones, Esq., Rev. James Philipps, and Rev. P. Phelps.
TRESPASS IN SEARCH OF RABBITS.
John Edwards and John Warlow were charged with trespass in search of rabbits by Mr. Vaughan P. Davies, [aged 43] of Skomer Island.
Mr. J. C. James appeared for the complainant and Mr. Price for the defendants.
Vaughan Davies deposed that on Sunday 4th of September he saw Edwards on Midland Island. Warlow was in the boat alongside the rock. Edwards had a gun in his hand, and was beating about for rabbits. He picked up a rabbit, and brought it to the boat. Vaughan Davies called out to them to bring the rabbit to him, but they went off.
In cross-examination, the Vaughan Davies said he had a telescope with him at the time, and was about 200 yards off. The defendants might pass that way to the fishing grounds at Grassholm.
The Bench fined the defendants £1 each and costs including the advocate's fee.

SKOMER ISLAND CLAIMS ANOTHER BOATING ACCIDENT
(Vaughan Davies is 53 years old). On Saturday at three o'clock in the afternoon on 16th August 1879, three men left Skomer Island in a small sail boat for Marloes, [Martins Haven] John Oliver, had been for some time employed on Skomer Island, and he and two young men, farm servants, intending to visit the mainland. There was a stiff breeze blowing from the north-west, and a heavy ground sea running at the time. The men have not since been seen or heard of.
Sunday the following day, the boat and oars were found thrown up by the sea near the place where they launched her. It is supposed that all three are drowned. Oliver is a married man. It is the opinion of Martins Haven fishermen that the boat capsized soon after they had left the Island. [Research shows the sinking took place on Rye Rocks, North Haven, Skomer Island]   Names of missing men are: John Oliver (aged 60 years; b. 1819), Thomas Charles (aged 17; b. 1862), and William Warlow (aged 16; b. 1863).

On Tuesday at Broad Haven the body of the boy Warlow was washed ashore, several miles from the spot where the accident is supposed to have taken place. His coat and hat of deceased were missing, but in his trouser pocket was a shilling that he had from his master Mr. Vaughan P. Davies. The body was interred on Wednesday at Marloes.

The inquest is deferred till next Friday in order to get the necessary evidence from the Island.

An inquest was opened in the evening at the Castle Hotel, Little Haven, before the Coroner, Mr. William Vaughan James. After taking evidence of identity the inquest was adjourned.

The bodies of the three men drowned by the upsetting of a boat at Skomer Island have now been picked up. Two were washed ashore at Broad Haven and the other at Nolton Haven in St. Bride's Bay. Neither the middle-aged man, named Oliver, or the two youths who accompanied him, knew much about the management of the boat.

SKOMER ISLAND MARRIAGES

On the Saturday 11th April 1868 at St. Martin's Church, in this town of Haverfordwest Mr. George James married Miss Ellen Codd, of Skomer Island. On Friday 15th October 1886 at St. Peter's Church, Carmarthen, by the Rev. T. Phillips, and the Rev. A. G. Edwards, vicar assisted by the Rev. R. W. F. Davies, brother of the bride, Charles Edward Davies, aged 27 [b. 1859 - d. 1930 aged 71] living at Brecon Old Bank, Brecon, the eldest son of Vaughan Davies, (age 60) Skomer Island, to Agnes Singers, third daughter of the late Frederick Davies, and granddaughter of the late Richard Spurrell, of Carmarthen.

On Tuesday 25th October 1887 at Llanstadwell Church, by the Rev. W. Jones, vicar of St. Mary's, Pembroke, assisted by Rev. H. L. Rumsey, vicar of this Parish, Edward Scriven, elder son of Edward Scriven of Wormleighton, Warwickshire, to Mary Alice, aged 26 [b. 1861 – d. 1944 aged 83] eldest daughter to Vaughan Palmer Davies, of Skomer Island, Pembrokeshire.

On Tuesday the 14th February 1888 at St. Martin's Church, Haverfordwest by the Rev. Canon Preedy, cousin of the bridegroom, assisted by the Rev. J. H. Poppelwell, William Fulshaw, of Earl Shilton, Hanckley, Leicestershire, to Annie Maud, aged 25 [b. 1865 – d. 1944 aged 79] youngest daughter to Vaughan Palmer Davies, [aged 62] of Skomer Island.

This wedding was the most Fashionable Wedding seen in Haverfordwest for many a year. Some stir was created in Haverfordwest on Tuesday by the marriage of William Fulshaw, of Earl Shilton, Hinckley, with Miss. Annie Maud Davies, of Skomer Island, Pembrokeshire. On account of the fickle temper of Father Neptune, it was necessary that the bride should leave her island home at a reasonable time before the day fixed for the ceremony. In order to be thoroughly independent of the ruling spirit of the "sad waves," Miss. Davies and her friends have for some time resided at the Castle Hotel, Haverfordwest.

It was from this hotel yesterday that the wedding party left for St. Martin's church, where the marriage was duly solemnized. The sun shone brilliantly while the bridal party stood at the altar. The scene is described by eye witnesses as one of unusual impressiveness' and grandeur.

The ceremony was performed by the Rev. Cannon Preedy cousin of the bridegroom, assisted by the Rev. J. H. Poppelwell, vicar. The groomsmen were Mr. Herbert Fisher, of Denant; Mr. Graham Harvey, of Broadmoor; and Mr. Davies, of Newton (uncle of the bride.) The bridesmaids were Miss. Davies, of Skomer Island; Miss. Wilkinson, of Penarth; and Miss. E. Fisher, of Denant.

After the ceremony the wedding party returned to the Castle Hotel, where the bridal breakfast was laid. The tables were spread for about 30 guests, and were laid out with admirable taste, the decorations being exceedingly effective.

The wedding presents were very numerous, and many of them exceedingly costly. The bride's trousseau was supplied by Messsrs. Greenish and Dawkins, of Haverfordwest. Honeymoon; the bride and bride-groom left by the midday train en route for London.

SKOMER DEATHS

You can die on Skomer Island but not be buried there, or on Skokholm or Ramsey Islands. Because there isn't any consecrated ground on these islands. If someone dies on any of these islands, then the body has to be taken over to the mainland for burial on church consecrated ground. The exception being Caldey Island, Caldey has a Monastery, church and consecrated ground.

MAGISTRATES COURT & PAYMENT OF SCHOOL RATES

April 1880.   The Magistrates were getting upset with costs, and had just been presented with a bill for £16 6s and the Clerk of the Court Mr. L. Mathias added: *'There is another Case which I have to bring before you bye and bye: a charge of 4s, by P.C. Griffiths for hire of boat to serve a school board order on Skomer Island'.*

[Mr. Vaughan Davies has been objecting to paying the school part of the rates, for some time and he wanted Skomer Island to change to another parish].

ST. MARTIN'S PARISH. December 1881, Vaughan Davies tried to move parishes, but it was decided that the Island of Skomer stays in St. Martin's parish.

NON-PAYMENT OF SKOMER ISLAND RATES - A NOVEL POINT

Basics of this case are 'Vaughan Palmer Davies' objected paying part of the rates, 'the school board part'. Then as you read on you'll see the problem, collector of rates has a point, he's got to go to Skomer Island, to collect the money, and he might be stranded on the island if the weather blows up, Vaughan says he might be stuck on the mainland if the weather blows up too, read on and enjoy.

These sessions were held in the Roose Petty Sessions Shire-Hall, on Saturday 8th March 1884, before Mr. Carrow, Mr. G. Leader Owen, and Mr. Joseph Thomas.

Mr. Vaughan P. Davies, (now aged 58) of Skomer Island, was charged by Mr. J. Roch Phillips, collector of rates for the parish of St. Martin's, with non-payment of rates.

Vaughan Davies: *In answer to the charge, said that the rates were not made correctly and in the second place that the rates had never been called for.*

Mr. J. Roch Phillips: *collector of rates; produced the rate books, and said he had served a demand note for the rates on Mr. Vaughan Davies on a fair day at Haverfordwest, but he declined to accept it. He afterwards sent him a letter; he enclosed the demand note in it, and registered the letter. He received no reply to his letter.*

Vaughan Davies: *objected to pay school board rates, which he thought was a reasonable objection, and suggested that he should make an application to the Local Government Board to be relieved from the School rates.*

Mr. J. Roch Phillips: *collector of rates. The rates had been properly made, and the defendant had not appealed against them.*

Vaughan Davies: *said there was a difference in the calculation as to the amount of rates, but that was not of importance, and need not be considered. It was probable he had received the demand note in the registered letter, but he must have missed it. He applied to the Local Government Board, and received a reply, from which he held he was relieved from payment of school rates from the 21st of July.*

Magistrates ordered Mr. Vaughan Palmer Davies to pay his rates in full.

Vaughan Davies: *He wished to know whether the collector was not bound to come to him for the money.*

Clerk of the Court: *said that was a point which he should like to have time to consider. He did not think the creditor was bound to go to the house of the debtor, and it might happen that if the collector went to Skomer Island, he might be detained there for some weeks.* (Laughter).

Vaughan Davies: *said that if I came to Haverfordwest, I might be unable to get back to the island for some weeks. The collector if he gets detained on the Island, he still gets paid for collecting the rates.* (Loud laughter).

Clerk of the Court: *said he would consider the question.*

The Bench adjourned the case for a fortnight.

Judgment of the Court

Vaughan Davies in Court for None Payment of Rates

The sessions were held in the Roose Petty Sessions, Shire Hall, on Saturday 22 March 1884; before Mr. Carrow, Mr. G. Leader Owen and Mr. Joseph Thomas.

In the case of Mr. J. R. Phillips, collector of rates for the parish of St. Martin's, v. Mr. V. Davies, of Skomer Island, the Court give judgment in favour of Mr. J. R. Phillips, collector of rates; ordering the rates to be paid by Vaughan Davies in full with costs.

[Vaughan Davies had lost; he then had to pay all rates owed, court expenses and other costs. I wonder if they did go to the island to collect. I know you'll agree with me when I say, what a character our Vaughan Palmer Davies was, I would have loved to have met the man, he really makes me laugh, with his dry humor, he could even made the whole court laugh out loud].

Plans Are Afoot For the Largest Yearly Show in Pembrokeshire
This reads Who's Who In Pembrokeshire:
The Dinner in early December 1882.
[Background; these gentlemen are the Largest land owners in Pembrokeshire, they met up to get the Pembrokeshire Show started, you see on the list Pembrokeshire who's who in the money, and land owners, you'll see our Vaughan Davies. The who's who of Pembrokeshire].
Lord Kensington M.P. presided at the dinner which was held at the Swans Inn, Haverfordwest. The following gentlemen were also present: Mr. C. E. G. Philipps, Lord-Lieutenant of the town of the county of Haverfordwest; Sir Owen Scourfield; Mr. William Davies, M.P; Mr. Fisher, Dennant; Mr. Scone, Haroldston Hall; Mr. Essex Harris, Scolton; **Mr. Davies, Skomer Island**; Mr. Joseph Thomas, Haverfordwest; Mr. Thomas James, Haverfordwest; Mr. Wathen, Marloes Court; Mr. Harris, jun., Rickeston; &c. The usual toasts having been given, the Chairman, in proposing "The Health of the Vice Chairman," (Mr. C. E. G. Philipps), stated that it was to be hoped that he would be able, in conjunction with the Lord-Lieutenant of Haverfordwest, to carry out the plan of having a large County Show at Haverfordwest.

HAVERFORDWEST ART CLASS, In February 1886, Miss Davies [Vaughan Davies daughter] of Skomer Island sent one of her oil painting to the Art Exhibition. On the day Lady Kensington came to distribute the prizes to the winners, a big cheer went up as Lady Kensington entered the hall. M.P. Lord Kensington was detained on business elsewhere. Miss Davies won a prize for her painting; she had won a few prizes over the years for her paintings that she had sent to exhibition.
[Can any reader help me; I would like dearly to trace any of the paintings by Miss. Davies of Skomer Island. Which daughter it is I cannot tell]

THE LOCAL NEWSPAPER PEMBROKESHIRE Herald dated Friday 28 September 1888, printed a letter from Mr. Vaughan Davies, he states:
Sir, -- There was a Woodcock caught on Skokholm Island on the 20th September, I believe it is the first of the season.
Yours truly,
Vaughan P. Davies. (Aged 62)
Skomer Island, Sept. 23rd, 1888.

VAUGHAN DAVIES OF SKOMER ISLAND asks Haverfordwest Board of Guardians, for a change of parish. A meeting of members of this Board was held in the Board Room on Wednesday 24th October 1888.
[As an insight into the times, before his request come up the Master reported (something interesting) that the number of paupers in the Haverfordwest House was 99: the number in the corresponding week last year was 108] Now let's move onto Vaughan Davies request.

The Clerk read a letter from Mr. Vaughan Davies, Skomer Island, in which he stated that it would be inconvenient to him to be included in the County Council list of voters for St. Martin's (to which parish Skomer Island belonged), and asked that his name be transferred to the list for Marloes or St. Bride's. The Chairman said that the Guardians had no power to deal with this matter. He suggested that the Clerk should be instructed to inform Mr. Davies that the Guardians had no power to transfer from one parish to another.

Mr. Walters said: Mr. Davies had better wait until the County Council is elected: they have the power to rectify their own boundaries.

PEMBROKESHIRE HERALD NEWSPAPER. Friday 8 March 1889 this advertisement appeared, Mr. Vaughan Davies is selling Skomer Seeds.......

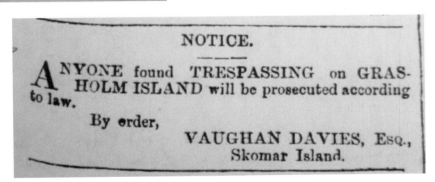

HALLETT'S PEDIGREE SEED OATS.

MR. DAVIES, of SKOMER ISLAND, supplies the Second Year's produce of HALLETT'S PEDIGREE BLACK TARTARIAN OATS for Seed, at 2s. 6d for 38 lbs, delivered at EAST HOOK, MARLOES, in purchasers sacks. Mr. DAVIES will deliver any quantity over 50 Winchesters at HAVERFORDWEST, for 2s. 8d. for 38 lbs.
Skomer Island, Feb. 29, 1889.

[THE PEMBROKESHIRE HERALD NEWSPAPER June 1890 carried these advertisements Vaughan P. Davies is now aged 64, and had just a few years left before leaving Skomer Island]

NOTICE.

ANYONE found TRESPASSING on GRASHOLM ISLAND will be prosecuted according to law.

By order,

VAUGHAN DAVIES, Esq.,
Skomar Island.

LETTER FROM MUMBLES 1895

"Pembrokeshire still takes the cake," wrote Mr. Vaughan P. Davies [he's now aged 69] living at 2 Church Park, Oystermouth, Mumbles. [He's now living at Oystermouth, Mumbles which is five miles west, of Swansea] these few words appeared on Friday September 1895 in a local paper

"I was the only occupier of the parish of Skokholm for many years. It had only one house, and I only occupied it for one month in each year." So that the Vaughan Davies Parish Council would be scarcely qualified to vote. Still, in parish meetings he could bring himself in from outside to act as chairman.

[Vaughan Palmer Davies had left Skomer Island in 1892 aged 66]

Mr. Vaughan Palmer Davies died on Monday 11th May 1914, peacefully with his family around him. Vaughan P. Davies (b. 1826 - d. 1914 aged 87).

[A year earlier Angelica Ellen Robinson had passed away on 25 March 1913 at Sunnyside, Narborough, Leicestershire]

Mr. Vaughan Palmer Davies, of Sunnyside, Narborough, Leicestershire, and late of Skomer Island, Pembrokeshire, and of 2 Church Park, Oystermouth, Mumbles, Swansea; who died Monday 11th May 1914, aged 87 years. The gross value of his estate being £1,388. Probate has been granted to his daughter Mrs. Annie Maud Fulshaw, and his son, Mr. Charles Edward Davies, Bank Manager, at Carmarthen.

While researching Skomer and our Vaughan P. Davies, I came onto this sad news. I was really saddened to learn this. 'I', or should I say 'we', we all have all taken this journey, we have followed Vaughan P. Davies and I think we really became part of his family. And how he made us laugh out loud some times. Remember that court case about rates, when he said,

"That if I came to Haverfordwest, I might be unable to get back to the island for some weeks. On the other hand the collector if he was detained on the Island, he still gets paid for collecting the rates". (Court burst out laughing).[Just Brilliant!]

Then this has to be the best one liner of Skomer Island ever, the one about nonpayment of wages, when the Magistrate Mr. O. E. Davies said this about Skomer Island:

"I think £6 is a very small wages to go on the island [then adding this one liner]:-

"I would as soon myself; be transported to the deserts of Siberia as go to Skomer Island."

Then the whole court burst out with laughter, [I burst out laughing as well] but it has to be the best description I have ever, ever heard of Skomer Island, just brilliant, just brilliant. We followed his family growing up, the marriages of his sons and daughters. Also the building up his farm by buying and selling seeds and cattle, then the sad deaths for his workers while crossing to the mainland. We saw good times and we saw bad times, we became part of the Vaughan Palmer Davies Skomer Island family. Now, with his death, I feel it's the end of an era, I hope you understand what I mean.

[Doing my research, I think I got to close to Vaughan P. Davies, I had forgotten the first rule of researching. Do not get close to the subject; sorry, but I had]

POACHING ON SKOMER ISLAND.

Cardiff Times Newspaper reports on Saturday 2 May 1908

Two Cardiffians [Cardiff] have been fined 10s and costs, a total of £1 10s 6d each, for landing at Skomer Island, Pembroke, in pursuit of seabirds in the close season. Skomer Island is occupied by Mr. J. J. Neale, of Penarth. [Note; the name of the occupier of Skomer Island is now Mr. J. J. Neale].

INTERESTING FACTS ABOUT SKOMER ISLAND.

- ❖ Skomer Island got its name by the Vikings; Skomer roughly translation means: short dagger or short sword.
- ❖ In the 12th century 'Skomer' was spelt "Skalmeye,"

❖ Anne Boleyn second wife of Henry VIII; September 1st 1532 Anne Boleyn became Marquees of Pembroke, this brought Anne in an annual income from Wales of over £1,000 per annum; this included rents from the islands of Caldey, Skokholm, Skomer, and Ramsey.

❖ June 1st 1533 Anne became Queen of England, and then in May 19th 1536 was executed.

c. July	c.	1501	Born in Kent, England.
September	1st	1532	Became Marquees of Pembroke.
January	25th	1533	Married King Henry VIII.
June	1st	1533	Became Queen
September	7th	1533	Baby Elizabeth born
May	19th	1536	Executed; by a Frenchman.

Anne's Age when executed between 28 - 35 years. Anne's date of birth is thought to be around 1501.

❖ Because of the amount of shipping losses in Jack Sound, shipping insurance companies would have a clause in their insurance saying; no insurance cover one mile before you entered Jack Sound, and till you were one mile past Jack Sound. This started commercial shipping not using Jack Sound.

❖ Captain Vaughan P. Davies married Ellen Robinson in Bombay in 1858, in 1864 when he was 35 years old, he leased Skomer Island, and for the next 30 years he farmed the island, with his wife.

SKOMER ISLAND HISTORY.

Around 4,000 years ago, living on Skomer Island were about 150 to 200 people. That has been worked out by number of the round houses and the estimated number of people per round house. Why would anyone want to live on Skomer Island 4,000 years ago? Let's start off with – It's got a sea view. But, seriously the sea view could save lives. What I mean is inhabitants could see who was approaching the island from a long way off. Times then were very rough and defence was of great importance. Skomer was a natural fortress with high cliffs which made it easy to defend. There were no dangerous animals on the island either. On the main land, the forests were so dense it was said that a man could go from one end of Britain to the other, tree to tree, without touching the ground. Britain was one big forest, with trees a metre apart. Light could not penetrate the tree canopy and the forest was a dark and frightening place to be 4,000 years ago. The mainland was not a safe place to be. Apart from the warring tribes, there were animals that wanted to kill and eat you, such as Cave Bears and Brown Bears, and the main animal that humans respected as their equal, the Wolf, some packs of Wolves could be 40 strong.

Living on Skomer Island you're never short of water; it is said these streams never run dry even in the longest of droughts. So there you have it: Nice round houses to live in, good defence, no dangerous animals and clean drinking water. As for food, the inhabitants were spoilt for choice: fish, birds, eggs, seals, shell fish, seaweed and a field system was also known to be on Skomer, so you had crops, and the animals were kept to eat. It sounds quite idyllic.

But there's always a downside to living 4,000 years ago. The tough lifestyle meant a life expectancy of about 35 years; you could die from a simple cut, or illness. On the main land you have dangerous snakes and animals' that wanted to kill and eat you. Skomer, there are no dangerous animals or snakes like Wolves or Adders. The good old British weather. Britain was going through a cold wet period 4,000 years ago [ideal if you're a tree]. British weather was a problem even that far back!

SKOMER & PIRATE PROBLEMS:

In the 16th, 17th and early 18th century pirates posed a big problem around the coast of Pembrokeshire. To plough Skomer Island fields with horse or oxen, and plough. The animal and plough were brought across from the mainland, and then once ploughing was finished, they had to be taken straight back to the main land. They would not be kept on the island longer than necessary. The pirates would steal the plough, and most likely, eat the horse or oxen.

A good example of the French eating Skomer Island animals occurred on the west side of Skomer. There is a place known as Bull Hole, and this is how it got its name in the late 17th century. French Pirates landed on Skomer Island and raided the farm house. They took the bull, which had been brought over to pull the plough, to the cove on the west side of the island, standing it at the cliff edge then pushed the poor animal over the cliff and into the sea. A waiting ship, took it aboard where it was killed, cooked and eaten. After that incident the cove was called: "Bull Hole."

SKOMER ISLAND SHIPWRECKS

Skomer Island's Boat Accident

Going to or leaving Skomer has claimed a number of lives over the years, on Friday 14th September 1827, as a small sailing boat (gig), was coming from Skomer Island, it was blowing fresh at the time, she was upset and sank, just at the entrance of Milford Haven, Mr. Philip Jones, of Houghton, near Neyland a respectable gentleman, of some property, and a boy, servant of Mr. Rowe, of the Island, were both drowned.

The boat a gig, belonging to Mr. Brown, Pilot of Hakin, has since been recovered. It is supposed they had too much sail on for a boat of her description.

FATAL BOATING ACCIDENT

On Monday 19th June 1837, a party of about 12 gentlemen from Milford, Haverfordwest, and neighbourhoods, went in the WATERLOO pilot smack, owned by James John Jun., to visit Skomer Island, from Milford, on a pleasure party, and anchored in a sheltered part of the island.

About four in the afternoon, they had all embarked from the island, and got the smack under way when, tacking, they got into difficulties owing to the head sails getting entangled, and the wind pushed them onto the Skomer Island rocks.

Many of the party escaped after undergoing a sound ducking, and some were severely bruised; but James John, the master and branch pilot, a boy named Thomas Thomas, belonging also to the vessel, an Irish gentleman of the name of Powers, who had been staying at the Nelson Hotel, Milford for three or four years past, and Lock, a block-maker at Hakin, were all drowned. – The body of Mr. Powers was picked up the same day. The vessel was totally wrecked and a good deal washed ashore.
A month later the bodies of Mr. Lock, block-maker, and Mr. James John, pilot, both of Hakin, have been picked up and entered in their parish, at Hubberstone.

THE BRIG THOMAS, of and for Chepstow, master Williams, was totally lost on Skomer Island, in St. Bride's Bay, during the tremendous gale on the 3rd February 1843. Very little of the wreck has been picked up. The body of a young man from 19 to 23 years of age was found near the spot, from which it is believed that the crew of the unfortunate vessel were all lost.

SKOMER ISLAND'S IDEAL SHIPWRECK.
This is the type of shipwreck they preferred on Skomer Island.
Saturday 11th April 1840 the SARAH of Liverpool, under the command of Master Doyle. On voyage from Bristol for Liverpool. Because of gale force winds and heavy seas, Master Doyle thought it best to call in and stayed at Dale Roads, in Milford Haven, till the gales past. Then she sailed out on Saturday morning, but she ran into thick fog and the winds died away. Then taken by the tide, and wrecked on Skomer Island. Now, why did Skomer Island folk like this sort of wreck? Well let's take a look at the ship's cargo the SARAH was carrying: Olive oil, "Wine", Gum, Vinegar, Cider, and Bale goods. [I bet Skomer folk said, you can keep the gum, but more wine next time].

Part of the cargo floated around St. Bride's Bay. I think the locals were kept busy in St. Bride's Bay for the next couple of days, cleaning up the beaches. They use to say, that on Skomer Island, "you could eat some exotic fruits; oranges, pomegranates, bananas and pineapples, furthermore drank the finest wines [I can't think why people said that?] Oh yes; and the SARAH crew, well they jumped into their rowing boat and rowed to Skomer Island, told the inhabitants of their plight, then mentioned they had a valuable cargo on board. Suddenly, with enthusiasm, they strongly, very strongly encouraged them for their own safety they must head right now for Milford Haven, before the next gale comes in. [It's good to see Skomer Island people thinking of the crews safety, especially with that gale that's about, any time soon, maybe today or tomorrow, next week, or? but it's soon. Could it have nothing to do with getting rid of the crew, no crew, no witnesses? Are you also wondering if it's anything to do with that valuable cargo? Wine? Surely not]

ECHO OF LIVERPOOL

Later in the year near High Cliffs on the south side of Skomer Island, the ECHO of Liverpool was wrecked, Master Hobbs. Bearing up for Milford, on Monday 23 November 1840, this brigantine was pushed by the dangerous currents onto the south side of Skomer Island, she became a total wreck. The crew had only time to jump into the rowing boat to save their lives. After landing on Skomer and looked after by farm servants of Mr. Lloyd Philipps of Dale Castle.

PERSEVERANCE of Carnarvon

On Wednesday 1st December 1845 the 45 ton sloop PERSEVERANCE of Carnarvon, North Wales, built in 1803 under the command of Captain Morris Evans, sailed from Falmouth, at eight o'clock in the morning for Dublin, with a cargo of sand for glass manufacturing and empty porter casks. On the following day; Thursday, a most tremendous storm arose, which continued without intermission for many hours. Friday, about five o'clock in the evening, she lost her bowsprit, jib, and foresails, bulwarks and stanchions, had her boat on the deck smashed to pieces, and the chain-cables washed over the side, she had become completely water-logged, [to name but a few problems. Oh, yes; I forgot to mention all this damaged was caused by hitting the South Bishops Rock].

I can now tell you this vessel was then completely at the mercy of the waves and currents, being driven into St. Bride's Bay then taken south into Jack Sound, where she struck rocks on the main land side just before midnight on Friday 3 December 1845.

In the short time before she went aground, William Roberts, one of the crew, was washed overboard. On the vessel striking, David Williams and Robert Evans were both drowned. Captain Morris Evans, watched in horror as the vessel was broken up underneath his feet into three pieces, the part he was standing on was carried onto the east side of Jack Sound [main land side] and cast onto the bottom of the cliffs, at deer park owned by Mr. W. C. A. Phillips, Esq.

The spot being rather lonely, with steep cliffs all round the poor fellow was left at the bottom of the cliffs until nine o'clock on Sunday morning before he was discovered, still at the bottom of the cliffs [that's 33 hours exposed to the winds, rain plus it's the middle of winter, let's be honest he's lucky to be alive]. Once pulled up the cliffs, he was unable to walk, from the bruises he had received, he was carried to the farm house of Mr. James Jones, farmer, who in a most kind and considerate manor, having sent for the Doctor. Captain Morris Evans was in a shockingly state, cut and bruised all over, from having several times attempted to climb the cliff, then getting so far up the cliffs, his strength give out and down he would fall. The crews four in number were all natives of Carnarvon, North Wales.

Let this be known; Pembrokeshire Farmer James Jones, when offered money for payment for food and lodgings furthermore for bring back to health the shipwrecked Captain; he would not take a penny.

[Photo: Captain Morris Evans was found sitting at the bottom of these steep cliffs]

DESTRUCTIVE STORM

From the various accounts received from different parts of the Kingdom, that this storm which visited South West Wales on Wednesday, and the hurricane of the following day, have been felt throughout Britain, particularly along the Pembrokeshire coast, and have been attended with the loss of a vast deal of property, besides human life.

About midnight on Wednesday 14th September 1842, the schooner FALKIRK, of and from Grangemouth, laden with cast iron beams, to be used in the building of fortifications at Pembroke Dock, in Milford Haven, came to anchor off Skomer Island. They were compelled to do this in consequence of the weather being thick and very dark, and perfectly calm. But before they could lower the anchor, the spring tide set her on the island, where she has become a complete wreck. The crew escaped into the rowing boat with only what clothes they could lay their hands on, and rowed to the nearest land, which proved to be a rock about 100 metres off Skomer Island. It was the calm before the storm, too surely announced by the peculiar atmosphere which precedes a tempest. Within an hour it came to blow hard form the N.N.W., accompanied by torrents of rain, the sea making a breach over the rock. The crew remained exposed holding onto the rock all night. At daylight, when the flow of the tide compelled then to again take to their rowing boat, and after much difficulty they safely landed on Skomer Island, where they were kindly entertained by the tenant of James Summers, Esq. The crew with the exception of the master remained by the wreck, the Captain left on the following day for Milford, to return with the steam tug boat SS TROUBUDOUR which took the crew off Skomer Island, to Milford.

Very little of the cargo can be saved, as the bottom of the vessel is knocked out.

ONE YEAR, EIGHT MONTHS LATER the local newspaper announces:
TO BE SOLD BY PUBLIC AUCTION.
(For the benefit of whom it may concern,)
AT HAKIN,
On THURSDAY, the 11th day of APRIL, 1844,
AT one o'clock,
About forty-five tons of cast iron,
Girders, Joists, and Bearing Plates,
of different lengths, saved from the Schooner FALKIRK
wrecked on Skomer Island.
The above are well worth the attention of Builders.
HENRY MERRITT.
AUCTIONEER.
Milford, April 2, 1844.

SLATE WRECK, but the dog finds heaven

The sloop LETITIA, of Llanelly, Master Davies, from Carnarvon, bound for Carmarthen, laden with slates, in coming through Jack's Sound, at 10.30 p.m., on Sunday 14th December 1845. She suddenly became unmanageable, in consequence of the south stream running very strong and the vessel having about an hour previous split her mainsail and foresail. She was thrown with great violence against the Midland Rock and sank in about five minutes. The mate and apprentice (the captain's son), leaped on to Midland Island, but before the captain could do so, a wave pushed the vessel off. He however, jumped off the bows and succeeded in swimming to the island safety.

As soon as the master jumped she went down stern foremost. The ships dog was also saved, Midland Island, for the dog was a dogs heaven on earth, the island is full of rabbits, and the dog was happily chasing rabbits, what the dog caught the crewmen would cook and eat, which was the only food the three crewmen tasted during the eighteen hours they were on the Midland Island. They remained on the Midland Island till the following afternoon, when they were picked up by a boat which was proceeding to Skokholm Island. As the local boat took off the survivors, and sailed for Milford Haven only one of the survivors sitting at the back of the boat was looking back sadly at Midland Island, the only one who did not want to leave Midland island, and that was the dog.

WRECKED AT PIG STONE BAY

Wrecked at Pig Stone Bay on the west side of Skomer Island on Saturday 21st May 1932.Schooner PERSEVERANCE. Vessel of 98 tons. Built 1882. Irish owned. Captain Rouney. While on passage from Ireland for Newport, South Wales to collect a cargo was wrecked at Pig Stone Bay, the crew of three took to rowing boat taking the ships dog with them and landed safely at Marloes Sands.

LONSDALE of Belfast. Sunday 23rd October 1938
Berehaven for Padstow. Captain J. Hegarty of 39, Orchard Street, Swansea. Owner Michael O'Sullivan of Swansea. Vessel of 500 tons.GT 221. Built 1904 by W. J. Yarwood, of Northwich.
Steamer ran out of coal in St. Bride's Bay. Coal loaded at Martins Haven, she then steamed for Milford, as she went through Jack Sound, her steering gear parted in heavy seas, she ran onto the east side of Middle Island.

[Photograph of the SS LONSDALE on the rocks on the north east side of Middle Island. Discovered the wreck in 1990, she's well broken up]

Captain J. Hegarty. The crew was all saved, by Betty Justin, her husband, T. R. Codd and by her father W. S. Stuart, owner of Skokholm Island, who used a small boat to bring the crew safely (four in their boat and towed the other two in ships long boat) ashore at Martins Haven. It was pitch dark when they got to Martins Haven, and they had to land by torches. (Wales own Grace Darling)
T. Potter, 145 Rodney Street, Swansea. (First Engineer)
A. Mattison, 4 Mount Street, Swansea. (Second engineer)
The other three from Ireland.

PEMBROKESHIRE NAME PROBLEMS

While researching Maritime History, I always come onto this problem of names of the rocks and islands off Pembrokeshire's coast. Their names seem to change every ten years or so, it's really annoying.

For example the island between Skomer and the mainland, has been written as 'Middle Island,' or 'Middleholm' or 'Midland Island' or 'Sailor's Rock' or even 'Broad Island.' Keeping this in mind with the next story.

SKOMER SAILOR'S ROCK DISASTER.

Seven young men left St. David's (Porth Clais), on Sunday 20th June 1866, in a pleasure boat. They were overtaken by a strong gale of wind, which bore them south towards Skomer Island, where they were seen late in the evening. On Monday evening the St. David's lifeboat went in search, but little hope is entertained of their being discovered, as none of them were capable of managing the boat in such a sea as that on Sunday.

One of the men was John Morgan, stonemason, of St. David's. The other six belonged to the Ordnance Survey Company.

A later report says: -- The seven men who left St. David's on Sunday on a yachting excursion, and whose non-return excited much grave apprehensions, have been discovered. It seems that the gale which sprung up after they started carried then across St. Bride's Bay, a distance of nearly ten miles, and their boat struck on Sailor's Rock, [They mean Midland Island] in Jack Sound, which lies between Skomer and the main land. Fortunately they succeeded in landing on the rock, where they lighted a fire, and made themselves comfortable for the night. Next day they killed some birds, which they roasted and ate.

Meantime their boat had drifted away and been picked up by the lifeboat which had been sent from St. David's in search of them. There was every prospect of their having to spend a second night on the rock when, happily, some Martin's Haven fishermen observed them, took them off, and landed them at Martins Haven. The six who belonged to the Ordnance Survey Company, immediately proceeded to walk to St. David's, a distance of 25 miles, which place they reached Tuesday morning. All their friends had given them up for as lost.

SHIP ON FIRE

The "SS FIONA" of Liverpool, caught fire on the evening of Thursday 10th April 1873; while on passage from Newport, South Wales for Liverpool, England with a cargo of coal.

The ship was cleverly run ashore at South Haven, on Skomer Island, where she sunk in a bid to extinguish the fire, which was confined to the after part of the vessel. The course thus adopted ultimately proved the saving of the ship, the cargo, and the lives of the crew, who, with the exception of the steward, who was rather badly burned, all fortunately escaped uninjured.

On the news of what had happened being brought to Milford by the Captain of the ill-fated craft, a steamer was immediately engaged by Lloyd's agent and dispatched to the scene of the disaster. On her arrival at Skomer every effort was made to save all that was possible from the wreck, and which was taken to Milford. This went on day after day, with eventual success, and on Thursday the ship was lifted by the aid of steam pumps and divers, and then towed into Milford, where she is undergoing temporary repairs to enable her to proceed to Liverpool.

The bottom of the steamer is so badly damaged that it is a wonder to many how she was ever got from such a place as Skomer Island, (where she lay with rocks through her) and taken safely into Milford Haven.

Lloyds Agent said afterwards: This case, indeed, does credit to those were engaged in saving such valuable property, and the success will be most certainly appreciated by the underwriters; so much for perseverance, skill, and appliances.

FISHERMAN'S PREMONITION

Sad drowning accident off Marloes. A remarkable story is told by Marloes villagers. On Friday 5th July 1895, Patrick Collins, a well built and strong fisherman met his death on the north side of Skomer Island. He was filled with for some time before the fatal day, with the premonition that his end by drowning was very near. Indeed, a few nights before the accident, he had a dream in which, he stated to his friends, he saw the fishing boat capsizing and himself drowning. Before going to sea in Warlow'sboat he declared that he was almost persuaded not to go in her; but he heeded not the premonition, and went, with his sad drowning.

CREW OF TWENTY PERISHED

Telegram from Lisbon, Portugal says. – Much regret has been caused by the news of the loss of the Lisbon vessel VENUS, which was seen to founder with all hands on Skomer rocks in the gale on Wednesday 9th October 1896.   The crew numbered twenty souls.

LIFE IS ONE CIRCLE.

In 1917 the newspaper Haverfordwest & Milford Haven Telegraph advertised; TO LET, On Michaelmas Day, [29th September] SKOMER ISLAND FARM – 100 Acres Arable, over 600 Acres rough grazing. Good Buildings. – Apply, Agent, Kensington Estate Offices, St. Bride's, Little Haven, Pembrokeshire. [The last time Skomer was advertised in the local newspaper "TO LET" was on Friday 19 July 1817, "100 years earlier" life is one circle].

HMS LEDA shipwrecked at Angle Beach:

HMSLEDA Wrecked at West Angle Bay on Monday evening 1st February 1808

[Painting by Harold Wyllie of the frigate HMS LEDA frigate under full sail. Built 1800 at Chatham Dockyard and had a crew of 284]

This frigate was fast, maneuverable and powerfully armed; she was equipped with 38 pounder guns. HMS LEDA was officially ranked as a 5th rate frigate, though in reality when handled properly, the ship was capable of taking on a ship-of-the- line at close range.

HMS LEDA was patrolling the Irish Sea, searching for French and American Privateers. These privateers were working for the French, or, more to the point, they were working for the 'Monster' Napoleon Bonaparte as he was known by the British. Privateers were licensed by the French government to take British shipping.
"Gales had been raging for days and the frigate had been badly damaged. She needed to head for Milford Haven to have the damage's repaired. As they entered Milford Haven pilot James Garretty, mistook Thorn Island for Stack Rocks.
James Garretty the Pilot ordered the helms man to turn starboard [right] she went straight onto West Angle Beach in gales force winds, with huge seas going over the

wrecked frigate. Captain Robert Honeyman ordered the masts to be cut away, and then all cannons to be thrown overboard. Nothing could save the ship, she became a total wreck."

[Thorn Island Fort, at the entrance to Milford Haven. Photograph taken on a summer's day, in 2014, but, when HMS LEDA arrived in February 1808, there was a bad gale blowing with poor visibility (about 150 yards) and heavy rain. In 1801 there was no fort on the island]

[This advertisement appeared in the Cambrian newspaper dated Saturday 6th February 1808] HMS LEDA has lost some of its not so happy crew!

> ## To Magistrates, Constables, &c.
>
> SEVERAL Seamen belonging to his Majesty's Ship Leda, which struck on the rocks, near Milford, on Monday evening last, having deserted, and are now straggling about the country, the Magistrates and Constables are particularly requested to apprehend every such Seaman who may be found within their several divisions, and immediately convey them to the nearest Rendezvous, or give notice to the Regulating Officers, who will take measures for their security.
>
> THREE POUNDS will be paid for every Deserter so taken, in addition to travelling expences.
>
> THOMAS NEW, Regulating-Captain, Swansea.

[It seems our press ganged men decided to leave HM Navy, while they had the opportunity, with all the confusion on West Angle beach. Normal practice of HM war ships was when near British land was to lock up the press ganged men below. You might be surprised at this. Press ganged men if given half a chance would jump over the side and swim for shore. I don't think they were too keen to be in HM Navy]

A Court Martial held on board "SALVADOR DEL MUNDO" Captain Robert Honeyman and his entire crew was acquitted of all blame. Court found that the Pilot was to blame. He had mistaken Thorn Island for the Stack Rocks and in the poor visibility with heavy rain, had laid the wrong course. [He turned right before he should have a simple honest mistake].

The Cambrian Newspaper on Saturday 27th February 1808; Announced: Sale by Public Auction, to be sold to the Best Bidders, this was to take place at Pembroke Dock-yard on 24 March 1808. The ship was said to be lying at West Angle Bay, near the entrance of Milford Haven. The navy was looking for £1,000 for the wreck. No one bide even close to this figure. The navy then used her salvaged timbers in the building of a few other war ships over the coming years, at Pembroke Dock.

Cambrian newspaper dated Saturday 12th March 1808. This really interesting advertisement about the HMS LEDA ships stores coming up for auction. Gives us some idea of what was carried on an average war ship of the day to feed 300 men in 1808.

ter of this Paper, Swansea.

MILFORD.

TO BE SOLD BY AUCTION,

On Wednesday, the 23d of March inst. at eleven o'clock in the forenoon, by order of the Honourable Commissioners for Victualling his Majesty's Navy,

THE following PROVISIONS and STORES, saved from the Wreck of his Majesty's Ship LEDA: 1119 Gallons of RUM, in puncheons, hogsheads, and barrels; 728 Gallons of RED WINE, in hogsheads and barrels; 670 Pieces (of 8 pounds each) of SALT BEEF, in casks; 1852 Pieces (of 4 pounds each) of SALT PORK, in casks; 4391 Pounds of FLOUR, in casks; 420 Pounds of SUGAR, in casks; 1088 Pounds of SUET, in casks; 313 Pounds of BUTTER, in casks; 80 Bushels of OATMEAL, in casks; 172 Pounds of LEMON JUICE; 43 Bottles of ditto; 3 Cases of ditto; 107 Gallons of VINEGAR, in casks; 210 Pounds of TOBACCO, in casks; 1710 BUTT STAVES; 400 PUNCHEON STAVES; 140 HOGSHEAD STAVES; 20 BARREL STAVES; 1060 HEADING PIECES; and 1706 IRON HOOPS.

For further particulars apply to Messrs. Thomas Philipps and Co. Contractors for Victualling his Majesty's Vessels in Milford; or to Henry Merritt, Auctioneer.

Let's do some sums, Rum: 1,119 gallons x 8 pints to a gallon = 8,952 pints, now let's divide by 300 seamen, why that's 29 pints of rum per seaman.

Wine, again let's do some more sums: 728 gallons x 8 pints to a gallon = 5,824 pints, divide by 300 seamen, and we have 19 pints per seaman. [Blimey! They must have been permanently drunk!]

In July 1808 the Superintendant of Quarantine, at Milford Captain John Williams, was presented with a handsome silver cup valued at 25 guineas, as a testimony of his conduct with his help and advice in saving much of the ship and lives. It was presented by Lords of the Admiralty.

OAK shipwrecked at Porthgwyn Rock, Solva:

SHIPWRECK AT SOLVA.

The OAK, of Belfast, a brig of 145 tons, under Master McConnell, and bound from Troon, Scotland to Cardiff, South Wales, was smashed to pieces in St Brides Bay at about 2 a.m., on Friday 17 October 1862. She had left Troon on Wednesday 8th September 1862. Because of unfavourable winds, put into Kingstown, Ireland. While sailing from there for Cardiff she was driven into the Bay by a violent gale from the W.S.W.

The captain let go of the anchor when he realised the vessel was approaching land, but the anchor dragged and she came broadside onto a rock on which the vessel, including the ship's long boat, were smashed to pieces. The crew abandoned the OAK, but without a long boat to escape in the only place they could go was onto the actual rock that had wrecked their ship. They held on all night, with waves sweeping over them.

About seven o'clock that morning, five men were seen on the rock by farm workers from St. Elvis farm. The survivors had spent the night on a rock at a little bay known as Porthgwyn, under St. Elvis farm, less than a mile to the east of Solva.

[Porthgwyn Bay, on a calm summer day, the rock 'centre bottom in the bay', is the rock the survivors held onto for over eight hours. The surf was coming up to the bottom of the cliffs. The island top left of centre is Green Scar. Let's be honest they were very lucky to be seen by the farm workers especially at seven in the morning]

Capt. J. Rees (Lloyd's Agent) was immediately contacted, and at once travelled to the spot with Manby's apparatus for saving life. But, unfortunately, in his haste, he took with him only three charges for the mortar, and they were wasted. [They were fired, and missed the rock] But he lost little time obtaining more. The fourth shot was fired, and it proved to be the lucky one. The line went straight over the rock and there was a chance for the crew to be saved.

The method they used to save those men was to shoot out a long line by mortar, and half way along this line was a lifebuoy. Those to be saved pulled the line with the lifebuoy attached and placed a person in the lifebuoy, and those on the shore pulled in the line.

Then, the line was pulled out. The crucial thing was not to let the line get tangled. The last man to put on the lifebuoy had to cut the line behind him, with no one to feed out the line it would surely get tangled up. Suffering from exposure and with their hands frozen, it was a very hard job to do, with waves coming over them.

Communication was established between those on the rock and the shore and having a line in place, a life buoy was attached to it. The survivors were signaled to draw it towards them, which they did as soon as they could.

The five crewmen were suffering badly from exposure. The life buoy arrived at the rock, but not one of the crew wanted to get into it and jump into the sea. The exposure had now got to them; they could not move their hands or hold onto the lifeline properly. In another hour they would be dead, that's how bad a condition they were in. They were starting not to care.

The mate, being the most adventurous, placed himself in the buoy and said, 'If I can do this, so can you.' And with that he jumped into the waves, and was pulled onto shore by the connecting line in just four minutes, shouting back to 'come on.' With the buoy pulled back to the rock, so the next man stepped into the buoy and jumped into the freezing water. By the time he was ashore, he was in a very bad state, two local men waded up to their armpits and kept his head up, as he had become unconscious; it was winter and he and the other survivors had been exposed to biting winds with waves going over them constantly for over 8 hours. This is how they arrived onshore, if it wasn't for those two men wading out, the survivors definitely would have drowned. The next was also brought ashore by this method, he also had become unconscious, with his head now underwater, again these two brave men David James of Solva and George Morgan of St. David's who were up to their armpits in cold winter seas, they lifted his head out of the water and saved another life.

[Once ashore they were hauled up these cliffs. This photo was taken on a summer's day, and the weather is perfect, you can imagine that morning, with surf reaching to the bottom of the cliffs, its winter, it's very cold]

Now, with only two left on the rock, the life buoy returned, it was now the turn of a 15 year old cabin boy, with the help of other crewman the buoy was placed around him. As he was about to jump, a gigantic wave covered them both. The boy was pushed under, and he was thrown back by the foaming sea onto the rock, and was left there for several seconds. The spectators thought he had been killed, but another wave floated him off, and he was soon landed. On shore, the two rescuers waded again into the surf up to their arm pits to get hold of each crewman. The crewmen did not even have the strength to save themselves and if it had not been for those two brave mariners from Solva and St. David's, going out to them in the surf, they would not have survived. Exposure by now had sapped all of their strength.

Now only one man was left on the rock he placed the lifebuoy over his head, and jumped – 'he must cut the line behind him if he was to be pulled to shore'. 'He did cut the line behind him'. As if repayment for the care he had taken of the cabin boy, and the other crewmen, an easier and quicker transit to shore followed.

Three of the survivors could not even speak, and two had fallen unconscious. They were taken to houses in Solva, I should say carried to houses in Solva, for they were in such a bad state. Given hot baths, dry clothes, and hot food and then put to bed. The survivors were in such a bad state, it was two weeks before they were fit enough to travel. They were given money and taken to Haverfordwest train station there they were put on trains and sent to their homes.

Mr. J. R. J. Nash, and Mr. W. R. Harries volunteered to seek for clothes for the ship-wrecked survivors, through the village of Solva. The result of their efforts was satisfactory. Sufficient clothing being obtained to clothe the five men. The good people of Solva, in 1862, were not that well off by any standards, but, still they shared what little they possessed.

Not enough praise can be awarded to John Howell, of Nine Wells, and George Griffiths, of Pointz Castle, Esqs, Doctors, for their kindness in attending to the poor sailors, also to John Williams, Esq., and Mr. John Owen, Solva, Samuel Williams, Esq., and Mr. W. Williams, St. David's.

The two brave mariners: David James, of Solva, and George Morgan, of St. David's, who ran out through the breakers, at great risk, to receive the men, so as to keep them from being knocked against the stones, up to their arm pits in winter temperature seas and surf. These two Pembrokeshire men were very brave men indeed.

The survivor's who stayed in local Solva homes, what did they have to pay the families for food, lodging's and for being nursed back to health? Let it be known that the Solva folk would not accept one penny, not one penny. "They are truly Pembrokeshire's Finest."

Tenby Twinned with OK Corral, Tombstone & Tenby shipwrecks:

WILD WEST TOWN OF TENBY

["WARNING; never cross the Mayor of Tenby, unless you're packing your six shooter!"]

Cambrian Newspaper, Saturday 6 April 1839; reports: -

GREAT SENSATION HAS BEEN CAUSED IN TENBY, owing to a duel, which took place on Cumfreston Farm, which lies just outside Tenby, at daylight on Monday morning 1st April 1839, between Mayor of Tenby Wm. Richards Esq., [b. 1796 – d. 1855] and Harry Mannix Esq. [b. 1798 – d. 1875] of the same place. Shots were exchanged and the Mayor received his adversary's shot in his side, and when hit fired in the air. The Mayor was taken to the farm-house, and then conveyed home in a post-chaise, accompanied by Mr. F. Smyth Esq.; his second. He now lies in a very precarious state, the ball not having been extracted by three or four of the most skilful medical men in the surrounding neighborhood.

Mr. Mannix and his second, Mr. Beecher, made their escape from the ground. The unfortunate occurrence took place owing to some altercation between the parties on Saturday last, relative to 'parish affairs'.

[The Mayor of Tenby did get better after the lead ball was removed, he lived another sixteen years. Another report says: he was shot in the groin; I bet that was Painful!].

ANOTHER SHOOT-OUT AT TENBY; [Now, 'The Wild West Tenby,' is definitely going to be twined with the 'Wild West O.K. Corral, Tombstone, Arizona']. And yes; it's the Mayor of Tenby 'again'.

The Cambrian Newspaper Saturday 10 September 1842 reports: - 'again!'

A HOSTILE MEETING TOOK PLACE AT TENBY, on Tuesday morning 6th September 1842, in a field near the town, between Mayor of Tenby Charles Cook Wells Esq., [b. 1801 – d. 1882] and Capt. Frances Rivers Freeling, [b. 1806 – d. 1865] Son of the late Sir Frances Freeling. Two shots were exchanged and both missed, happily they then both agreed 'Honour had been done', and shook hands.

[This is off the record, don't tell anyone I said this: but, I've heard through the grape vine, that when a new Mayor of Tenby is sworn in, they place around their neck 'the Mayors chain of Office', then slung around their hips are two pearl handled Colt 45s, with locally made leather holsters; they go nicely together: chain of office and two pearl handle Colt 45s.

But, remember it's only hear say? You did not hear this from me!]

TENBY SHIPWRECKS

A fine schooner, she might be American, sank on Monday, 23 October 1820 in Tenby Roads.

The following most melancholy event occurred, during a heavy gale of wind, accompanied with rain, from the W.S.W., in Tenby Bay. A fine schooner, with a figure head and painted ports, having rounded the easterly point of Caldey Island, while the crew, by their maneuvering the vessel, betrayed a total ignorance of the coast and Caldey Road anchorage places. Two Tenby pilot-boats immediately put out to sea in order to render them assistance.

With a gale blowing and, at the imminent peril of their own lives, the two Tenby boats continued on. They had proceeded about a mile from the shore, and then saw the schooner being struck by a heavy sea, which went clear over the vessel, and smashed her stern boat to pieces.

On seeing the tremendous breakers on the Woolhouse rocks, the crew, it is supposed, were too afraid to come near the shore, and consequently bore away in another direction towards Caldey.

It being late in the evening, there is too much reason to apprehend that the vessel was stranded on the opposite side of the bay, [Caldey Island sands, the crew must inevitably have perished].

One of the pilot boats returned safety to Tenby, while the other, when within a few hundred yards of the shore, was, by a sudden gust were instantly turned over. The sister pilot boat went out instantly having seen the sinking; sorry to say notwithstanding every possible exertion to save them, five brave Tenby men, who had thus been thrown into the sea, and were benumbed with cold and exhausted by fatigue, sunk, to rise no more.

That three of the unfortunate men have left wives and children to deplore their untimely fate. Two bodies were recovered from the sea later that day.

KENT OF LIVERPOOL

Wednesday 24 November 1830.   The brig KENT of Liverpool, Master Johnston in charge and sailing from Africa for Liverpool, was very much damaged by a gale, having lost her main mast and her rowing boat. She managed to get into Caldey Roads, but buy then she had lost both her anchors and cables. She tiered up to another ship which had to hold them both on her anchors. [That's okay, if the winds don't increase and change directions for the worst.] Friday arrived and guess what: the gale is getting worst, and add to the problems, there was a change in the direction of the wind, with the increase in wind strength, anchors started to drag both vessels. Now the Captain has to make a decision fast--only one ship can be saved. Orders were given: "Cut the ropes holding the KENT alongside!" The KENT was let go! She was driven by the winds across from Caldey Roads to the sands at North Beach, Tenby, opposite Caldey Island and from the tremendous seas; she was speedily pounded to pieces.

Her cargo consisted of about 1,400 casks of oil, which floated ashore, and have been secured, about "half, of the teeth, and nearly the whole of the redwood."

[What they really meant was Elephants tusks when referring to 'teeth'.]

The KENT of Liverpool, was a very large brig of 416 tons, and belonging to Sir John Tobin, of Liverpool, and, it is said, was not insured.   Who was Sir John Tobin, of Liverpool? I've come across two other shipwrecks where his name pops up as owner. Going out to Africa was the FREDREICK wrecked at St. David's Head February 1833, and returning from North Carolina with bales of cotton the LANCASTER wrecked on St. Patrick's Causeway, Cardigan March 1835.

Articles saved from the KENT, were placed on other ships and continued their voyage to Liverpool. These were 1,299 casks (small barrels) of palm oil, 78 barrels of a thick greasy matter like butter, used in the manufacture of soap and such, 64 elephant teeth, [Tusks] and 1,088 pieces of redwood.

How safe was it to have a nice gentle cruise to West Africa in the 1830's? Well, if you're thinking about it in the 1830's "Think again!" Just look what happened to the crew of the KENT, and this was not uncommon in those days. She sailed with a full crew of healthy young Englishmen from Liverpool. A month later they arrived off Sierra Leone, West Africa still with the same healthy young crew.
"Two weeks later, they are all dead!" Yep! All Dead! Only the master was still alive. With another crew found and her cargo loaded, she sailed back to Liverpool, England, having left the bones of the previous crew on Africa's unhealthy shores. Now, why would young healthy men want to be crewing on such dangerous voyages? Well, it was all about money: they were paid about four times more wages. And, why were only young men were picked to crew such voyages to darkest Africa? The truth is they had a better chance of recovering from illnesses. But, not this time.

What caused the deaths of these young, healthy men? It was Yellow Fever, plus the heat, poor food, not forgetting the drinking water. Let's take a look at "Yellow Fever." First off, how did it get its name? Simply, the skin of the sufferer turned Yellow in colour.
In 1830's they did not know how you caught Yellow Fever. [That's not helping the situation is it?]
Yellow fever is a serious viral illness with no cure. It is contracted through the bite of female mosquitoes found in areas in the South American rainforest, and throughout Africa. The mosquitoes pick up the virus when they bite a monkey or person who has Yellow Fever, and then pass it by biting and infecting someone else.

- In people who develop symptoms, the incubation period (time from infection until illness) is typically 3–6 days.
- The initial symptoms include sudden onset of fever, chills, severe headache, back pain, general body aches, nausea, vomiting, fatigue, weakness, jaundice, bleeding, and eventually shock and failure of multiple organs. [Then finally death, as you can see, it's not a nice way to die].

TENBY MARKET DAY 1834

Well before I begin, and I'm going to be frank with you, this story always upsets me; maybe I've been doing too much research. Once something very strange happened to me I think it was around the year 1987. I had been researching for months, eight hours, six day a week a day at the Library then once home, on the computer, typing up that day's work. At the end of a long day's research, as I left the Library, I actually thought, no lies, no messing you about, I actually thought, I was in the 1830's. I was looking for horse and carriages. I must admit this did frighten me a lot. I did not do any research for a long time after that event. [This is the first time I have mentioned this]I must get back to the story. As I was saying, this story has always upset me. See what you think?

TENBY MARKET DAY, SATURDAY, 27TH **DECEMBER 1834**, was full of excitement and jolliness. It was market day, all the stalls were brightly coloured, Christmas had just passed, and everyone was out for family fun, the market after Christmas at Tenby was always a big success. Music was everywhere, dancing in the square, children had never seen such colours and so many people dancing and so much laughter, for today was a special day, mothers were taking their children around the stalls, though they had a few pennies on them. But, the children had to pick some brightly coloured bangles, it's the sort of thing you know, children liked; for their mums were saying, "Your father will be back from Caldey Island this afternoon, and with his wages you'll get that bangle or that brightly coloured ribbon." Christmas in the 1830's: the child would only get one present, in large families children would get nothing, and most of the presents such as a little girls dress were hand me downs, but altered to fit the child, as for boys, toys were usually made of wood by their Dads. On Christmas day the meal was prepared by the whole family helping, (if it could be afforded a Goose, or chicken) the table to brighten it up, as its Christmas; with holly on the table. The meal was not large.

But, their fathers had found a week's work with a 'Bonus' if they finished the job on time, to be fair they had worked long into the nights to get this quarrying of stone job finished by the date of the Tenby Market fair of the 27th. Now they were expected to be back at Tenby, by midday at the latest.

At Caldey Island, a party of 13 Quarry workers and farm labourers, together with two women, left Caldey to return to Tenby. The owners of the Island Abbot Kynaston, had just paid the men their wages, and bonus, but, warned them against attempting the crossing because of a strong easterly wind and heavy swell that was running. However, with the extreme poverty of the time, almost all of the men had needy families anxiously waiting for them, and they decided to disregard Abbot Kynaston advice.

To be fair they did wait till after three in the afternoon, but, remembering they promised to be at Tenby early in the afternoon. They were late and the day was getting on, it would be dark soon and their families were waiting for them, plus, they had money in their pockets and it is market day, the best market day of the year. The passenger-boat which plies between Tenby and Caldey Island was waiting, with no time to waist they boarded her and set off for Tenby, once off the island the sail was hoisted, and they headed with the winds towards Tenby, towards the waiting families. Looking back they could see the gathering gloom of a winter's afternoon. As the boat nearly reached St. Catherine's Island, Tenby families had now come down to the beach wondering why they were so late. Now, the families, mothers and children could see the ferry boat coming; children started waving and shouting to their fathers everyone was shouting and waving, everyone was so excited, aboard the ferry boat they were waving and shouting back--when suddenly disaster struck. Eye witnesses on shore who had been nervously watching the boats progress reported that she broached to in the trough of huge wave, shipped water heavily over the side and sunk immediately.

A six oared gig was launched from Tenby and battled to the scene of the accident through heavy surf. Tragically there were no survivors.

Tenby beach was full of wife's, children, families and friends, all waving with excitement then right in front of them the ferry boat sank; 16 Tenby people were on the ferry boat, not one survived. On the beach were the most dreadful scenes of despair. As the news spread, people were leaving the market and rushing to the beach, in minutes the market was empty and silent. You can imagine the scenes on the beach, next to St. Catherine's Island.

The accident left seven widows, 33 children and four aged relatives without any real means of support. Mrs. James has eight children; another, Mrs. Lewis has six children. Later, six of the bodies were recovered, upon all of whom inquests have been held, and verdicts of accidental death, returned. A fund was immediately started for the dependants, and a week later already £150 had been received'.

A subscription for the relief of the widows and children has been entered into, and donations were thankfully received by the Rev. Dr. Humphreys, Rector of Tenby; donations came as far afield as the Rev. Hugh Williams, of Llantaff; Mr. W. Lewis, solicitor, Bridgend, and Mr. H. S. Coke, solicitor, Neath.

Swansea Town 1st February 1835. Collected for the relief of the widows and children of the unfortunate persons who were drowned on the 27th of December 1834, in crossing from Caldey Island to Tenby, and that upwards of fifty pounds has been collected for this truly charitable object. They hope shortly to announce a large increase to the list.

APOLLO OF ILFRACOMBE

This advertisement appeared in the Cambrian Newspaper on Saturday 4 August 1838:-
"For Sale: brig APOLLO. 114 tons. Built Bideford 1821. Carry 117 tons. Apply Ilfracombe."

Over a year later: Tenby Friday 19th November 1839 – The brig APOLLO, Master Mason, from Newport, South Wales to Cork, Ireland, took shelter for a few days in Caldey Road, when she thought it was safe to carry on with the voyage she drove out of Caldey Roads on Friday morning, as she was doing so, the gale came back with a vengeance. The strong winds pushed her on shore on the sands to the south of this town, crew and eight passengers saved, four women, one man, and a child drowned.

In the words used at the time, "Great praise is due to our Tenby boatmen for the bravery and promptitude they evinced in rescuing the survivors, which they affected by hauling thirteen of them through the sea by ropes to the boats, as the sea was too heavy to lay along side."

The master's son and a passenger attempted to gain the shore in their boat, when she was upset, but they succeeded in reaching shore by swimming. The passengers were chiefly Irish labourers, who came on shore in a very destitute condition, and who, with the crew, were treated with the greatest hospitality.

The body of the female was soon washed ashore, and every means tried to resuscitate her, but without effect. The newly-formed Ship Wrecked Fishermen's and Mariners Society at Tenby Town, promptly met, and appointed a sub-committee to attend to all their wants; they were in consequence provided with good food and lodgings, clothed and given a free passage to Waterford, per Milford Packets, and supplied them with other assistance.

The bodies of three women and the child have been found and decently interred. In the pocket of one of was "a certificate of the good contact of "Marbarry," signed by Thos. Fenton, dated at Stoat, March 28th 1839. – Upwards of £80, has been collected by some spirited Tenby gentlemen to reward the boatmen and others that were conspicuous in rendering assistance.

The vessel still holds together, and it should become moderate, may be got off by discharging the cargo of coal.

CANMORE OF SWANSEA

Tenby, North Sands Friday 24th January 1862, the barque CANMORE, of Swansea, about 300 tons burthen, laden with coals from Swansea, South Wales for Malaga, Spain ran ashore on the North Sands of Tenby on the morning of the 24th, where she now lies.

The whole day a strong gale was blowing from the S.W. and the previous night, she was lying at anchor in Caldey Roads. At day-break the Captain found that she was dragging and drifting towards Wool House Rocks. He slipped his cables, let her wear round clear, and then tried to reach Tenby Pier, but failing to do so he ran her in on the North Sands, where she was comparatively in smooth water. Hopes are entertained of getting her off as she is not much damaged. Sadly the gales have shifted direction, with strong force winds and waves have done their damage, the vessel is now a complete wreck.

Vessel had been bought by Mr. Thomas Twidle Drysdale, who had moved to Swansea, in July 1857. He had bought the barque CANMORE, of Swansea for £600. After she was wrecked, he was paid by the insurance £428.8s.5d.

In 1868 they started building a Fort on St. Catherine's Island at Tenby. Forts had been erected all over the south coast of England, and in the Bristol Channel, now they are building them around southern Pembrokeshire coast. The cost of this building project was 'ridiculous'.

The forts were built during the Victorian period on the recommendations of the 1860 Royal Commission on the Defence of the United Kingdom, following concerns about the strength of the French Navy, and strenuous debate in Parliament about whether the cost could be justified. The name comes from their association with Lord Palmerston, who was Prime Minister at the time and promoted the idea.

The forts became known as "Palmerston's Follies," partly because the first ones, around Portsmouth, had their main armament facing inland to protect Portsmouth from a land-based attack, which gave the impression that they faced the wrong way to defend from a French attack. They were also criticized because by the time they were completed, any threat had passed, largely due to the Franco-Prussian war of 1870, and because the technology of the guns of the day, had become out-of-date. They were the most costly and extensive system of fixed defenses under-taken in Britain in peacetime.

Amongst those that stand out around south Pembrokeshire are the forts in Milford Haven, on Stack Rocks, and Thorn Island, and at Tenby on St. Catherine's Island. There are many other Forts to numerous to mention around the Milford Haven area.

Prime Minister Lord Palmerston:
Henry John Temple, 3rd Viscount Palmerston,
KG, GCB, PC.
(b. 20 October 1784 – d. 18 October 1865),
died in office aged 80

ST. CATHERINES'S FORT WITH SUSPENSION BRIDGE

[That must have been a sight, the suspension bridge between the Castle Hill and St. Catherine's Island. This was to allow the workmen easy access to the island while building the fort]

Tenby; St. Catherine's Fort Building smack wrecked. At nine o'clock on Wednesday evening 19th August 1868, the smack PEARL, belonging to Mr. George Thomas, Government Contractor, for the fortification on St. Catherine's Island, was driven ashore on the South Sands. The vessel was lying alongside the jetty on the north side of St. Catherine's Rock, discharging her cargo of limestone, when a gale suddenly came on from the North-East, and as the crew tried to haul the smack off for the purpose of coming into the harbour, the rope parted, and she was driven on the rocks at Castle Point, her mast coming in contact with the suspension bridge between Castle Hill and St. Catherine's Island, doing great damage to it.

The smack has become a total wreck, and the loss to Mr. Thomas will be very great. The crew fortunately was saved, having come on shore in their own boat soon after she struck.

DECEMBER 1868 at the building of the St. Catherine's Fort, Tenby, builder William Jenkins died, fell of a ladder and died on the spot.

ONE YEAR LATER

One year later one of the Fort Building Smacks was wrecked at Tenby: On the Wednesday 29th September 1869, the smack MORNING STAR, of Milford, was beached on the South Sands, for the purpose of taking in a cargo of sand, for the use in concrete making for the fort now building on St. Catherine's Rock. At the time the weather was fine, and only a light breeze blowing. Towards evening, however, the wind shifted, and blew strongly, and the sea drove the vessel high on the beach. She is now high and dry!

When the high tides again set in, she was pulled down the beach some fifty yards, and then they commenced again to load her with cargo of sand. Again, most unfortunately the wind blew with violence, and from Saturday to today she has been gradually breaking up.

Sorry to have to say, Thomas James, of Milford, was both master and owner, has lost everything he was possessed of, and at an advanced age finds himself in a state of absolute poverty, bereft of the savings of hard work and toil. "Subscriptions will be thankfully received at Mason's Library, Tenby".

SOLDIER DROWNED
Soldier Drowned: St. Catherine's Fort Tenby, 1st November 1874. An inquest was held a few days later, the artillery soldiers name was Patrick Stanton age 22; he was a native of Galway. It seems he was late getting back with the tide in so he must have waded to the fort, next morning the soldier's boots and cane were found on the beach. His body was discovered 100 yards away. Inquest verdict 'found drowned.' The jury also recommended that some form of method of getting soldiers to and from the fort when the tide was in.

FOUNDERING OF A BRIGANTINE OFF TENBY.
On Sunday evening 2 Mar 1873; the brigantine JUNO of Whitestable, Master Herbert Goldfinch, with seven seamen aboard, foundered whilst endeavouring to get into Tenby Harbour. The vessel, which is laden with copper ore, from Plymouth to Llanelly, was boarded by the Llanelly Pilot (No 3) off the Woodhouse beacon, in Carmarthen bay, about 10 a.m., but, there being too much sea on the bar, the pilot took her into Caldy Roadstead, when, as the tide was very low, she grounded on the Highcliff Patch, where she remained for about two hours, striking heavily and the heavy ground sea making at times a clear breach over her.

As the tide began to flow the vessel drifted off, and about half-past three she got again into deep water, when it was found she was making water very fast, and fears were entertained that she would founder. A gig from Tenby went off, but the master refused the offer of assistance, as there were already pilot on board.

Just at this time, the screw steamer SS LLANELLY, of Llanelly, Captain Charles, from Liverpool, England for Llanelly, South Wales came round Caldey Point. Signals were made from the pilot boat, and the steamer came to the assistance of the distressed vessel, taking her in tow, and succeeded in bringing her within a cable's length of the pier head, she foundered at 6 p.m.

The men succeeded in getting their clothing and personal belongings out, and into the pilot boat, before she went down. Attempts will be made to get her into the harbour with the next tide, but should a gale spring up, it is feared she will go to pieces.
The occurrence was witnessed by some hundreds of persons, both from the Castle Hill and South Cliff.

Mary Celeste and Dale Village:

MARY CELESTE

Remember the story of the MARY CELESTE? That's the ship that was discovered in 1872, with no crew on board! The whole ship's crew had just disappeared!
I know you're wondering about why the MARY CELESTE story is connected with Pembrokeshire, read on and all will be revealed?

New York, USA: Late on Saturday 2nd November 1872 the MARY CELESTE'S cargo was loaded and made secure. She was loaded with 1,701 barrels of industrial alcohol for Genoa, Italy. [Before you think 'Alcohol', this is the stuff you don't drink, it industrial alcohol, one drink and you head would exploded! Well not exploded, you would just die from drinking industrial alcohol].*She* sailed with Captain Benjamin Briggs in charge; an experienced Master also aboard was his wife Sarah Briggs and their child, plus seven seamen. [In total 10 people]

MARY CELESTE was a square-rigged brigantine, a medium-sized ocean-going ship with two masts. She plied the oceans of the world as a cargo-vessel, transporting goods across the Atlantic Ocean.

[Spouse Sarah Elizabeth Briggs (nee Cobb) b. 20 April 1841 aged 31. They married in 1862. With Sarah was their daughter Sophia M, then nearly two years old, b. 31 October 1870].

[Captain Benjamin Briggs of MARY CELESTE, b. 24 April 1835 aged 37]

December 5th 1872, Captain Morehouse of the DEI GRATIA, sighted Captain Briggs's ship halfway between Portugal and the Azores islands, and was disturbed by the way that the MARY CELESTE seemed to be careening out of control. The DEI GRATIA attempted to hail the MARY CELESTE, with no response. Finally a boarding party was sent to investigate. They found no crew aboard, two cargo hatches open, charts missing together with the life boat, plus, one of the mast ropes was cut at the top; this was trailing behind the ship.

The crew had just disappeared?   Some of the crew of the DEI GRATIA was put aboard and the both then sailed to Gibraltar. Later the Captain and crew of the DEI GRATIA were paid salvage money.

MARY CELESTE was returned to the owners, and continued her voyage to Genoa. Shortly after she was sold – at a considerable loss – and over the next 12 years the vessel changed hands no less than "17 times."

In late 1884 an ageing and rather unkempt MARY CELESTE was bought by Gilman C. Parker and loaded with fright, which was insured for $30,000. The vessel sailed for Port-au-Prince, Haiti. But she never arrived. On the 3rd January 1885 the MARY CELESTE ran aground and caught fire, on the razor-sharp coral reef of Rochaelais Bank in the Gulf of Gonave, off the coast of Haiti.

Parker put in an insurance claim. They found that Parker had loaded the ship with rubbish – not the valued cargo he had insured – he had deliberately run MARY CELESTE aground, and then set her alight. Case went to court, then case dropped because a legal technicality. Insurance never paid out. A short time after, Parker went bankrupt, and he died in poverty and disrepute. One of his fellow conspirators went insane and was placed in a mental institution where he ended his days. Another killed himself.

[Brigantine: DEI GRATIA of Digby, Nova Scotia]

The DEI GRATIA Story

The DEI GRATIA was a Canadian built in Bear River, Nova Scotia 1871.   Named after the Latin phrase for "By the Grace of God." DEI GRATIA became famous in 1872 when, under the command of David Reed Morehouse, he discovered the mystery ship MARY CELESTE, found abandoned and without any crew near the Azores. DEI GRATIA was sold to Irish owners in 1881.

Now we have move forward to 1906, and Dale, Milford Haven: After breaking her moorings in a South-east storm.   On Friday Morning, 27th December 1906, the brigantine DEI GRATIA, which had been flying signals of distress from midnight, was sighted off Dale, apparently drifting in strong winds towards Dale Beach! Mr. James Stanley despatched a messenger to St. Ann's to inform Mr. Rees, H.M. Coastguards, within the short space of 38 minutes summoned the rocket brigade and horses necessary, and had this apparatus at Dale, a distance of three miles.   Great praise is due to this capable officer for his promptitude. As it happened, however, the life-saving apparatus was not needed, as the vessel had drifted on to the Black Rocks, on Dale beach, where the crew were able to get ashore fairly easily.

It proves what could be done in case of emergency. Praise is also due to Mr. Lees, of Snailston Farm [near St. Ann's Lighthouse] and his men for the expedition's way the horses were got ready, despatched, and yoked to the apparatus.   To see the fully equipped brigade bounding over the road reminded one of the fire brigades in the metropolis.

[The vessel ashore is the famous DEI GRATIA; she was the ship that found the MARY CELESTE, in 1872 without her crew in the Atlantic Ocean]

[Photograph taken 1906; Salvage steamer alongside the Brigantine DEI GRATIA, at Black Rock, Dale, Milford Haven. Brigantine DEI GRATIA broke her moorings on Friday 27 December 1906]

Dale Village and the Sweating Sickness:

Monday 7th August 1485 Henry VII arrived at Mill Bay, [Mill Bay is to be found at the entrance to Milford Haven between the village of Dale and St. Anne's Lighthouse] with his small army of French and Scottish mercenaries.

Henry was heading into battle with Richard III, and on the way some 5,000 Welsh joined him. The Battle of Bosworth Field took place on 22 August 1485. Henry won the day and the throne of England, he was 28 years old.

But, what happened at the village of Dale after Henry VII had passed through on his way to Bosworth? The village of Dale was visited by a strange sickness; it's believed the mercenaries soldiers brought it.

[Henry VII, born at Pembroke Castle in 1457]

- ➤ 1st Time: 1485: first symptoms showed themselves a week after our Henry VII had passed through. One minute your okay, then you're sweating greatly and death comes in less than 24 hours. The sickness became known as the 'Sweating Sickness'.
- ➤ 2nd Time: it arrived was 1506: again same symptoms. Sweating and death in less than 24 hours.
- ➤ 3rd Time: arrived in 1517: Symptoms the same. Sweating, then death, quicker this time in 3 hours after first symptoms showed.
- ➤ 4th Time: in 1528: Returned with same symptoms Sweating then death in less than 6 hours.
- ➤ 5th Time was 1591: Returned for the last time, the Sweating Sickness. This time the Sweating Sickness stayed for over five months.

Same sickness reported at Shrewsbury in 1591, which carried away 960 persons. Half the inhabitants of many towns fell sick. The outbreaks usually lasted about two months.

Interestingly: if you started sweating but survived for 24 hours then you would recover. Sweating Sickness; only came in the summer months, once the cold weather arrived it disappeared. Children and old people were less susceptible to it. It carries away the young and healthy aged between 15 and 30.

Symptoms Recorded of the Sweating Sickness
- ➢ Inward very hot (Sweating)
- ➢ Skin; Burning hot
- ➢ Unquenchable thirst
- ➢ Restlessness
- ➢ Sickness at stomach and heart (though seldom any vomiting)
- ➢ Headaches
- ➢ Delirium
- ➢ Faintness and excessive drowsiness
- ➢ Pulse very quick
- ➢ Breath short and labouring
- ➢ And then death

In 1871 the local Pembrokeshire news paper looked at these symptoms and the experts said that the Sweating Sickness was similar to the Plague [Black Death]. The Plague occurred a number of times in Pembrokeshire. It arrived the first time in England in 1348. The first signs of it in Pembrokeshire were in 1349, when half of the Pembrokeshire's population died. Actually, half the population of Wales and England died. But the symptoms are nothing like Sweating Sickness.

Let's look at the signs of the Plague 'Black Death'.
- ➢ Swelling appearing in groin or armpits, as large as an apple
- ➢ Black or red spots
- ➢ Developing a rash and pain all over the body
- ➢ Feeling tired and lethargic but the pain made it difficult to sleep
- ➢ Temperature of the body increases and this affects the brain and the nerves
- ➢ Speech is affected and the victims become less and less intelligible
- ➢ And then death

The average time of death from the first symptom was between four to seven days. It is thought that 75% of those who caught the disease died.
Pestilence has hit Britain before; the chronicles of 'Brut y Tywysogion' records for 1197: There was a great pestilence throughout the island of Britain, and the tempest killed innumerable people and many nobility and many princes, and spared none. 1197 saw the deaths of a number of Welsh Princes and men and women, estimates are that half of the population of Wales died.

Paddle steamer boat trips to the islands with a difference:

PEMBROKESHIRE ISLANDS BOAT TRIPS

Let's go back to the 1840's. Even in those days there were boat trips around the Islands off the Pembrokeshire coast: Caldey, Skomer, Skokholm, Grassholm, and as far as the Smalls, aboard the paddle steamer STAR.

Today, visitors are only allowed to bring back memories of the boat trip by taking photos with their cameras. But, in the 1840's – this was when cameras were still in their infancy, easy to carry box cameras had not yet been invented – what memories could be taken home with you? Back in those days instead of taking a camera, why you would take you're 12 gauge shotgun and shoot away happily on Grassholm Island? Yes, you read it correctly, shoot away happily on Grassholm Island, and then you bring back memories by how many dead puffins, gannets, guillemots, razorbills and seagulls you had shot!

Can you imagine calling at the boat trip booking office today, for a trip to Grassholm Island to see the Gannets, and asking questions like: Do I need sun screen? Do I need a hat? Which, would you recommend I take -- my automatic eight shot 12 gauge, or my twin barrels 12 gauge shotgun? Should I take 50 or 100 cartridges? Will you be selling shotgun cartridges on board the boat? Oh, yes, and will I need sun glasses? This is the advertisement about Grassholm Boat Trip in 1844

THE STAR,

Capt. WILLIAM REES, Commander,

This advertisement was published in the Pembrokeshire Herald Newspaper on Saturday 19th July 1844:

THE STAR under the command of Captain William Rees, Sail from the Ship-dock, near Haverfordwest on Thursday 1st August 1844. And proceeding to cruise round the islands, making Grassholm the place of debarkation, where Puffins, Gannets, and Gulls shooting may be enjoyed to satiety [satiety means: glutted state, feeling of having had too much] and returning in the evening, so as to reach Ship-Dock Quay about half-past seven.

Then as you return to harbour, The Gentlemen of the Amateur Harmonic brass Band have kindly intimated their intention of joining the merry throng, so their gaiety and good humour are engaged for the day.

The advertisement added: "Fun and frolic who shall dare to mar, whilst gallant Rees commands the Star?" And the cost, of this fantastic boat trip: "Saloon 3s. Steerage: 1s. 6d. Children under 12 Half-Price." But you have to bring your own shot-gun, well what do you expect for 3s. Forgot to add this, I know you'll be interested, especially with all this shooting going on: "Refreshments of every kind may be had onboard." We'll come to 'Refreshments' in a minute!

Well, that's one of the best advertisements I have ever read, I was wonder if they still do those trips? Seriously; they did stop these shooting parties being landing on Grassholm. Why? Was it their consciences? Did they feel this was upsetting the seabirds? No, simply they had problem getting the passengers on and off Grassholm Island. A number of passengers fell into the water while stepping off or getting back on the longboat. If you've been on one of the boat trips around Grassholm Island, you would have noticed the size of the waves hitting the rocks, one minute it's flat calm, the next you have big waves. And no-one wanted to drop a very expensive 12 gauge shotgun and cartridges in seawater. Let's not forget the wording "Refreshments of every kind." They had a lot to do with it as well.

"Refreshments of every kind," 'Gentlemen', after too much "Refreshments of every kind," these were of an alcohol nature, before landing and started the shooting, some gentlemen in their enthusiasm, and with too much "Refreshments of every kind," would shoot happily away and hit the paddle steamer with lead shot; this made the passengers who were watching the shoot, dive for cover!

It's not good publicity to have one's passengers - shot.

Let's move on to 1857; with the growth in the South Wales population, there was a market for boat trips. They even lay on special trains from Swansea. This is one of the advertisements: You'll notice they don't give a time for the return train journey, the train only left when the steamer returned back at Neyland. Sometimes it was up to two hours late returning!

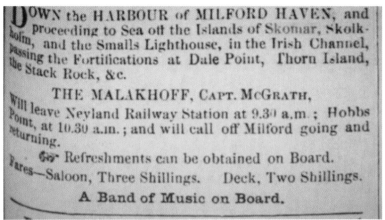

DOWN the HARBOUR of MILFORD HAVEN, and proceeding to Sea off the Islands of Skomar, Skolkholm, and the Smalls Lighthouse, in the Irish Channel, passing the Fortifications at Dale Point, Thorn Island, the Stack Rock, &c.

THE MALAKHOFF, Capt. McGrath,

Will leave Neyland Railway Station at 9.30 a.m.; Hobbs Point, at 10.30 a.m.; and will call off Milford going and returning.

☞ Refreshments can be obtained on Board.

Fares—Saloon, Three Shillings.   Deck, Two Shillings.

A Band of Music on Board.

This one of the advertisements that appeared in the local papers

MARINE EXCURSION DOWN THE HAVEN

The inhabitants of Haverfordwest are now to have a treat, already enjoyed by the denizens [inhabitants] of Swansea, Merthyr, Cardiff and Pembroke-dock, of a marine excursion down the Haven.   With special laid on trains bring the customers to Neyland. On Monday 10th July 1857, a train will leave Swansea Station at 9.30 a.m., and on its arrival at Neyland the paddle steamer MALAKHOFF will be in readiness to convey passengers down the Harbour, off to the islands of Skomer and Skokholm, even as far as the Smalls Light-house in the Irish Channel, Dale Point, Thorn Island, and Stack Rock.   The train will be in readiness to convey the passengers back immediately on the return of the paddle steamer.   Should the day prove fine the appliances of enjoyment will be numerous, and we have no doubt the excursion will be a monster one. Captain Mc. Garth certainly deserves a bumper.

Fares – Saloon, Three shillings. Deck, Two shillings.

They even have a "Brass Band on board." I bet the brass band went down well with the Puffins, Guillemots, Razor Bills and Gulls on Skomer Island. Can you imagine the scene as the paddle steamer steams into North Haven, at Skomer Island.   Now, by popular request the Brass Band will play the 1812 Overture, with added real cannon fire! BANG! BOOM! BANG! And then for the passengers delight, the Captain would sound the ships steam whistle, so all the passengers could enjoy watching the sea birds of North Haven flying around – "In Sheer Panic!"

Vendome shipwreck story & The CAVE OF DOOM:

SS VENDOME SHIPWRECK

Joseph Garnon was born at Fishguard, Pembrokeshire in 1858. His story starts on Wednesday 8th December 1886, when Joseph was then 28 years old, with his brother Thomas, both single men and a married man named Edmund Purtill, born 1837 aged 49. Edmund was master and owner a small fishing boat of about 2 tons, built in 1880, he had named her "POLLY" of Fishguard. On that day there was a gale blowing, but the winds are coming from the south, which was offshore wind. They would be quite sheltered as long as they did not go too far from the shelter of the cliffs.

They headed from Fishguard for Penrhyn Erw-goch, to pick up their herring nets. As they got near to the nets, they went just a bit too far from the shelter of the cliffs, the wind caught them, and they were, unfortunately, blown off shore, and were unable to regain the shelter of the cliffs. The boat was blown towards Pwllgwaelod, on the Dinas Island.

There signals of distress were observed and the Goodwick Lifeboat was launched without a moment's delay.

The wind had come around slightly from a south-westerly direction; which meant the Lifeboat almost flew before the wind, with all sails set, after the drifting boat POLLY. When the Fishguard Lifeboat reached within a short distance from her suddenly the Fishguard Lifeboat was capsized by heavy seas, she should right herself in seconds, but, it's in shallow water, and her masts had stuck in the seabed, thus preventing the Lifeboats self-righting properties coming into use. The Fishguard Lifeboat crew clung to the upturned hull and life ropes.

Shortly after this the drifting boat POLLY, which by this time had got into very rough waters, was also capsized, and the three occupants thrown into the sea.

On the capsized POLLY, the three men could all swim, and each man secured the help of a floating oar, but after a desperate struggle in the boiling surf Purtill and Thomas were overcome and drowned. [We must not forget it is the middle of winter, and the sea temp was only 4c]. Joseph Garnon swam for shore, with the seas covering him, but, he did reach shore, more dead than alive; in a completely exhausted and insensible state, he could not speak for hours.

In the mean while, the Fishguard Lifeboat righted herself, keeping to the cliffs well out of the gale force winds they rowed back to Fishguard. The whole of Wales had been hit by this storm; a number of ships were wrecked. One 150 ton sailing ship safely arrived at Milford Haven, then as she rounded Thorn Island, under full sails; she sank, just like that! No survivors. There was a tug close by, and they could not find any survivors.

Joseph Garnon had survived the sinking of the POLLY, but he was in a very bad state, he had managed to crawl up the beach, then completely exhausted just lay there. When he was found he could not speak or walk, a horse and cart had to be used, which took him home.   He was in such a bad state, he had to stay in bed for a week, it was another week before he could walk.

Now we move on to 1888 and Joseph Garnon is now aged 30: he has signed on the SS VENDOME of London, the Captain Arthur Parry [Photo], who's from St. David's.

Captain Arthur Parry
was from St. David's

SS VENDOME of London. She had traded many years between Dynevor Colliery, Neath, South Wales and France her career had been a varied one. A few years ago she collided with a vessel on the French coast and remained under water for two years. Most of the crew reside at Neath, South Wales.   Launched on 18th February 1882.Steamer of266 tons. Could carry a cargo of 150 tons. Length 155 feet: Wide 23 feet 8 inches: Depth of hold 13 feet 2 inches: 1 Boiler.
Owner O. Robinson & H. Dansey of London.

In the early hours of the morning with force 5 winds from the south-west, the Captain was asked to come on the Bridge, for they were not sure where they were, but he would not leave his bunk: There was one slightly small problem or should I say a large problem, the helmsman did not know where he was, or what course to steer! Then at five o'clock on Tuesday 4th December 1888, the steamer SS VENDOME," commanded by Captain Parry, struck a rock. It appears that the "SS VENDOME," was on her return voyage from Ramsey, Isle of Man, where she had taken a cargo of Neath Valley Coal, now she was returning to Neath, South Wales, and in the darkness which prevailed on Tuesday morning she run onto a rock. And nobody knew where they where?
With the steamer now on the rock, her crew of eleven, with great difficulty, launched the boats, and succeeded in leaving the vessel. Crew saved nothing but what they wore, she was stuck on a rock, then minutes later, she slipped off the rock and sank

into deep water. With just the top 6 feet of her mast showing, the two rowing boats kept near each other and kept near the top of the mast showing, for they still had not the faintest where they were. It's the middle of winter; daylight is around 8 a.m. At last it was getting lighter and with daylight, they could at last see around them, all they saw was just cliffs. Then crewman Joseph Garnon, started to say, I'm sure I know this place? This is where Joseph Garnon put his lobster pots down; he knew this area well. Wrecked 5 a.m. Tuesday 4th December 1888. Cargo: in ballast. [No cargo]

[Photograph by the Author Jim: She had hit the rocks known as Tri-Maen-Trai, where the white water is to the right of the photo, just South of Strumble Head; Joseph Garnon; knew these rocks well, for he had put lobster pots down in this area]

They arrived at Fishguard Harbour at 11 a.m. Fishguard give them the warmest possible welcome, and showed them much practical sympathy.
The Captain and crew then caught the first train for London, but, Joseph Garnon, he just walked home, as he only lived down the road. So there are the Garnon family, just about to serve the Sunday roast and who do you think walks in why 'Joseph Garnon'. I bet that was a good family story for years. (Joseph Garnon was born in Fishguard 1858 – he died at Fishguard aged 58 in 1916)

Intelligence reached Neath on Tuesday that the SS VENDOME, belonging to the Dynevor Colliery Company, Neath, she had gone down off Strumble head, near Fishguard. The crew, consisting of about 15 persons, were saved in their own boats.

The steamer registered 480 tons, and was returning empty from Ramsey, IOM, where she had been with a cargo of coal.

The Board of Trade Inquiry.
The Court found that the stranding of the vessel was due to the absence of the captain from the deck, and the want of supervision by him. There was however no evidence as to whether the deviations of the compass (which were satisfactory instruments) had been properly ascertained. No proper measures were taken to verify the position of the vessel at 4 a.m., on the 4th of Dec., proper courses were not set and followed, and proper allowance was not made for tide leeway.
He had his certificate suspended for three months, by the Board of Trade.

Diver Bruce Jones Research material September 1980; Captain Arthur Parry of St. David's:
Sometime after, Captain Arthur Parry was captain of another steamer. While rounding Cape Horn, off South Africa, the steamer sank suddenly.
It was two years before his wife (living in Nun Street, St. David's), ever found out. Another Captain of a steamer being close by had seen her go down, off Cape Horn, and it is he who travelled to St. David's, and told Captain Parry's widow, the circumstances of her husband death.
Captain Arthur Parry left a wife and two small children. Wife's name Lillian. They had two children Billy born 1882; I believe Billy died young.
Captain Parry's daughter when grown up; adopted a girl, Hilda and she was the one who told Diver Bruce Jones in the autumn of 1980 this story, of what had happened to the Captain; she even had a photograph of the captain. Hilda Davies, use to live in Nun Street, St. David's.

The story of the shipbuilder of the SS VENDOME.
Built 1882 by D. Baxter & Co., of Sunderland, Yard No. 23.
In 1982, Shipwreck Researcher Tom Bennett supplied me with the Baxter shipbuilder Story: -
Baxter builder of the SS VENDOME was brought up in North Scotland and was at various Scottish shipyards before raising money from his family and coming to Sunderland to open up his own shipbuilding business at North Sands Point on the river Wear. He did well and brought his son into the business but the son and the office manager dipped their hands into the till and cleared out with the result that the father went bankrupt in 1884.
The father returned to Scotland and later went off to America in search of his son. When he did find him on the west coast the son was dying and after his death he brought the body to the east coast for burial where the family had settled. From then on the Baxter's were an American family and there are many of them still in shipbuilding to-day.

SS VENDOME WRECK DISCOVERED

Let's move forward to August 1980: Now its 92 years after the sinking of the steamer and we have two fresh faced young Divers who are about to search for this forgotten shipwreck.   Young Diver & Shipwreck Researcher James Hedley Phillips and even a younger Diver Bruce Jones, its Sunday 31 August 1980.   Shipwreck Research Jim says; she had hit this rock and sank here, it's as simple as that.   ["Here are another couple of months searching" I thought to myself]   The planned Search & Location method was; for a Diver to be towed on an underwater sledge, what that means is a rope from the boat 60 metres long to the sledge & Diver.   This way the Diver just hangs on to the sledge and is towed at a speed about 2 m.p.h.   The boat takes the Diver around the site.   This way the Diver uses hardly any air, covers five times more area than a Diver swimming around would.   It's simple and effective.

So here we were, at the supposed wreck site, I said to Diver Bruce "I'll pop down just to see what the visibility is at 30 metres."   Reason of this is you need a minimum of 8 metres to be towed safely.   Say you had 10 metres underwater visibility, then being towed you could see 10 metres on one side and 10 metres the other side, and 10m in front; now you can see the benefits of sledge Diver towing.

As I kitted up, Bruce said, "I'll pop down with you", I agreed saying, "once we hit the bottom we'll have a quick look around and up, okay", "Yep" said Bruce.   Arriving at the sea bed, the underwater visibility was about 10 metres.   The seabed was littered with boulders the size of caravans. "Great" I thought.   Signaling to Bruce, let's go up. He signaled back let's look around these boulders.   I pointed at my watch, meaning "we don't have time!"   He signaled back "Come on, only one minute. "   Okay, I said; One minute and no longer!   So he led the way while I followed muttering under my breath "This is a "fearful" and "we are wasting of time!""We won't find anything! Youngsters today!"   So we swam between two large caravan size boulders, with me still looking at my watch, following and muttering.

"There was the wreck!" "Just like that!"   It had taken us just three or four minutes to locate the SS VENDOME shipwreck.

On this one dive I personally stacked port holes four high, 'two stacks'.

Back on the boat Diver Bruce said "Did I hear you moaning, just before we discovered the wreck." "Never!" I said; "Bruce, I was enthusiastically following you and saying, this is a brilliant idea of yours Bruce; to swim around these rocks!   You probably could not understand me, or miss heard me because of the depth of water."   Cough!

Thanks to young Diver Greg Evans the GPS position of wreck SS VENDOME is: - N52 00.477   W5 05.349

[Diver Jim recovering a port hole right next to the boiler 1980. I just picked it up, and turned to the Diver cameraman, and click. Just like that. I didn't even have time to put my gloves on!]

Over the following days and weeks I recovered a strong box with coins; glass oil lamp; compass stand; china mug, brass bits and bobs, then on the 9th September 1980; The Ship's bell was recovered, with the wording SS VENDOME 1882 written on it. [That was a nice surprise, over the years I have recovered two bells 'SS VENDOME'; and 'SS IERNE'; (off Gower) just the top part of the bell SS CAMBRO (Smalls)].

[Photograph by Diver Howell Lewis of Cumtawe Sub Aqua Club. Jim cataloguing the items salvaged]

The recovered 12 port holes, off the SS VENDOME; to raise money for the shipwreck projects I placed a classified advertisement in the Sunday Times Newspaper and sold the lot, I also recovered china mug, some penny and half penny coins, [Bruce recovered the strong box brass key] brass compass stand, floor tiles, glass oil lamp, and brass oil lamp holder etc. [Receiver of Wrecks was informed].

71

[Photograph Bruce Jones. Some of the items recovered, dead eye, port hole, china mug, bottle still corked and full of Blue ink, bottom of oil lamp, Strong box brass key to strong box, (strong box was found with some coins) and some beautiful floor tiles]

IT CAN BE VERY DANGEROUS DIVING ON SHIPWRECK!
[I cannot watch horror movies, for example the movie 'THE DEEP', I didn't watch that movie till it had been out for at least ten years and 'JAWS' well, that was at least 15 years, so you will see how this event would go down well with me, and we won't mention the movie 'THE FOG'].

THE STORY OF THE CAVE OF DOOM!
We had now been diving, the shipwreck SS VENDOME for about two weeks. On this day my job was to move down the port side [left side] of the wreck heading to the deep part, the bows section. Arriving at the port side I slowly headed down looking for anything interesting. At a depth of about 35 m, I could see just off the wreck a small cave, I went over to have a look with it being dark inside the cave I switched on my underwater torch, on entering, and looking down at the floor, searching for anything of interest. I had moved right inside this cave and still nothing on the floor from the wreck, as I was about to turn, I was some way in the cave by now, I noticed just in front of me, what appeared to be a telegraph post, but this telegraph post was pointing almost straight up? I moved closer and then I noticed it was a shiny bluish/gray colour, looking even closer, now I'm only one foot away, I was just about to touch it, when I noticed a fin all the way down one side; that was constantly moving, moving my torch beam slowly to the top of the telegraph pole, which by now, I started to doubt very much that it was a telegraph pole, that I was looking at. Suddenly I saw a head on the top, the size of a dirty great big Alsatian Dog; I was looking at the biggest CONGER I had ever seen! [And over the years of diving shipwrecks, I've seen really big ones, but, this was by far the biggest! Believe me; it was big, with big teeth as well! The worst bit is I was only one foot away!]. I mean it

was the size that gives you nightmares!   It was opening and closing it mouth, and the size of these teeth, they would put a Saber Tooth Tigers to shame.   Doing everything in my power; to control my breathing, my heart rate, and above all to control my panic, I thought the best option was too very gently retreated!

After the dive while sitting in my Avon inflatable ACE, drinking tea; I told Diver Bruce Jones the story, head the size of a dirty great big Alsatian Dog with even bigger teeth than a Saber Tooth Tiger!   Well, would you know he did not believe me, "where's the trust gone, I don't know, youngsters today?"

So in the afternoon, Bruce said, "show me this cave with this fictitious conger lives." "Okay I would" I did say it in an annoying way!   So over we went, and then at about 35 metres right in front of us was "THE CAVE OF DOOM!" I pointed and give the signal "BIG TEETH!"   So in he goes head first, I waited for the Conger to eat him as a snack!

[Diver entering the CAVE OF DOOM]

In he went all the way into "THE CAVE OF DOOM!"   There was no conger in there! It had gone. So out came Bruce, giving me that look of; "Stop messing about" so I went, inside "THE CAVE OF DOOM," looking towards the top was a large hole, that's why the conger 'that's the one with big teeth' was facing upwards, that was his exit hole.

I went and got on with my job, and Bruce went to his; about five minutes later, Bruce came over swimming about 30 mph, and pointing towards the ships boiler, signaling BIG TEETH OVER THERE!

On the boat, we chatted, Bruce confirming the head was the size of an Alsatian Dog, and confirming its teeth are bigger then a Saber Tooth Tiger! "See" I said, "Have you ever known me to exaggerate?"   Cough!

Bruce said it came out of a large pipe next to the boiler, next day I had a look for this pipe, finding the pipe, there was no conger to be seen, switched on my torch and looked right inside the pipe, it was empty. Taking my Divers knife out, I measured across the pipe, now my Divers knife is one foot long, point to the handle tip fitted in the pipe with an inch or two to spare. That's a big conger I thought. Leaving the pipe I got on with my job.

Later in the day we dived again and part of my job was to check under the boiler, so over I went underwater visibility was about 10 metres. Looking under the boiler I found nothing of interest, as I rounded the ships boiler right in front of me was that pipe. To my horror, the conger's head was sticking out of the pipe. I stopped about eight feet away, and was about to back off, when it slowly started to come out, and out, and out. It kept coming out 'straight', not bending just straight and so slowly. All I could do was just watch this happening in front of me. It came out as I said straight, then it gets worst, much worst, slowly it's whole body started to turn, it was turning slowly "Towards me!" Now look, I've done thousands of dives on wrecks, and I can say this is honestly the first time I have ever, ever, actually put my hand on my Divers Knife Handle, ready for action!

Now our heads are about two feet apart, he was looking at me, and I was looking at him, I'm trying my best to look non threatening. Like a regular guy; someone you could trust. By the way, part of the conger was still in the pipe, so how long he was I don't know, and I don't care.

There was the Conger looking straight into my eyes now let's not forget we're two feet apart; while he kept opening and closing his mouth, and, not forgetting its head was the size of a dirty great big Alsatian Dog with dirty great big teeth! I don't think I was breathing, I honestly just could not move. All I did was to look right back into it eyes, I could see the congers eyes were cold, unfeeling, my eyes were scared. All the time I was doing everything I could, to look even more 'non' threatening! Then, he started to move; thank goodness it was moving slowly backwards into the pipe, I don't think this guy, rushes for any one!

I boldly backed off, and went quickly around the boiler the other way, and got on with my job. After that dive we never saw the conger again, like I told Bruce; It was the way I stood my ground, the way I looked so cool, the way I looked him straight in the eye; then the conger must have noticed how I slowly moved my hand over the knife handle, [just like one of those spaghetti western films] This conger could see; "I was the sort of Diver you don't mess with!" Anyway, that's what I told Diver Bruce Jones. Then Bruce said something very childish, "Or it could have been that whimpering sound you were making."

[As I have always said "Remember, no one can hear you scream under the sea! Or whimper!"]

Animal sea stories:

DOG OVERBOARD. During the last cruise of the DOVE cutter from Milford Haven, on 8th November 1825, a little spaniel dog jumped overboard, (as he was in the habit of doing) unobserved by the crew, 20 miles from land, near the Smalls. About 17 hours later the spaniel was picked up by Mr. Palmer, at St. Ann's Light, in a very weak and exhausted state; but with proper care he was in a short time recovered.

VOYAGE OF A CAT WITH NINE LIVES

Among the passengers who arrived at Tenby by the paddle steamer BRITON, on Saturday evening 27th April 1878, from Bristol, was a fine black cat.

The animal had been observed by the crew on board the boat just as the vessel was starting, but was lost sight of soon afterwards. When the paddle steamer BRITON arrived at Tenby, and was alongside the wharf, a piteous wail was heard from the interior of the port [left] paddle-box.

On examination, one soaking wet black cat was found perched upon a narrow ledge close to the wheel, as nearly drowned as it consistent with an animal reputed to have nine lives.

The poor creature had no doubt been there during the whole of the voyage, and the wonder is how it lived to reach Tenby.

SAVING LIVES OF SHEEP

I myself have been involved in saving lives well, really it was three sheep. A local St. David's farmer came up to me one day at Whitesands beach while we were launching my boat, and asked if I could save some of his sheep. We would find them about three feet above the high tide on a ledge at the bottom of Gesail-fawr cliffs, about one and half miles north of St. David's Head. As we were leaving the beach, the St. David's farmer said, "I'll see you alright financially," adding loudly, "only, if you save my sheep that is." With this in mind and thinking to myself "what an honest St. David's farmer he sounds," we set off to save some poor sheep, plus, we would be getting a 'Huge Financial Reward' from this generous farmer. Arriving at Gesail-fawr cliffs, we could see why these sheep were stuck! The Ledge was easy to get down to, but impossible to get back up from, and it was only 3 feet above high tide. Some long juicy grass must have attracted them. Well, the grass was no longer 'long' or looking 'juicy,' as they had eaten it so fine - it looked like the top of a pool table. These three sheep were looking thin and weak. Because I had worked on farms while a young man, I just said to my fellow brave divers, "Go and get them." From their faces of these brave deep-sea divers, I could see they had never dealt with "dangerous sheep before," I then shouted words of encouragement: "Think of the Huge Financial Reward we're going to get from the farmer!" That didn't work either, so I had to get on the ledge myself, and bravely, boldly (not thinking of this huge financial reward, waiting for us at Whitesands, from the St. David's farmer) I caught the first one, she was very weak, I think they were nearing the end. Once all three were aboard, myself and my fellow 'brave' Divers headed to sloping rocks where we could land them, and they could walk up the slope to freedom. As I was driving along the sheep were now walking and looking around the boat, one was standing at my right side, and I think was pointing it hoof saying in sheep talk of course; "watch your speed; look out for that rock; do you have to go this fast; are we there yet."

We had more of a problem getting them off, they just did not wanted to leave. I think these sheep never had so much excitement before, and they were getting a boat trip, I bet all their friends [sheep] were jealous.

Now, for that 'Huge Financial Reward' which was waiting for us at Whitesands Beach, from the St. David's farmer; "Strangely, I never saw him again?"

MARS shipwreck and the long horn cattle:

WRECKING OF SS MARS OF WATERFORD

The SS MARS had done the voyage many times before: Waterford, Ireland to Bristol, England. Bristol's population was growing rapidly and with it came a demand for more and more food. Ireland had become a major supplier of cattle, pigs and butter, but, especially pigs.

During my research I realized that if the ship had been sailing from Ireland to Bristol, then I could bet my bottom dollar part of the cargo would have been Pigs. "Bristolians seemed to like there pork a lot."

The SS MARS had been built in 1844 as an iron paddle steamer but was converted to screw and single propeller just a few years later, at a considerable expense to the owners: Waterford & Bristol Steam Navigation Company. But, her paddle wheel boxes were left in place because it was felt she would keep here balanced better.

With the well experienced Captain at the helm Captain Blinman, this 373 tons steamer, with a crew of 23 and 30 passengers, set sail for Bristol with her cargo: Boxes of eggs, Barrels of fish, live chickens, 10 horses, 137 pigs and 180 horned cattle.

Thankfully, there were survivors of the sinking to explain what happened.

The following account of the loss of the ill-fated steamer has been obtained from Irish crewman James Case, and, he does not account from the precise circumstances of the wrecking, but, it does give us the best description of what James Case, went through as she broke up and sank. Now let's James Case tells it in his own words, this is his statement:

The "SS MARS," left Waterford at very near to her advertised time, 10 o'clock on Tuesday morning 1st April 1862. After they had been at sea some time the weather thickened, and although the wind was not very high a great deal of sea got up. As night draw on the thickness increased and it became very dark, and for many hours they did not see a thing.

James Case describes Captain Blinman as having been remarkably attentive to the working of his ship, and seemingly anxious, and it was remarked that he did not go below for more than five or ten minutes during the whole of the afternoon and evening.[Captain Blinman, whose father had died when the "FROLIC," paddle steamer that was wrecked on Nash Sands, near Swansea in 1831].

Captain Blinman ordered the patent log [this was the method they could see the speed of the steamer] *to be kept out, by means the ships progress is self registered, and so things went on till approaching 8 o'clock in the evening, at which time the ship must have been nearing the Welsh coast – unfortunately nearing it more rapidly than anyone on board could have been aware.*

Somewhere about that time Massey's log was taken in, for James Case had seen it hanging on the rail of the quarterdeck. [Since the sixteenth century, sailors had determined the vessels speed by using a log. This was basically a rope with knots tied at intervals along its length. With a board attached to the end to create drag, the log-line would be thrown overboard and allowed to run out for a certain amount of time. The number of knots counted off during certain amount of time, indicated the speed. The unit of speed at sea is therefore the knot, one knot equal to one nautical mile per hour. Edward Massey, received the first patent for a successful mechanical log]

At 8 o'clock the watch was change, and it became the turn of me, and Joseph Cross, the other seaman who was saved, and some of the other poor fellows who were drowned to go for what sailor's call their watch below. [They would get something to eat and some rest].

At about 10 or 15 minutes after 8 o'clock in the evening the vessel received a tremendous shock, and it at once became evident that she had struck on a rock. The vessel at the time she struck was going; James Case supposes about 9 or 10 miles an hour. [Struck at 8.15 p.m. Tuesday 1st April 1862].

[Photo of Crow Rock, Linney Head, near Milford Haven. SS MARS struck near this rock. With such cliffs, there is no chance of survivors climbing these]

I heard the Captain to call out "Hard-a-Port!" [Turn the wheel hard left] *and in a few moments after, "Reverse!" and it is believed that the engines were then reversed.*
As may be supposed, all at once became confusion. The sea broke over the sides of the ship and poured down the hatchway into the engine room, and it soon became evident that she must become a wreck. James Case believes that the boats were then hurriedly resorted to.

Myself and Joseph Cross, with assistance, got a very small boat and succeeded in getting her afloat, and into that he, his messmate, two of the firemen, brothers named Suttod, a youth, who was about to emigrate to Australia, and a drover named Kane, got aboard. Another drover was approaching to get into her but was too late.
The "SS MARS" went down as near as James Case can guess, in about five or six minutes after striking. Just before she became engulfed Joseph Cross seen a women, who he is certain was the stewardess, Mrs. Way, she was standing on the paddle box wringing her hands. [In them days it would be quite common to see, the wringing of hands, you don't see people doing that now-a-days].
The rowing boat was floating and was being tossed about by the heavy ground swell James Case and his companions heard the Captain and others shouting to them as if to urge them to keep near, but whether they were clinging to the wreck, to some floating fragments, or had succeeded in getting into the lifeboat they were unable to say.

But although providence had so far favored their efforts as to enable them to get into the rowing boat and get clear of the wreck and rock, the dangers and difficulties of the unhappy men were by no means at an end. They were without light, food, or rudder plus the seamen had very little clothing on.   The rowing boat in which they were tossed violently about, while the risk of capsizing was every moment increased by the drowning Long horn cattle, some of which swam about, occasionally thrusting their heads over the boat, and threatening it and its occupants with instant destruction.[Half a ton, of frightened Long Horn Cattle, trying to get into the 12 ft rowing boat].

It was very dark with rough seas and surf, the greatest difficulty was experienced, by means of a couple of oars, in keeping the boats head to sea, [They had to keep the bow of the rowing boat towards the incoming surf, or she would have turned over] *so as to prevent her being swamped. Luckily, James Case was a very good seaman, and he hit on a plan for keeping something like steering way on the boat by lashing an oar through the rudder-hole.*
In this were the occupants of the boat passed the long hours of the night tossing about at the mercy of the elements, not knowing where they were, and praying rather than looking for deliverance.

They suffered greatly from exposure to cold and wet, and after a time Case, and Joseph Cross's hands became so benumbed that they could hardly grasp the oars, in their power to use which alone their chance of reaching the coast lay. Break of day enabled them to see where they were, and they made desperate efforts to get their boat to the coast.
This at length they happily succeeded in doing, and landed ultimately at St. Govan's Head, greatly exhausted, but with hearts over-flowing with gratitude at having been spared.
Once on the coast they received assistance from the Coastguardsmen, and others. They went to Milford where information of the wreck was given to them. Since then they have been sent on to Waterford, and it was in that City that James Case, give the narrative from which this is prepared by his aged father, then sent onto Bristol.
[The steamer SS MARS had hit Crow Rock, Linney Head, south of Milford Haven under full steam].

Surprisingly, more survivors were turning up along the Pembrokeshire coast, including cabin passengers Dr. Blist, of Portlaw, on his way to Bristol; Captain Russell, with his wife, child, and servant, who were coming to Bristol for their departure for India; Miss Combes, residence unknown.
Deck passengers: There were 15 persons entered as passengers on deck, of whom the following were known to have survived, and who were all pig dealers: Messrs. Cooper, Belcher, Wilshire, Kerwick, Brien, and Molly.   Those are described as residing at Waterford.

The loss of the SS MARS of Waterford was the third major shipping disaster on the Pembrokeshire coast in only seven years. Just two years before on 28th February 1860, the paddle steamer NIMROD of Cork, had been wrecked at St. David's Head, and all 45 aboard went to a watery grave. And on 5th February 1856, the 2,000 ton American sailing ship GREAT DUKE was wrecked near St. Govan's Head with loss of 29 crewmen out of 32.

St. David's Head, Queen Victoria and the German Kaiser:

The German Kaiser (Wilhelm1) his Government ministers were asking the British Government ministers questions, Queen Victoria (who is related to the German Kaiser) she also was asking questions to her Prime Minister Benjamin Disraeli, and he was asking his Ministers, H.R.H. the Prince of Wales, Lords Commissioner's of the Admiralty, Board of Trade, and Post Office Authorities, were all getting involved as well, and all asking questions?

Left
[The German Kaiser Wilhelm1 (b. 22 March 1797 d. 9 March 1888, aged 90)]

Right
[Queen Victoria
(b. 24 May 1819
d. 22 January 1901 aged 82)]

[British Prime Minister Benjamin Disraeli (b. 21 December 1804 – d. 19 April 1881 aged 77)]

Why would such powerful people and two Government Departments of Germany and Great Britain, all be interested in; "St. David's Head, Pembrokeshire?"

Let me tell you how it all began: -- it all starts on the 7th May 1875 on the Scillies Isles. The German Transatlantic steamer SS SCHILLER, New York, USA for Hamburg, Germany, was wrecked with a great loss of life, 320 German passengers perished. Cause of sinking was in thick fog she struck the rocks. Just over a year before on 28th March 1874 the ALARIC of Liverpool, on voyage from Pensacola, Florida, USA for Liverpool, England she had struck the Hats & Barrels off the Pembrokeshire coast, this fully rigged ship had turned upside-down and then drifted with the current into St. Bride's Bay. Finally sinking on Green Scar, about a mile south of Solva, with the loss of 22 British lives.

SS SCHILLER: The Kaiser's German Government was asking the British Government questions, HM Queen Victoria, (who is related to the German Kiser), was asking questions of her Prime Minister Benjamin Disraeli.

Question being asked by the two most powerful Governments of the day: What was the British Government going to do about this great loss of German citizen's [320 lives lost], and how was the British Government going to stop this happening again.

This is the British Governments Answer: August 1876 to Build "Lookout Post at St. David's Head" [They built them all over the South West England and Pembrokeshire coasts].

Now everyone's happy; The German Kaiser (Wilhelm1) and his Government ministers are happy, the British Government ministers, Queen Victoria (who is related to the German Kaiser) her Prime Minister Benjamin Disraeli, Government Ministers are happy, even H.R.H. the Prince of Wales, Lords Commissioner's of the Admiralty, Board of Trade, and Post Office Authorities are all happy. All these powerful people and powerful Governments are all happy. Now, any shipwreck could seen by anyone of these lookout posts, from Cornwall to St. David's Head. Problem solved, well, not really; just there is a slight problem with this 'brilliant idea,' let's see now; first off as long as the ship did not sink at night, or in fog, or in bad weather, or in poor visibility, or in a gale or even a storm, or the two men on watch were looking in the right direction at the right time.

St. David's Head it all went ahead, and this is the announcement made in Pembrokeshire: We are in a position authoritatively to inform the people of Pembrokeshire that the Lords Commissioner's of the Admiralty have definitely settled upon having a Coastguard station at Saint David's Head, and by their Supt. Division Officer, Capt. C. D. J. Odevaine have fixed upon Llaethdy Peak, Carn Llidi as the spot where to build a look-out house and signal station upon and no doubt such a commanding altitude [593 feet, that's about 200 metres above sea level] will be very advantageous one, in order to detect at once anything that may be wrong in the offing, from Bardsey Island on the Welsh coast, Carmsore Point, the Connemara and Vinegar Hills, Ireland, can very often be seen with the necked eye, and no doubt on a clear day a radius of some 50 or 60 miles can be scanned over through a good telescope such as the Coastguard men generally have to use. [They really must have good eye sight to see over the covertures of the earth, let me now be honest with you, ask anyone from St. David's and they will tell you; to see the Connemara and Vinegar Hills, Ireland, or even Bardsey Island or I really should say the tops of them, this is only possible say at the best once a year, if you're lucky. This idea of lookout posts is based on politics and not local St. David's knowledge].

Of course the Admiralty have the power to command and compel landowners to sell or lease land for such sites, but in this case, hitherto, they have not threatened to use compulsory powers, and the matter, I understand, has been left in the hands of Mr. Samuel Williams of St. David's as principal commoner to negotiate with the fellows who are five in number, one of them being no less a personage the H.R.H. the Prince of Wales, who has a small interest in the property. And they were quite pleased to sell or lease the land; after all it is their patriot duty to do so.

Consideration of having telegraph wire communication with the Lighthouses on the Smalls and South Bishops Lighthouses are in the planning stages – the Lords Commissioner's of the Admiralty, Board of Trade, and Post Office authorities Departments were are now fighting to see who will take charge of such matters'.

Great News on Tuesday 15th April 1879 [Four years after the wrecking of the SS SCHILLER the German Transatlantic steamer New York for Hamburg, Germany; was wrecked on the Scillies Isles on 7th May 1875 with a great loss of German lives, 320 perished]; that the watch Tower on Llaethdy Peak, Carn Llidi is now completed, and has been handed over to the officer in charge of H. M. Coast Guard Station.
It will be some comfort to think that no human being will have the misfortune to spend another winter without shelter on such an exposed spot, for some years to come.

Now let's take a look at the wrecking of the fully rigged sailing ship ALARIC of Liverpool, with its cargo of wood. Her voyage was from Pensacola, Florida, USA to Liverpool, England. Captain Roberts. Owner: Mr. O. Owens of Liverpool. Vessel of 1,262 tons. Built 1860 at Ruddock, New Brunswick. Crew of 22 all drowned. Lost in gale conditions.
She was first sighted bottom up, one mile west of the Green Scar Rock, off Solva, on Monday 30th March 1874. On Monday morning at about 6 a.m., a large ship was seen drifting into St. Bride's Bay, bottom up, supposed to have struck and capsized on the Hats and Barrels, near the Smalls, and fears are entertained that all hands have perished. The wreck was brought up about three miles west of Green Scar, near Solva.

Capt. Rees, Lloyd's Agent, had the report about 8 a.m., on that day, and with his usual promptness and intrepidity proceeded at once from Porth Clais, with a crew in an open boat, then blowing fresh and the sea running high, and got alongside the wreck at about 10 a.m., having discovered the position of the ill-fated vessel, made for Solva to report the same to the several underwriters, and telegraph for steam tugs, which unfortunately did not arrive until Tuesday evening when the LASS O'GOWRIE, came into sight, the wind was still blowing too hard for her to render any assistance, and during that night the wreck drifted, and came into contact with Green Scar rock, where she began to break up; it was then discovered that she was laden with timber, and amongst the floating wreck was found the name of the unfortunate vessel, ALARIC of Liverpool.

On Wednesday they had a go again of towing her, the tug took her in tow and went for Solva, but, the sea still running very high, with a stiff breeze blowing on the coast, and when near the harbour's mouth in consequence of some of her gear becoming entangled she was cast on the rocks, where she now lies, and from the present severity of the gale is likely to become a total wreck.

Wood from the wreck is all along the coast from Porth Clais to Newgale.

Some of the ships beams and wood washed ashore were taken and used in the City Hotel, St. David's.

On Saturday18th April 1874 a letter was published in the Dewsland Newspaper of Solva:

To the Editor of the Guardian.

Sir, -- In your valuable paper of the 4th inst., I read a report of the wreck in St. Bride's Bay and the promptitude of Captain Rees and his crew, and no doubt much credit is due to those noble men to go out in an open boat on such a rough morning; but you do not say a word about the Life-boat and Captain Hicks who got together his brave men to man the boat, and the short time they took to reach the wreck, in hopes that they may be the means to save some poor fellow that may be still be clinging to the lost ship.

I think these men deserve share of the praise, and also that it should be made known that Captain Hicks in a hurry to get the boat out met with an accident, and has since lost part of one fingers.

Yours &c. J.

[The Coxswain of St. David's Lifeboat had lost part of the top of his finger, but, still he carried on, and stayed at the helm, till they returned to shore, he then allowed his finger to be seen by the local Doctor].

Another letter to the Dewsland and Guardian Newspaper dated: Saturday15th July 1874.

To the Editor of the Guardian.

Sir, -- I will thank you to insert the following report in your columns with suggestions offered by the use of telegraph communication between the Smalls and Bishops,

thence on to the Life-boat station at Solva and St. David's. For information of so many shipping disasters I am Indebted to Capt. Rees, Lloyd's Agent, St. David's.
I am, Sir,
Yours &c.
G. H. JONES. Engineering Surveyor, Portmadoc, North Wales.
[Talk again of some communication between the Lighthouses of Smalls and the South Bishop's too the mainland].

The ill-fated ALARIC, which was lost with all on board on the Hats and Barrels, distance 3 ½ miles from the Smalls, according to the report of the Smalls light-keepers who were eye witnesses of the melancholy disaster. The crew was seen clinging to the rigging for three hours before the vessel capsized. It is probable the poor crew had lashed themselves to the rigging, hoping some passing vessel might observe their perilous position – they had the ensign up as a signal of distress.
The weather was too thick at the time no one could see the unfortunate ALARIC, from the mainland between St. David's and Solva, the distance being 22 miles or thereabouts to the Smalls from the life-boat stations.

It is not likely that had there been a Telegraph between the Smalls and the Bishops, thence on to St. David's, an alarm might have thus been given. Life-boat would have gone off, and been nobly instrumental in saving the lives of the crew of the ill-fated vessel. [Not forgetting that the St. David's Lifeboat would have to row over 20 odd miles, straight into a south westerly gale].

Imagine being a Lighthouse Keeper on the Smalls and all you could do is just watch the sad scene of seamen holding onto the wreck. These were witnessed both from the Smalls and by the Bishops Light-keepers. Vessels lost and their crews disappearing in the angry waves. There was nothing you could do, what an awful situation to be in.

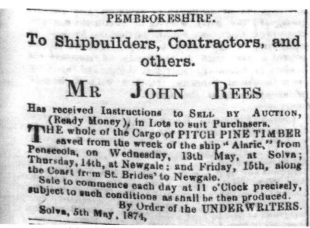

[This advertisement appeared in the local newspapers late April 1874]

Lately five vessels are known to have been lost between the Smalls and Bishops Rocks within the space of the last three years; two large derelict ships were seen drifting by, they looked abandoned, but the Lighthouse men cannot be sure? Had there been direct communication between the lighthouses and the mainland, at least there might have been some hope? Thus, there is now a big push for the Telegraph.

G. H. Jones, the Engineering Surveyor, at Portmadoc, North Wales. Was now pushing even harder for communications he said: "It is highly important the Board of Trade Authorities should at once direct their serious attention and devise some means of saving a further sacrifice of valuable lives".

KYNOCH on the Hats and Barrels:

SS KYNOCH OF LIVERPOOL

Wrecked Sunday 11 May 1902, on the Hats and Barrels Reef.

The Hats and Barrels have been the scene of several wrecks. Navigation at the spot is very difficult.

The steamship, owned by the Garston Steamship Company, drifted on a strong tide against the reefs, situated between the Smalls and Grassholm Island off the coast of Pembrokeshire, at nine p.m. and foundered within half an hour. The SS KYNOCH, which was bound from New Milford to Kinsale, Ireland, was a fish carrier, and had a crew of ten.

The men took to the boats just in time to save their lives, and reached Milford Haven the following day. One of the firemen was reported as having been seriously injured.

The captain refused to make a statement beyond saying that:

"THE MATE WAS IN CHARGE WHEN THE VESSEL STRUCK."

Smugglers caught:

SMUGGLERS CAUGHT OFF CALDEY: Arrived at Milford, Wednesday 26th April 1815, the Customs cutter, under the command of Captain Prosser, with the smuggling cutter MARY of Guernsey, Captain Phillips, with his crew of ten. She was captured on Tuesday, after a very long chase in Caldy Roads; The MARY had on board about 600 ankers [8 ½ gallon casks, barrels] of Brandy and gin, which have been secured in the Customs house store. All the captured smugglers have been sentenced to five years in the Royal Navy, and just so happens at present in Milford, one of His Majesty's ships, will be pleased to except these men on her three year cruise, which she sailing in a few days. The extra crew will be delivered over to the Navy on the day she sails. They will be brought aboard in irons, on both wrists and ankles, and then they will be placed in the bottom of the ship hold, still in chains and only then brought up on deck once out of sight of land.

SMUGGLER VESSEL SUNK north of Lundy Island, in May 1830. Vessels for days after kept finding barrels of brandy floating off Lundy, the vessel NILE, picked up 26 barrels. The schooner ASSIDUOUS of Brixham, recovered a number of brandy barrels too, the following day she was found with her sails ripped to pieces her main mast had been carried away and drifting without any crew to be seen tendering the ship. Thinking the ship had been abandoned she was boarded. The crew was found so drunk and asleep on the cabin floor, with no one working the vessel.

SMUGGLERS CAPTURED at Aberpwll Cave, Abereiddy Bay: On Tuesday 23 July 1844. Smuggling – A large quantity of tobacco, upwards of 3,000 lbs was lately seized, by information, [Someone got a reward!] from a cave in a slate quarry, at Aberpwll, near St. David's Head, [about 4 ½ miles north of St. David's Head] by the ARROW cutter, and taken to Plymouth. The landing was affected by a celebrated French smuggling cutter. A person from the neighbourhood of the quarry was made prisoner, [Again from information received!] and the prisoner will be brought to trial at Haverfordwest.

Haverfordwest Trial: On Tuesday, 30th July 1844 [Just Eight days later, that's swift justice for you], William Watt's, the prisoner who lives near Aberpwll, who was apprehended by the crew of the ARROW, cutter, on suspicion of being concerned in the late smuggling transaction at Aberpwll, in the county of Pembroke, was brought before a bench of Magistrates, assembled in the Guildhall, Haverfordwest.
Mr. Potbury, from the Solicitors of the Customs Office, London, attended on behalf of the Crown and ably stated the case and laid down the law. Mr. Cozens a Solicitor in Haverfordwest appeared for the defendant. A lengthened trial of upwards of eleven hours, [Which was quite long in them days] during which time several witnesses were examined on both sides, the Magistrates retired to consider their verdict, when an acquittal was pronounced.
It appeared that the defendant had successfully proved a really good alibi. Mr. William Watt's was acquitted.

[With the Crown Solicitors having lost one case, they were not going to lose the next case as well! They moved this trial from Haverfordwest to Pembroke]. On Saturday 4th August 1844 came before the Magistrates at Pembroke. John Yelland Ellery, from Stonehouse, Plymouth, having been recognized as one of the smugglers. It seems the customs men seen this gentleman 'Ellery' on the smugglers boat, but, somehow, he had escaped. They had caught him a few days later. The trial went on all Saturday, and then adjourned till Monday.

Monday: John Yelland Ellery was brought before Magistrates at Pembroke, on Monday 6th August 1844, charged with the offence of being on board a vessel on the high sea, the said vessel having on board 3,664 lbs, of tobacco, in illegal packages.

Again Mr. Potbury appeared on behalf of the Crown and again Mr. Cozens [who had won an acquittal for Watts] for the defendant, this time there are too many witnesses i.e. Customs Officers, who said, 'they seen him on the smugglers boat, his defence was; "It was someone who looked like me, it wasn't me honest; I swear on my children's lives." After a patient hearing, the Magistrates convicted the defendant, and sentenced him to six months imprisonment in the county goal. But, in consideration of his age and bodily infirmities asthma, they relieved him from hard labour, which, under other circumstances, they would have inflicted on him.

Fishguard shipwrecks:

On Tuesday 16th February 1836; the schooner, TREVER of Chepstow, with a cargo of iron, was wrecked near Lower Fishguard.

A letter give the following, distressing account --

This morning, about four o'clock, the schooner "TREVOR" of Chepstow, Master David Evans, laden with iron, and bound from Newport, South Wales, for Runcorn, [near Liverpool] came ashore here, and sunk within about a cable's length [200 metres] of the rocks.

The crew and Master's daughter, she had only been taken on board yesterday.

In about three hours after the vessel was discovered, with the crew and masters daughter in the rigging, the sea was making complete breaches over the vessel. The

young woman, who was about 18 years of age, was observed by spectators to fall into the sea, and was seen no more.
The crew, of seven in number, were rescued by the life-boat, through very heavy surf, and brought in much fatigued, where every kindness was administered to them.
[Schooner wrecked between Saddle Point and Goodwick Sands]

Fast forward to January 2014. I was shipwreck researching and getting nowhere, while trying to find a certain wreck. "Days had been spent getting nowhere, just a big blank, and so, as always happens to me, my mind began to wonder. I sharpened my pencils, move around in my seat and began to read up about Skokholm Island, and came across a letter about the battle of the Alamo in 1836, Texas, did you know that there was a Welshman fighting at the Alamo, and he had arrived only a few years before in the USA. This is not what I was supposed to be looking for – and then out of the blue six words just jumped out at me "Wrecked on the Cow and Calf." Just these six words woke me up. I was looking for another wreck and there, a wreck I had dived on all them years ago.

It all came back to me, the summer of 1982. That summer I had been busy salvaging the wreck LEWIS, which had sunk about 3 miles south west of Porth Clias, in March 1894. I had located the LEWIS in August 1980, and in 1982 I was fully committed to the salvage project of lifting her valuable cargo of good Welsh roofing slates. A fellow Shipwreck Researcher and Diver, Tom Bennett called around to see me. He said that after I had finished for the season with the LEWIS wreck, he would show me another slate wreck off Fishguard, on the Cow and Calf Rocks. It also has a cargo of slates. Tom had no name, or date, of this mystiques slate wreck.

Sunday 19 September 1982, Tom, and I were at Goodwick loading up my boat "ACE" with our diving gear, before heading for the Cow and Calf Rocks, just outside Fishguard Harbour. The wreck is right in the middle of these rocks. It was one of those perfect days for diving, and the wreck is in shallow waters, which was a real treat for me. All my dives that summer were all over 30 metres and staying down for 65 minutes at a time. Arriving at the rocks, 'Cow and Calf' we kitted up and over the side we went. Tom showed me around the wreck site, we found plenty of broken slates. The non broken slates were 16in x 8in, the underwater visibility was about 10 metres, and I think the deepest we went was about 12 metres. The wreck site is well covered in seaweed. Tom showed me the anchor winch, just next to the winch I recovered the lead shot, used to give the captain the depth of water they were in. They tied a line to it, threw it over the side and counted the knots on the line till the lead shot reached the bottom.
The number of knots that passed through your fingers gave you the depth. One knot might represent five fathoms [one fathom is 6 ft or about 2 metre], plus putty would be stuck to the bottom. Whatever the seabed was made of would be stuck to the bottom,

like sand, gravel, mud. Now-a-days we just look at the echo sounder; it's much simpler and faster.

[Cow and Calf Rocks, and in the distance is Dinas Head. The wreck lies between the big rock and the rock going to the centre of the photo]

Once we finished looking around the wreck site we headed up to the surface, and while in the boat drinking our tea, Tom asked me what I thought of the wreck site. "Well Tom," I said, "it's not worth putting time into salvaging her, but we'll have to find out her name, adding 'it should be easy to find the name especially with a cargo of slates." That was in 1982 -- it's only taken 32 years to find the name, and what happened to her that fateful day in 1878.

The shipwreck is the schooner CHARLOTTE, of Portmadoc. Wrecked on the Cow and Calf, Fishguard on Monday night the 7th October 1878. The schooner was built 1852 at Portmadoc. She was a 62 ton vessel, her owner R. Humphries from Carnarvon, North Wales, was also her master. With her cargo of Welsh slates, she was on voyage from Portmadoc, Wales for Stockton-on-Tees, England.

A terrific gale hit the Pembrokeshire coast on Monday night 7th October 1878, and drove the schooner onto the Cow and Calf Rocks.

As soon as her perilous position was seen the No. 1 Lifeboat belonging to the National Lifeboat Institution, and stationed at Fishguard was launched and went out to her assistance.

The boat had a difficult and dangerous service to perform. She and her gallant crew behaved admirably, and eventually the shipwrecked crew of the CHARLOTTE were safely landed at Goodwick by the lifeboat at half-past three o'clock the following morning. The vessel and cargo of slates were a total loss.

A week later Captain Humphries wrote to the local newspaper paper:

As Captain of the schooner CHARLOTTE, a 62 tons schooner from Portmadoc, bound to Stockton-on-Tees with a cargo of slate, writes Captain Humphries praising in the highest terms the conduct of the coxswain of the Fishguard lifeboat (Mr. James White), who with his able and willing crew put off to the assistance of the schooner which, in the gale on the 7th inst., was driven on the Cow and Calf Rocks, in Fishguard Bay.

At great danger to themselves, they succeeded in rescuing the whole of the crew from a most perilous situation.

The paper added; we must not forget to thank the sailors and others from Fishguard and Goodwick who have on many urgent occasions placed themselves under the able command of Mr. White and thereby had been the means of saving many a poor shipwrecked sailor.

Grassholm Island:

YES, WE ABANDONED HER! But sorry, we don't know where we were, but, if it's of any help, we did drift onto a small island, with sea birds flying around, they are called Gannets; does that help?

Everything was going so well as the SUCCESS, under the command of Captain Perry as he headed down the English Channel, on her voyage from London for Liverpool with her valuable cargo of Porter and general goods. [Porter is a dark style of beer originating in London in the 18th century. The name 'Porter' is thought to come from its popularity with street and river Thames porters]. SUCCESS having sailed from London on the Saturday 23rd April 1814, she came around the Cape Cornwall on the Saturday 30th, and at 11 p.m. of the Sunday 1st May in calm seas a very thick fog set in. Without any wind she just drifted all night, and then she gently came into contacted with an Island.

The crew finding her in such a perilous situation without the least apparent prospect of saving her, and not knowing where they were, took to their boats, and entirely deserted her. All night and most of next day they just rowed east, still in a thick fog. In theory if they kept rowing east then they should hit land. In fact, they had rowed almost into Milford Haven. At the entrance they were picked up by the DILIGENCE, a Customs Cutter under Master Dobbin.

Captain Perry and crew were asked some awkward questions and it went something like this:

Question: Captain Perry, where did your ship SUCCESS with it valuable cargo sink?
Answer: Well, she did not sink really, we, well, hum, sort of abandoned her!
Question: Captain Perry, was she sinking when you abandoned her?
Answer: Well, hum, not really, but, there was a small island, and we sort of drifted onto it!
Question: Captain Perry, This Island you sort of drifted onto. Can you show me where she lies on the chart?
Answer: Well, it was somewhere west of Milford Haven, oh yes, and there were sea birds looked like Gannets flying around the island.
Question: Captain Perry, apart from Gannets flying around this island, what else was on this island?
Answer: Oh yes, we also seen lots of sheep on the island.

Let's go over the clues again:
1: An island that lies west of Milford Haven?
2: With Gannets on the island and flying overhead?
3: Sheep grazing on this island?

The island is Grassholm. Gannets everyone knew about, but sheep? Well yes, Grassholm used to have sheep. About 30 sheep were placed in the spring, and taken off in autumn.

Back to the story of the supposed shipwreck, SUCCESS. Now, it's Tuesday morning, the fog is clearing slightly, and two vessels set off in search for this valuable shipwreck as well as the salvage reward. They were customs cutter DILIGENCE together with the SANDWICH, a Post Office Packet. As they are about to leave the Haven what do you think they saw coming into the Haven why the SUCCESS, being towed in by the VENUS, under Captain Tindleton. The SUCCESS was in a very shattered state. It appeared the vessel must have drifted off Grassholm on the following tide and the VENUS discovered her many miles south of Grassholm. Her strange appearance was strange, with most of her sails set in different directions. First, they hailed her, but receiving no answer, fired a gun, after which Captain

Tindleton, sent crewmen on board. They towed her into harbour to claim the salvage money. A meeting of the Magistrates was held on the following day, convened for the purpose of the salvage claim. The magistrates have handsomely rewarded Captain Tindleton of the VENUS for all their exertions.

SALVAGE & JUST REWARDS: When I [Jim] was about ten years old, my dad used to get telegrams now and again for the amount of salvage money they were going to get. As I got home from school my mum would say, "Take this telegram down to your dad, it's the telegram he's been waiting for." Off I would trot to Swansea Docks, to find my dad's tug boat. The tug boat was quite easy to find, mum said, "I had to look for a tug boat that's the same colour as our living room." No need to wonder too where my dad got the paint from.

Once aboard I would find myself sitting with a mug of tea, amongst salvage men. There language was always just perfect, never once did I ever hear any sort of bad language [not like today's salvage people, but, when I search for wrecks there are never any bad words allowed to be spoken]. Aboard the tug, it might have something to do with someone shouting 'Graham's boy is here!' Then it was all polite society talk. The crewman with hands the size of shovels said to me, 'pass the milk, thank you young Sir.' The one who I always thought looked like Long John Silver would say 'Arrrr, Sugar, my dear young fine gentleman Arrrr.' And the mate, my dad said he always gets in fist fights for money, would say, 'The 'situation demands another brew.' Once all the Salvage crew was sitting around the table, dad would read out, the telegram, and they all would shout together "HIP, HIP, HOORAY, and JOLLY GOOD SHOW!" That's how Salvage men talked in those days. Then dad would show me around the tug boat, let me sit in the captains chair, then get out the charts, which I could read up to a point.

As for my just reward, boy, oh, boy, I would get a whole "Shilling," Wow! "One Shilling," that was a fortune in the late 1950's. Happy memories.

Let's return to the Pembrokeshire Islands and the question of sheep grazing. Most of the islands off the Pembrokeshire coast had sheep placed on them. Grassholm had 50 sheep, then west of Ramsey the South Bishops 30 sheep, Daufraich 20 sheep, Carreg Rhosson 20 sheep, and Ynys Cantwr 20 sheep, Ynys Bery 50 sheep. The last two are on the south side of Ramsey Island. As you enter Milford Haven, just on the right is an island called Sheep Island you can guess how it got its name. These sheep, apart from having a nice sea view, were not troubled by flies or other pests. It was said the meat of these sheep tasted much nicer. Some families would have nothing else but these island sheep to eat. The farmer got a much higher price for Island Sheep. In all, about 250 sheep grazed on these islands.

In 1814 Grassholm Island had about 50 Gannets. Even in 1930's the number had grown to only about 5,000. But in 2014, there are about 90,000. [Count them, if you don't believe me!]

Sheep have been placed on the islands possibly going back to medieval days till around the 1880's, when the practice stopped.

Grassholm Island was once known as Grass Island. In 1693 Captain Greenville Collins, said about the island "It's a high, small island and green." Sheep on Grassholm but, do not put on the island ewes in milk, as the milking sheep require more water.

On the higher part of the island are the remains of a stone compound used for collecting the sheep possibly from medieval days. The centre of the island was chosen as a location to keep the sheep away from the cliffs. 20 sheep would remain all year round, and then more were brought in the summer.

The practice of putting sheep on Grassholm Island ceased but in 1865 Skomer Island Farmer Captain Vaughan Palmer Davies, started to use Grassholm again.

How many Gannets nest on Grassholm?

In 1802; we have no record of Gannets recorded nesting on Grassholm Island.

1802 = not one Gannett recorded
1814 = 10 Gannets
1860 = 20 "
1872 = 24 "
1883 = 40 "
1886 = 500 "
1890 = 600 "
1905 = 800 "
1935 = 5,000 "
1964 = 60,000 "
2014 = 90,000 "

WRECKS ON GRASSHOLM

I have 25 named shipwrecks, from small sailing coasters to large steamers. As for unknown wrecks, say another 50.

In Jack Sound alone I have 40 known shipwrecks, and there could be 100 more.

"We certainly have a lot of shipwrecks around and off the coast of Pembrokeshire.

A total of over 3,000 known shipwrecks, and how many unknown, well, but, let's say, as a Shipwreck Researcher my educated guess is on top of 3,000 known, another 3,000 unknowns. That's 6,000 wrecks of the coast of Pembrokeshire. [These are my calculations, and with over forty five years of research, I speak with some authority].

The schooner ELLEN was wrecked on north side Grassholm Island on Sunday 15th October 1871. She was built at Conway in 1858. 93 feet long. 140 tons. Her voyage was from Portmadoc, Wales for Hamburg, Germany. All the crew was saved except the Master Thomas Davies. A search was made, and then a few days later his body was found in the wreckage, he had been eaten by the ships rats.

RATS: I'm sure you would like to know all about rats on the Pembrokeshire Islands: well interestingly, there are no rats on Grassholm Island, but all the other islands have a rat problem. Rats love sea birds especially their eggs, and then they like or attack the chicks and even attack the adult sea birds. Every now and again when the rat problem is getting to an 'unacceptable' level; they bring onto the island the 'RAT TERMINATOR' [I do met some of the most interesting people with my research, but I must say the RAT TERMINATOR; really was a very interesting chap] now his job is to get rid of these pests. This is what he explained to me; how it's done. It's very interesting, and I know he would what me to share it with you. Rat Terminators have a sort of 3 inch plastic pipe by 3 foot long, I think he said they then place it about a foot or two off the ground, of course only the rat can get to it, after all you don't want to kill anything other than a rat. The poison is placed in the centre of the tube. Then every day they are checked to see if the poison has gone, if so he replaces it. Now I'm not talking about one or two traps, there would be 500 or even more of these poison traps, placed all over the island. At first as you can imagine the poison go's from most, then day by day less and less is taken. Till finally none is taken. They are checked for a month or more after, just in case some poison goes! This can take up to four months.

How do rats get onto the islands, in the first place? It's thought they may be brought in with bags of feed for the animals or in bales of hay. Then we have shipwrecks these are the worst for introducing rats to all the islands. When the steamer SS SZENT ISTVAN was wrecked on South Ramsey in 1908, the crew reported seeing rats swimming to the island from the wreck. Proof of this can be found on the north Pembrokeshire border an Island called Cardigan Island, in Ceredigion. Once Cardigan Island had all manner of seabirds happily living there, they had been coming to this island for thousands of years, nesting birds such as Guillemots, Razorbills, Kittiwakes, Manx Shearwaters, and my favorite sea bird - Puffins. There they were these happy sea birds minding their own business; then without any warning and without any sort of invitation; out of the blue on the 15th March 1934 the SS HEREFORDSHIRE. CRASH! BANG! Straight onto the island. She was a complete wreck, not only did the crew abandon ship, but the rats also, in vast numbers.

[Cardigan Island, Ceredigion. Cardigan Island is to the west of Cardigan Town]

Within two years, the rats had decimated the sea bird life of Cardigan Island. The authorities sent in the Rat Terminator in the year 1985 and he has eradicated every single rat, but still today, [2014] the Puffins, have not returned to Cardigan Island as most of the other seabirds have. Now let's pop over to Grassholm; they had the same sort of thing happen; 10th July 1910, the SS DALSERF crashed into Grassholm Island on the south side, as the crew climbed up the rocks onto the island, they reported seeing rats also climbing up with them; I'm talking about hundreds of rats! [I knew you would like this story] You can imagine what they were going to do to the Gannet population on this island! Furthermore it's in the middle of July and the young chicks were still sitting on the nests! Let's move on one year later, the question is: "are there any Gannets left? "

Well, the Gannets are quite happy, but it's the rats that are missing? Not a single rat to be seen? It's believed that the Gannets killed them. Have you seen the beaks on a Gannet! So that's why Grassholm has not got a rat problem!

Let's change the subject from rats to cute bunnies; rabbits. Rabbits were introduced to the islands, by the Normans, in 1358, they also introduced them to Ramsey, but, before this they were already introduced to the islands of Caldey, Skokholm, Skomer even to Grassholm, strangely none survived on Grassholm. They have survived and are still living quite happily on all these islands except the island of Grassholm. It's thought it may have something to do with the Gannets! You can also see why when the Gannets took over more of Grassholm, the Puffins moved out. It's not because of the 24 hours of Gannet noise, and boy are they a noisy sea bird! It's to do with Gannets poo. This poo comes in great quantities in a small area, the chemicals in Gannet poo, kills the grass, where there isn't any grass the rain washes away the earth.

So the Puffins cannot build their homes or should I say dig their burrows.   That's why there aren't any Puffins on Grassholm anymore.

Back to shipwrecks: This 167 ton streamer SS MERSEY, of Maryport, bound from Maryport to Antwerp Germany while in thick fog she went and hit a rock about 100 metres to the north east off Grassholm Island, on Saturday 12th August 1876, her cargo was iron ingots. Built by T. R. Oswald of Sunderland 1867. Two men belonging to her took to the rowing boat and were picked up by the "SS ANGORN," 20 miles north and were taken to Waterford.   Only once the two men were picked up did the authorities know of the shipwreck! A telegram sent from Waterford to Lloyd's Agent at Milford on Monday requesting that a steamer should be sent out to search for the crew.   Capt. Jackson, the agent, immediately dispatched the Trinity House yacht ARGOS.

No survivors were found. Captain Robertson of the SS MERSEY and fourteen men have perished.   Out of 17 crew 15 were lost. She hit the rock, with her cargo of iron ingots and she sank taking 15 crewmen with her. The rock she hit is now called: Mersey Rock.

MARY sinks, who do you, believe?:

THE WRECK OF THE MARY

[This is interesting, two accounts of the same sinking. Here we will see both parties use the media of the day, i.e. the weekly newspapers. Who do you think is telling the truth?]You are now the jury:

We have received the following letter through the hands of the respected agent for Lloyd's (Frances Harper, Esq.,) and we are proud of the opportunity of holding up to scorn and condemnation of the civilised world the conduct of the heartless savage who left his fellow creatures to perish, when he could have so easily rescued them from their perilous situation: --

"TO THE EDITOR OF THE INDEPENDENT
Maryport, [Cumbria] *January 2nd, 1848*
"Sir, -- Having returned home since the loss of the brig MARY of Maryport, an account of which has appeared in most of the newspapers, as having been seen to go down on the 14th December 1847, about 12 o'clock 25 miles N.W., of the Smalls Light, by the crew of the schooner SPECULATOR, Capt Williams, of Milford, who further states that the crew had taken to their boats, but the sea was so bad he – Captain Williams could not render any assistance.

As I think it is right that the heartless conduct of the master of the schooner SPECULATOR should be sent through the world, I thank you, Mr. Editor, to give the following facts and particulars of the case a place in your columns.
At the time the MARY went down, the schooner SPECULATOR, and eight on the MARY's crew in the long-boat; and one man in the jolly-boat were so close to the schooner, when I asked Capt. Williams for a rope, Capt. Williams replied that he would stand by us.
But instead of doing so, he proceeded on his course to Waterford, leaving us with only one oar in each boat to the fury of the waves. We had the schooner within sight till dark. At midnight on nearing Tacumshane shore, a distance of upwards of 50 miles from where the SPECULATOR passed up, a sea struck the long-boat, and five of the men were washed overboard, four of whom perished. The boat was then thrown bottom upwards, with two of the men and I were underneath her and in that situation we remained till the boat broke up.
Had the sea been as bad as Captain Williams represents it, I feel confidence that Captain Williams might have saved the whole of the crew, with the exception of one man, who sank with the vessel.
I am, sir, yours truly
WILLIAM COCKTON,
"Late Master of the brig MARY, of Maryport."
Wexford Independent.
The newspaper added this: (*Captain David Williams, of the schooner SPECULATOR is not a native of Milford, but resides at Cwmeglwys, near Dinas, in the county.*)

The reply in the local paper; PEMBROKESHIRE HERALD. Saturday 10 March 1848
Sir, -- A statement having appeared in your paper to the effect that I had neglected to make any effort to rescue the crew of the brig "MARY," of Maryport while in their boats, in consequence of the sinking of their vessel, on the 17th of December last. Be pleased to allow the insertion of the enclosed declaration, as I wish to show that there was no real ground for the charge brought against me.
I am Sir, yours truly, DAVID WILLIAMS,
Master of the schooner "SPECULATER," of Milford Haven, March 9, 1848.

COUNTY OF PEMBROKE, (to wit.) We, David Williams, master of the schooner "SPECULATOR" of Milford, William Samuel, late mate of the said vessel, do solemnly and sincerely declare that on the 7ᵗʰ of December last, on our voyage from Newport to Waterford, when about 25 miles W.N.W., of the Smalls we saw a brig which proved to be the "MARY," of Maryport, standing to eastward.

Upon coming within about a mile of her she lay to with a signal of distress flying. We then ran down to leeward of her, and hove our vessel to in order to save the crew; before we had hove to we saw a boat leave the brig with one man in her, the boat much damaged; after we had hove to we saw another boat leave the brig, which we expected would reach us, but she failed to do so, as it seems the men in her had but one oar, of which we were ignorant. Having fastened lines to our fender, we hauled our vessel on the wind in order to stay, with the hope of picking them up, but she would not stay, and in making the attempt she was struck with a heavy sea, sprung her topsail-yard, and in consequence of her falling rapidly to leeward, the boat drifted to a great distance from us.

Our vessel was deeply laden, there was a heavy sea, and she was making so much water that it was with great difficulty we could keep her free. Under these circumstances we were utterly incapable of making any further attempts to rescue them, which we should most gladly and heartily have done, had it been practicable. We made this declaration for the purpose of contradicting the reports circulated in the newspapers to the effect that we had refused to make any effort to rescue the crew of the "MARY" from her perilous situation; and we make this solemn declaration, conscientiously believing the same to be true.

(Signed)   "DAVID WILLIAM and WILLIAM SAMUEL"

"Declared before me, this 2ⁿᵈ day of March, 1848, (Signed) "H. LEACH,

"One of her Majesty's Justices' of the Peace, for the County of Pembroke.

[Now you've read both accounts, which do you, believe?]

Newgale shipwrecks:

SHIPWRECKS ON NEWGALE SANDS

A French vessel outward bound from Bordeaux, while still off the French coast, was attacked and captured by British Privateer ship LIVERPOOL. The French ship was taken as a prize along with its valuable cargo of brandy, wine, general merchandise plus some boxes of silver coins. The Privateer put aboard her newly acquired prize a crew, with orders to sail straight to Liverpool. So the PRINCE with her prize crew aboard waved farewell to the mother ship, and sailed for Liverpool. When off the Pembrokeshire coast she sailed into thick fog, and lost her bearings. Anchoring off Skomer Island, she waited for the fog to lift. During that night a south westerly gale came up and blew her across St. Bride's Bay onto Newgale sands. PRINCE the prize ship with all these lovely goodies aboard was wrecked on Limpet Bed, Newgale Sands. She went to pieces in the pounding surf in the early hours on Wednesday 10th August 1757.

In 1992, some coins were found, on Newgale Sands, when sand levels were low, and they proved to be 'French silver pieces of eight.'

THE SCHOONER COSSACK, of Harrington, Master Walker, with its cargo 190 tons of mixed timber, and pine wood, from the Bay of Chelure for Dublin, went ashore on the morning of Thursday 4th December 1823. The crew was saved. It is remarkable that the persons on board the COSSACK did not see a vessel or the land during their whole voyage. Off Pembrokeshire with it being thick weather they hove too, and gradually drifted to the place where they were stranded. Over the days she became a complete wreck.

In the meantime she was plundered by local, country people, and one man (who was detected in carrying away some of the stranded articles), has been committed to the County Goal, by the Rev. Mr. Harris, and Mr. J. Stokes, Esq. But, for the attendance of Messrs. Saul. Starbuck and Co. merchants, and Agents for Lloyd's, assisted by Officers of the Customs, everything portable would probably have been carried away. The plunderers went as far as to fire their flintlock guns at the night watchman.

ANN OF SUNDERLAND

At one p.m. Friday 17th January 1840, the ANN of Sunderland was driven by gale onshore at the North West end of Newgale Sands, near the bridge, and has become a total wreck. When she was broadside to the waves, the crew was able to get into the boat under the lee of the vessel, and arrived on shore with loss of only their clothes. Under the command of Master Nixon, her voyage from Gloucester, England for Leghorn, Italy in ballast. This 278 tons brig went to pieces over the coming weeks. Vessel about a year old.

NO CREW ON ABOARD

A brig, under full sail, was seen drifting. Furthermore, it looked as if no crew on aboard. As she near the east end of Newgale Sands the onlookers could see that it was true -- she did not have a crew on board!   On Wednesday 8th February 1871, about 5 a.m., the weather being foggy with a light breeze from S.S.W., and the vessel touched the Newgale Sands. She proved to be the TARRAGONA, of Whitehaven.

Great fears were entertained by the on lookers, with no crew aboard and as none in sight that they had drowned. But, before the tide had ebbed from her all together, the crew, consisting of eight men, arrived on the spot. It appears that the crew abandoned her about 3 a.m., and got into Little Haven about 8 a.m. With the seas and winds calming down, the whole crew once again jumped into their rowing boat and headed for the North side of St. Bride's Bay, searching for their ship, only to discover her on Newgale Sands, unharmed and in perfect upright position. She was just sitting there, patiently waiting for the return of her crew.

15 days later, on Wednesday morning 22nd February 1871, the brig TARRAGONA was safely got off Newgale Sands and towed into Milford by the steam tug RANGER of Llanelly.

VITULA shipwreck and the lost 5 men of St. David's:

FIVE ST. DAVIDS MEN MISSING AT SEA

The 146 ton brigantine VITULA, of London, under the command of Captain James Roberts, left Fowey, Cornwall at 11.30 a.m., on Saturday 9 December 1882, destined for Weston Point, Chester, England, laden with 248 tons of china-stone clay. At 9.30 p.m., on Monday 11th, with the tide being at last quarter flood, the weather dark and a fresh breeze blowing E. by S., but with a smooth sea, the vessel suddenly struck forward, and climbed on what proved to be a reef close to the North Bishops.

Captain Roberts had been in his bunk since 9 p.m. He rushed on deck, and, finding water rushing in at the fore peak [narrow hold at bow], and the vessel listing to port [left], he ordered the lifeboat out, and all hands left the sinking vessel, which was now falling even more to port, and in a very dangerous position. All night they were taken by the tides and wind. On Tuesday, at 8 a.m., they landed on Aber Mawr beach on the west side of Ramsey Island.   Arriving at Ramsey farmhouse, where they were attended to by Mrs. Williams, from the Grove Hotel, St. David's - her husband was farming the island as well as running the Grove Hotel.

Two hours after arriving at the farm house, the ship's Captain and mate, with five men from St. David's, who included Mr. W. Arnold, of Penarthur, and Mr. Tom Williams, ventured out. They borrowed Mr. Arnold's boat, and off they set for the wreck on North Bishops Reef, to see what could be done about saving the ship.

From only half a mile from the wreck they could see her stern was under water, and, being unable to reach her because of worsening strong off shore winds and tides, they were pushed west, out into the open ocean.

Unable to regain land, they drifted further offshore. News of their disappearance spread, and the St. David's lifeboat was launched to rescue them. The lifeboat searched around the Bishops and Clerks islands and rocks, but they were not seen.

Anxiety in St. David's was high. The lifeboat was launched again, and the whole of the Bishops and Clerks rocks were surveyed on the Wednesday evening, but, again, without any success. Hopes were that the boat and crew had been picked up by a passing steamer. All Mr. Arnold was worried about was his boat. It was a substantial one.

On Thursday morning a telegram was received from Kingstown, Ireland, saying that they were all safe and comfortable there. For days afterwards, the wreck of the VITULA could be seen resting upon a curious, flat ledge on the southernmost rock outlying the North Bishops. It could be seen plainly from the Cross Square, St. David's.

The missing men had been picked up by the brigantine JENNY LIND, of London, and taken to Ireland.

All this happened in 1882, but for many years, from the 1830s, a fierce paper war controversy had been waged as to the North or South Bishops rocks being the more suitable for a lighthouse being built on. Many still say the South Bishops Lighthouse should have been built on the North Bishops. These are their words from a local newspaper:

"It was very unfortunate that in that case the "South had it," as since, we do not almost care to reckon how many vessels (known) have been cast away on those dangerous rocks. It was at that time, we well remember that the South Bishops was to be the Pharos [Beacon] to guide the trade to Milford, the Milford of Shakespeare, the Milford that was to be (out as not), Liverpool, Bristol, Newport, Cardiff, Swansea, &c., had then due notice to shut up shop, &c., but they all increase whilst "blessed" Milford dwindles. Can there nothing be done concerning the "North Bishops?"

A lighthouse on South Bishops Rock had been hinted as a path to more trade for Milford Haven that would lead to more regular work and not just work that was seasonal. It did not happen, and afterwards most of the local population still had access to only seasonal work.

Porth Clais harbour's history:

George Owen in Elizabethan times writes on the talking of the trout from the river 'Alan' which runs into Porth Clais Harbour', he says, "*For bigness they exceed any in those part's, and for tameness against nature, that they were not afeard at the sight of many people looking on them, and approached almost to men's hands to receive any thing that should be cast into the broke for food.*"

What George Owen is taking about; tickling trout, I've seen trout being tickled and caught this way when I was a child, what happens is you put your hand in the water and slowly very slowly move your hand under the trout and very gently you tickle it belly, once your hand is fully under the trout, you lift your arm up throwing the trout onto the bank. This takes practice with a lot and lots of patience, I've have never seen trout in the 'Alan,' but I'm told by locals that in the early 1950's there was still Trout in the river. In 1982, we used the Alan river, [really it's a stream], to wash Welsh slates, that we were salvaging off the wreck LEWIS. While washing the silt off the slates, and standing in 6 inches of water, now and again you would see eels up to half metre long swimming upstream. At first seeing them we'd jump in the air. You got use to them swimming around you feet, good job we had wellies on.

[Overlooking Porth Clais Harbour is this house which uses to be Pen Porth Clais Inn. Master George Lile of the smack LE COURIER wrecked at the entrance in 1879, used to lodge there at the Inn]

[Photograph taken in 2014, you can see the harbour wall had been repaired recently]

What's in a name: "PORTH CLAIS HARBOUR?"
I've always found the name 'Porth Clais', an interesting name, 'Porth Clais' has been spelt in many ways over the centuries. One of the oldest is 'Portclys', it means something to do with a fortified spot in that neighbourhood. It's a name borrowed from the English 'Portcullis,' that comes from the Latin "Portaclaus. So there we have it the name Porth Clais comes from the word Portcullis

Who built Porth Clais Harbour Wall? In 1968 I was told it was the Romans. Then in early 2014, I came upon this, in a letter written to Browne Willis, dated April 23, 1722, "Davies and his brother, one of the cannons of St. David's Cathedral, having contracted an enthusiastic partiality for the place of St. David's, and have entered deeply into its interests, and left behind them many proofs of their indefatigable zeal to rescue St. David's, the brother writes of his brother the Cannon who is now in residence is hastening to build up the pier at Porth Clais".
He writes: This Porth Clais, being the nearest accessible creek to St. David's, where every-thing was landed that served for their convenience or luxury of the place, a pier at a very early period had been constructed of the most durable masonry, and on a plan well calculated to repel the violence of the sea, which, on southerly winds, engulfs itself into this little estuary, and to form a safe harbour for the small craft that shelter there".
So from this 1722 letter we can see that the harbour wall existed before 1722, his brother then in residence at St. David's paid for it to be rebuilt, as he says "*was hastening to re-build up this pier,*" so we now know that it existed before 1722, this last material reparation it has experienced I believe, until the 1980's re-build. So maybe we can say its 1600 century or medieval, or can we go far back as the Roman Builders? Porth Clais was a very important port in its day.

Before Porth Clais harbour wall was built and re-built in 1722, all the small fishing boats and other commercial vessels moored there were at the mercy of gales, especially from the south. With nothing to stop these waves they would go straight up the harbour smashing to pieces any wooden boat. With the harbour wall, in place it made a lot of difference.

I have seen what storms can do at Porth Clais, with the harbour wall, re-built in 1722. In August 1979, we had the Great Fastnet Gale. That evening was so calm, with a beautiful sunset. Then without any warning, in the early hours 'all hell broke loose' this gale caught out seamen in the Fastnet Race, off Southern Ireland. Fifteen were drowned. We ourselves were in the middle of search and locate shipwrecks in Ramsey Sound. Luckily I had brought out my boat that night for some maintenance then in the morning planned to put her back in the water. With storm force winds the camping fields of Porth Clais Farm at dawn, looked what I can best described as, after a major battle had taken place. Everything was flapping in the winds, everywhere were tents turned inside out or flattened, plastic sheets, sleeping bags, saucepans, tables, chairs, all the necessities you need for a camping holiday, blown across the fields; and this is the middle of August. Some tents were never seen again.

I also witnessed waves so big, that just on the east side of Porth Clais Harbour entrance, the waves were from the south-west going all the way up and only stopping when they reached the hedge. Now that's not a gale, that's not a storm, that's what I would call a full blown hurricane.

The winds went from south westerly to more southerly, they came straight into Porth Clais Harbour, and the harbour was at this time of the year full of local and holiday-makers small boats.

We went down to the harbour to help but all you could do was watch. It was just too dangerous. Looking at the harbour wall, huge seas were coming and surfing up the harbour, going around the bend and straight over the road bridge, almost into the car park. Small boats were being smashed to pieces, the ones left on the moorings that is. I'm not talking about waves but surf, coming up the harbour about 4m high that's about 12ft high.

SHIPWRECKS AT PORTH CLAIS HARBOUR

In the Dewsland newspaper dated 26 November 1870; Mr. Samuel Williams of St. David's wrote that the BETSEY had been wrecked at the entrance of Porth Clais around 1850. As you look out of the harbour, on the west side at the point, [Right Side] in 1970 I located a big anchor, I think it is still there.

[Porth Clais Harbour, photograph taken about 1890. You can see the habour wall just behind this Ketch, and the state it has fallen into in 1890's]

In Porth Clais Harbour about 6 o'clock on Tuesday morning 4 January 1876 a fire was observed on the smack "CATHERINE," the property of William Jackson, lying in Porth Clais harbour; by a man named John Thomas, one of the crew. An alarm was given, which soon assembled the persons residing near, and after a time, a number of the citizens of St. David's.

The fire broke out in the bow, and some men got on the stern and tried to get the fire out under by pouring on buckets of water, but their efforts proved of no avail. When it was seen that they could not save her, and as the tide was coming in at the time, she was scuttled. Unluckily this was not carried into effect until the mast had fallen and her bows completely burned out.

She was insured. There are many rumours out as to how the fire occurred, but they cannot be depended upon. A week later Samuel Prosser, mariner, of St. David's, for loss of clothing, by the burning of the smack CATHERINE, at Porth Clais, has been awarded £2 15s 0d by the Shipwreck Benevolent Society.

THURSDAY MORNING 9th October 1879, while making for a small creek, named Porth Clais, a 21 ton smack with its cargo of culm [coal dust] from Little Haven named LE COURIER of Hakin, Milford Haven; built in 1857 at Hakin. On her approached to the entrance, the wind died away and she drifted onto rocks, at the entrance to the harbour where soon after she was abandoned, and the vessel was dashed into matchwood.

Master George Lile of Pen Porth Clais Inn, which overlooks Porth Clais Harbour and Mate William Mortimer of St. David's escaped in a small boat with some difficulty. The owner of vessel was Mr. William Williams of the Grove Hotel, St. David's.

Weekly Mail Newspaper on Saturday 8 April 1905 reports with these BIG headlines:

LLANELLY SHIP WRECKED.
DISASTER OFF PEMBROKESHIRE.
THE CREW SAVED.

About five p.m. on Saturday a schooner was seen in St. Bride's Bay, Pembrokeshire, making for Porth Clais Harbour, near St. David's. At this time it was blowing a south westerly force 5, fresh breeze and a heavy sea was running, the schooner was seen near Porth Clais (which is a very dangerous harbour to enter especially in rough weather), and in doing so she struck a rock near the entrance. In a few minutes the vessel foundered, the crew of two having barely sufficient time to take to the boat.

The schooner proved to be the CONFIDENCE, of Llanelly, culm-laden, for Porth Clais, St. David's. She was in command of by Captain Owen of Trevine. The CONFIDENCE was a small vessel of 90 tons, and will become a total wreck. Built: Lytham St. Anne's, Lancashire in 1856.

Wreckers - you are warned:

WRECKERS & PLUNDERING a warning no less from the Bishop of St. David's. The background to this story is the Bishop of St. David's was getting grief from the authorities for the church in not speaking up against this practice of plundering of shipwreck goods, around the welsh coast.

In December 1816 the Bishop of St. David's wrote an open letter to be read out at every Welsh church service in every sea port or near the coast. The cruel and unchristian-like enormity of plundering wrecks; and that they will, for the future, preach to them on this subject, once a quarter, or, at least, twice every year, and press strongly on their consciences the flagrant criminality of this inhuman practice, so disgraceful to them as Britons and Christians – to the enlightened country of which they are natives.

This is the open letter that was read out in Churches around the coast of Pembrokeshire: So they have been warned, but, another thing to add, if you were caught, you could be hanged, if hanged then no clergy would be allowed to be present, and to read the Bible over your dead body. WOW; the church is really getting tough. I bet that put the jeepers up the congregations.

Clergies to Read out loud this Circular Letter:

"Wreckers" Can you now impiously consider every unfortunate vessel driven upon your coast as a "God-send?" If you believe there is a God, or a future state, in which your souls will be doomed to suffer for your enormities on earth, banish from your minds the blasphemous idea. Expiate your former crimes by sincere contrition, and a steady determination to aloft for the future a line of conduct directly the reverse of the past. When the winds of Heaven place in jeopardy on your part of the coast the lives and property of your less fortunate fellow creatures, let all your energies be exerted to save and protect both; let there be no intermission, no relaxation of your efforts, till all shall be done that may be in your power to accomplish.

Your first care, in cases of wreck, should be the preservation of the crew, your next, that of the vessel and cargo; -- in the former you will generally be successful, in the latter less frequently so. But whatever you save should be watchfully guarded and restored to its owners, who will, in most instances, compensate you to the extent of your services, or of their own means. Rewards thus obtained will be far sweeter to your feelings than the produce of pillage and robbery; should you be detected in such excesses, and the facts be proved, the penalty is Death – ignominious Death! You cannot expect mercy, the frequency of your crime calls loudly for 'severe examples'.

WOW! Hell and Damnation just before Christmas too. The Pembrokeshire congregations, after giving this a lot of deep thought and soul searching, 'did not take a blind bit of notice,' and carried on with the old practice that had been going on for a long, long time.

Now, let's hear the Pembrokeshire folks reason's for acquiring these items washed ashore: they will give it to you straight, eliminate the essence and clarify the logic: let's start off with wreckage coming ashore; First off, these items washed ashore, they can be very dangerous to: fish, seals, crabs and sea birds, It's been proved that these poor sea creatures could cut themselves; [do you need more, you do?] They are of no use anyway, the best example is sacks of flour washed ashore, seawater soaking wet on the outside, but, the flour is dry in the centre, now who would buy these bags of flour, then who would want dead pigs washed ashore, these were acquired, then transported to the Pembrokeshire kitchens, cooked straight away to stop infection and germs, and to clean up the beaches. Let's look at wood off shipwrecks, what can you do with it anyway, bust or sea water soaked, has made it useless, who wants bust –sea water wet wood. [How's that; what, you still want more!]

Let's now look at the cost of recovery of anything of value, once ashore, it could be at the bottom of cliffs, only to be got by boat, the dangers of this are the seas, seas coming straight in from the North Atlantic Ocean, once recovered, then it has to be transported, (and we all know the cost of transporting), take a found item to the receiver, as the finder legally you must be rewarded and your expenses covered for finding and handing in to the receiver. By the time the owners of the cargo had sorted it all out, the costs and time; let's be honest, it was not worth all the effort financially. That's what Pembrokeshire folk say.

Smalls Rock Lighthouse:

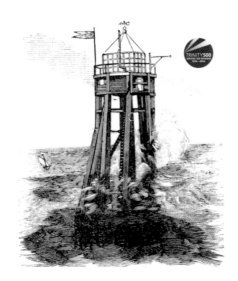

The Smalls Rocks are right in the way of the main shipping route for Liverpool. By then Bristol was the 2nd main port after London. With the growth of the Lancashire textile manufacturing and iron industry, Liverpool was fast overtaking.

The Smalls Rocks lays 20 miles south-west of St. David's Head. The highest part is only 1 metre (3 foot) above the highest spring tides. I'm always asked "How many Shipwrecks are on the Smalls Rocks?" 160 known shipwrecks and most likely about another 200 unknown shipwrecks.

[Henry Whiteside's design of the Smalls Lighthouse, 1776.
Thanks to Trinity House for use of drawing.]

John Phillips advertised for Lighthouse designs and chose one submitted by 26 year old Henry Whiteside, a musical instrument maker from Liverpool. Henry Whiteside's design was simply five wooden pillars and three more of cast iron, with a hut of timber, 4.5 metres [that's 13 ft across for two men to live in for one month] in diameter. Top room was the lamp room, with windows all the way round, plus, an iron hand railing and walkway all the way round, so they could clean the windows. It stood 20m high (66ft) and had a door on the north-east side of the hut, with a pulley bock above the door to pull up supplies. From the rock a rope ladder went up to a trap door that was in the middle of the 13 foot room. In 1773 [aged 27] Whiteside arrived at Solva. He built the structure temporarily at Solva, and then transported each piece by boat [20 foot with one sail come rowing boat] to Smalls Rock. From 1773, Henry Whiteside erected the structure and the first light showed 1 September 1776. Solva is a small fishing village about 25 miles from the Smalls.

Because of Whiteside's planning the parts all just fitted together it just took three years to put together on the Smalls Rock. On 1st September 1776 a light was showing, for the first time on the Smalls.
Why on pillars and not of solid granite structure? It was all about cost and building time. A granite structure would take six times longer to build, and cost 20 times more. This was in the days of oar and sail only. The wind is free, but it never blows in the right direction.

The excavated holes for the pillars to stand in were dug, well really they drilled and blasted. This work was done by Solva coal miners. When the timber poles had been placed in the 10 feet deep holes, the gaps between the pillar and rock was then filled with two to three tons of molten lead and pebbles. Eight were dug out this way [let's do some sums just on the lead needed: 8 pillar holes; 10 feet deep; 3 tons of lead each; why, roughly that's 24 tons of lead, 24 tons of lead that had to be transported 25 miles offshore, in a 20 foot sail come rowing boat. Next the miners moved on from pillars holes to another hole this one was a lot bigger: 10 ft x 6 ft x 6 ft again this is dug out of solid rock. This hole was made to hold coals, oils and fresh water in wooden barrels. Over the years, Whiteside had to keep drilling and blasting more holes as he needed them, in total I have counted 30 holes plus the box hole. That gives us a rough amount you have to transport 25 miles of 70 tons of lead and about 30 tons of pebbles.

After the two Lighthouse keepers moved in they discovered straight away, in rough sea conditions, but much worst in gales, in their wooden cabin, the top part swayed one to two foot one way and then the other way. Imagine that, in a 13 foot by 13 foot wooden cabin 60 ft above the rocks, 25 miles off shore, and let's add it's blowing a gale. Mr. Whiteside added wooden pillars these were placed at an angle, against the straight pillars, to stop this swaying movement.

By December it was obvious that the structure was incapable of withstanding the sea forces and in January 1777 Whiteside (age 31) and his blacksmith proceeded to Smalls to repair and strengthen it. While on the lighthouse, they encountered a period of severe storms. They were stuck in the 13 foot x 13 foot room [that's four men don't forget] and they were getting desperate. Running out of water did not help. By February, their only hope was to get a message ashore. Whiteside wrote three letters and placed each letter in a small cask (barrel) and then tossed them into the sea. The next day one was picked up at St. Justinian's in Ramsey Sound. It begged for "immediate assistance to fetch us off the Smalls before the next Spring tide or we fear we shall all perish, our water near all gone, our fire quite gone and our house in a most melancholy manner." The Letter said:

To Mr. Williams.
Smalls, February 1, 1777
Sir,
Being now in a most dangerous and distressed condition upon the Smalls, do hereby trust Providence will bring to your hand this, which prayeth for your immediate assistance to fetch us off the Smalls before the next spring or we fear we shall all perish; our water near all gone, our fire quite gone, and our house in a most melancholy manner. I doubt not but you will fetch us from here as fast as possible; we can be got off at some part of the tide almost any weather. I need say no more, but remain your distressed

Your Humble Servant,
Henry Whiteside,

We were distressed in a gale of wind upon the 13th of January, since which have not been able to keep any light; but we could not have kept any light above sixteen nights longer for want of oil and candles, which makes us murmur and think we are forgotten.
Ed. Edwards
Geo. Adams
Jno. Price
We doubt not but that whoever takes up this will be so merciful as to cause it to be sent to Thos. Williams, Esq., Trelethin, near St. David's, Wales.

Interestingly, one of the other message casks was found in Galway Bay, Ireland, months later.

After the storm of December 1777 drastic repairs and alterations had to be made. But, John Phillips did not have the money. He extinguished the light and sacked the keepers.
Then in September 1778 in stepped Trinity House, they repaired and maintained the light-house, collected the levy' -- all ships that passed the lighthouse had to pay lighthouse dues. The bigger the ship the more they paid, and all the major ports had lighthouse dues collectors.
In view of Phillips' services and his losses, he was granted a lease in June, 1778 for 99 years at a yearly rent of £5. Then more gales damage the light in 1807, 1812 and 1832. The pillars had to be replaced or strengthened a number of times, with the storm damage, even Mr. Whiteside kept adding new pillars. Also, without warning to Captains; it might be months with no light showing.

[At high spring tides, the Smalls Rock is only 3 feet above sea level. You can see why ships Captains could not see the rocks, till the lighthouse was built]

Tending the Light
At this time, the job of tending the Smalls Lighthouse was not an especially arduous one, aside from the physical circumstances. As Ivor Emlyn described in 1858, "The Light-keepers had little to do in lamp cleaning and filling the oil ready for the next night. Captains and ship owners were content with paying dues for a dim light, as at this time only 4 lamps with glass reflectors were used. In 1817, the number was increased to 8; and again to 16, with silver reflectors, patented by a Mr. John Wilkinson, of London.
In 1800 the annual consumption of oil did not exceed 200 gallons. In 1858 there are seven-and-a-half times that quantity burned -- 1,500 gallons.
Smalls Lighthouse description in 1801, as a "raft of timber rudely put together." But, it survived for 85 years (1776 to 1861). Whiteside's design of raising a super-structure on piles so that the sea could pass through them with "but little obstruction" which has been adopted for hundreds of sea structures.

Background in supplying the lighthouse, with change of men and supplies, below is a drawing; this will help in the understanding how the supplies shipped and landed. This is Eddystone Lighthouse, but the same principle was adopted in the supply of the Eddystone and Smalls.

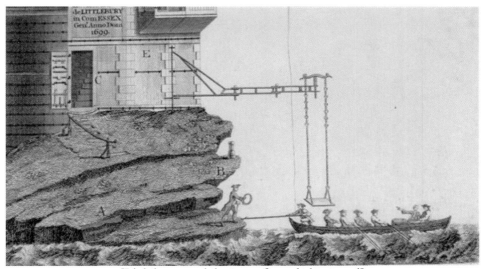

[Lighthouse and the type of supply boat used]

The supply boat had oars and one sail. The oarsmen would keep the boat in the same position and the supplies would be pulled by rope and pulley blocks. Size of boat 20 feet [7 metres] one man at the bow with a long pole to keep her away from the rocks, four men at the oars to row forward or backwards at the command of the captain, who you can see him sitting and steering at the back with one man to sending up supplies. Just where the bow man stands with his pole, you can see the rope which was used to send up the supplies. That seat dangling above the first rower, there was not one on the Smalls, the keepers had to jump off or jump on, but if calm, then they could just step off or on.

THIS IS A VERY FRIGHTENING STORY

The death of Light keeper Thomas Griffith (labourer) in 1801 and the suffering of Thomas Howell (Cooper) [barrel maker]. Both men were married and had families, Griffiths lived at Solva.

Normal working practice of Smalls light-keepers involved two men spending one month on, but this time in 1801, it was impossible to change light-keepers, with a gales blowing for the whole of "two months".

A few days after the two men had been put onto the Smalls, a distress flag appeared at the Light-house. No way could you know the exact problem, just the distress flag was flying. Ships passing would see the flag then report what they saw, once they arrived in harbour. The Smalls Lighthouse supply boat found it impossible to get near the rock, with large waves and surf going over the rocks with gale force winds blowing. Every time they tried the men on the supply boat could see on the walk way gallery a figure of a man waving them to come on, come on -- it was even impossible to get close enough to hail him. But, he just kept waving them to 'come on.' The gales did not ease off, sometimes Henry Whiteside had to turn back half way there, or just outside Solva Harbour, that's how bad the sea conditions were.

The wife's and relatives of the Light Keepers, Howells and Griffith, all they could do was to wait at Solva, watching from the cliffs as the supply vessel came back, looking to see if the keepers were on board. When close enough the faces of the crewmen would confirm to them all they needed to know. But every night the 'Smalls Light was lit', every morning the light was extinguished. The lighthouse keepers were still doing their jobs.

Then after two months of gales at last the sea was calm enough for the supply vessel crew to land on the Smalls Rock -- with no one to greet them? You can imagine that normally the men would be waiting and eager to get off and return to shore. Quickly, Henry Whiteside and two crewmen climbed the rope ladder. As they lifted the trap door, inside they could hear two men talking.

On climbing through the trap door, they found Thomas Howells sitting with his back to them talking to him-self and answering him-self. Then he turned around and looked at them, and what the three saw before them was not the dark hair healthy man Thomas Howells who they had put on the rock just two months ago, but, a man with pure white hair, who had not slept for months, unshaven, un cut nails, unwashed, dirty, smelling, starving, wearing the same clothes for the last two months, and who had gone completely mad. Let's remember this is 1801, "what would you have done in these circumstances, for a start you'd be frightened at the sight before you." Let's recap, let's take a good look at what is in front of these three men.

Firstly, they were 6o feet above a Rock, on pillars, and to leave you had to climb down a 50 foot rope ladder. They were in a room that was 13 feet by 13 feet with a man who was known for his bad temper, a strong man who liked to fight. On top of all that he had gone completely mad. This is a very dangerous situation.

What would you have done in this situation, just think, you also have to get him down a 50 foot rope ladder. So [please don't get upset] they tied him up, and then lowered him down by rope and pulley to the waiting supply vessel. Interestingly he did not do anything or say anything, as they tied him up, or as they lowered him down? Whiteside and the two crewmen then went up onto the gallery, walking around on the south side of the walk-way they discovered to their horror Thomas Griffiths lashed to the railings in an almost sitting up position. He had been dead for some time; in addition the body had been attacked by gulls. They had attacked his face, [gulls always go for the face]. The dead man's arms were by his side, in the gale force winds his arms had been blown about, that's how it looked to the crew of the supply vessel, as he bide them to "come on, come on." Griffith's body was wrapped up in the supply boats spare sail, and lowered down to the supply vessel. Then Henry Whiteside, quite wisely, changed light keepers; before they had time to think "what's going on here!" With fresh supplies oil for the light put on the rock; the supply boat pulled away 'quickly,' leaving two lighthouse keepers to contemplate "do I really want to be a lighthouse keeper on the Smalls, after what I just saw!" Smalls supply boat now headed back to Solva.

Over the following weeks they slowly found out from Thomas Howells what had happened on the Smalls Lighthouse.

After they had been on the Smalls for just a day Griffiths had complained of being unwell, Howells then put up the distress flag.

That night Griffiths breathed his last and died in his bunk. Howells worried that if he put the body in the sea, with his reputation of being an argumentative fighting man, he might be arrested for murder. So he decided to make a coffin, by using the wood from their bunks and the doors of the kitchen units. Placing the body in the coffin, he would keep the body until the boat arrived. With the distress flag flying that would be anytime soon. After a while the body started to smell. Inside a 13 x 13 ft size room, it became unbearable. Howells took the coffin outside, up onto the walkway gallery, and tied the coffin to the railings. Days later the gales blew the coffin to piece so Howells tied Griffiths' body to the iron railing in an almost sitting position. The arms and body was blown about by the gale force winds. It was this swinging the supply vessel's crewmen had thought they had seen, a man waving them to; come on. After a week in this position the body had moved and his right hand started to tap the window as the winds blew. This is what Howells could hear, Griffiths hand hitting the tapping with every strong gust of wind, tap, tap.

Strong gusts of wind which would then be followed by tap, tap, tap, all the time the winds were howling with the movement of the tower as it swung with the gale.

Thomas Howells had been alone for two months on a lighthouse 20 miles from shore, with gales constantly blowing. Imagine the noise of the winds howling, the lighthouse 'swaying one or two feet' and just waiting for that; tap, tap, tap. It had started to affect his mind. He started to sleep with the Bible under his pillow, all night he would lay awake just waiting. As the winds increased he'd wait for the inevitable tap, tap, tap, as if Griffiths wanted to be let back inside. In daylight when he went up to the lamp room he could see, tied to the railings, the back of Griffiths body, and his arms moving with the gale force gusts of wind. As dusk fell he would go up to the lamp room and light the lamps. At dawn, he had to return to lamp room, to put out the lamps, and then refill the oil lamps ready for the next night. While he would not be looking at the body, he could see the white fluttering of gulls attacking the body, attacking the face.

It is hard to imagine what Howells had undergone, both mentally and physically Thomas Howells friends did not even recognize him on his return back to Solva.

But, let's not forget that Thomas Howell's is a "Hero;" yes, a Hero. He still did his duty, as a Lighthouse Keeper, he had kept the lights burning at night for two months, by himself. He had saved many a ship's crew from those waiting, unforgiving, rocks.

After this incident, Mr. Henry Whiteside decided that three Light-keepers will be stationed on the Smalls lighthouse, and should a death occur, the body was to be put in the sea, with two witnesses, to write statements on how the death occurred.
Some say, because of this, Trinity House on all lighthouses around Britain, placed three men instead of two.

LOST; ONE SMALLS SUPPLY VESSESL LOST
This advertisement appeared in the Cambrian Newspaper on Friday 4 February 1805.
Henry Whiteside has lost his supply boat -- she had broken from her moorings at Solva:

[This is the size of boat that was used to build and supply the Smalls, its 20 long. Solva to Smalls; they were sailing out 25 miles - offshore. What can one say but, Wow!]

LOST, a large BOAT, with the inscription
SMALLS branded on several parts on it, and on the
Oars belonging to it, on the 5th January last, from the
vessel which attends the Smalls Lights.
A Reward of TEN GUINEAS will be paid to any person
Who will give satisfactory account of her being found in a
state fit for use, by applying to Mr. Henry Whiteside, at
Solva, Pembrokeshire.

SMALLS LIGHT DAMAGED

The Smalls Lighthouse was so materially damaged by the violent storm on the 18th October 1812, when part of the house-pillars were washed away, all the light house windows were broken, the lantern's were completely destroyed to add to the problem, parts of the lower room floor was washed away, by really big waves. It was impossible to show any light. The three men were eventually taken off, by the agent Whiteside's supply vessel and landed at Solva. They had lived since 18th of October till the 12 November, that's 25 days and nights; in a corner of the room, nailed up with boards. Luckily they were in the corner where there food was stored, at least had plenty to eat. This was a once every 100 year storm, the worst storm known in living memory, giant 20 metres waves which pushed the floor into the ceiling. With just a small part of the floor left, which they managed to board up with bits of broken wood from the flooring, at least they had food. Three men living in the corner of what's left of your 13 x 13 foot room, with storm force winds blowing and giant seas. Add to this the light-house swaying back and forth! The reason for this swaying of the 60 feet high Light-house? A few upright pillars had gone completely and others had split. By now they were living in 5 foot square part of the floor, 60 feet above the rock looking down they could watch foaming waves breaking right below. For 25 days and nights. Just once or twice a wave came up through the floor, entering the room itself. One wave washed away all their food stores, leaving them to eat; saltwater soaking bread, and a big piece of cheese.

On the 12 November 1812, they were all rescued by the Supply Boat.
In February 1813 plans were afoot for Trinity House to purchase the Lease of the Lighthouse on the Smalls, and planned, if successful, to repair and present wooden building for immediate accommodation; and afterwards, if found practicable, to erect a stone building, on the plan of Eddystone Light-House. But, if not, to build a more substantial one on the former plan. It is expected the Light will be again shown in the month of April. [Smalls was not repaired till June 1813]

MEANWHILE; 50 MILES TO THE WEST of the Smalls is another small rock called; Tusker Rock, it's near to Waterford, Ireland, and men were busy employed erecting Tusker Rock lighthouse.
Twenty four men were on the rock when the same storm struck without warning, on 18th October 1812. With waves completely covering them, all they could do was to

hold on, during the night the waves swept away 14 of them to their deaths and a further five died later.

Some of the expensive Smalls Light-house oak beam pillars were completely washed away, and Mr. Whiteside wanted them back.   This appeared in the CAMBRIAN NEWSPAPER. Friday 7 November 1812
WHEREAS information has been obtained
That some of the OAK BREAKWATER PILLARS from the SMALLS LIGHT have been thrown on shore on the Coast of South Wales: whoever will give intelligence thereof, so that they may be recovered, to Mr. Whiteside, of Solva, Pembrokeshire; or to W. Humphreys,
Of the ship a-ground, Swansea, shall receive salvage thereon;
But any person concealing the same after this notice, shall be prosecuted with the utmost rigor.

CONSEQUENCES: OF NO LIGHT SHOWING ON THE SMALLS

London Docks 17TH December 1812: John Owens master of the brig FORTITUDE of London, had done this final checks, the valuable cargo of general goods, was well stored and well secured down below in the holds, his crew of 14 hands, were all experienced seamen, he did have one passenger an invalided seaman, who he was taking back Liverpool; this was in total 16 souls onboard.

With the Thames River flowing downstream, two rowing boats towed the FORTITUDE down the Thames and then into the open sea -- her voyage had begun. Thursday 17th December 1812. The brig was bound from London to Liverpool, but this is not the best time of the year to sail around Lands End then north past the Pembrokeshire coast. To seamen, the Pembrokeshire coast was not considered a safe passage during winter months.

Off Pembrokeshire there were islands, rocks and reefs, but as it was winter thankfully you did not have the problems of the Privateers. Being winter, they wisely stayed in port. But there were other dangers to content with, such as the islands of Skokholm, Skomer, Grassholm and a 10 mile long reef called Hats and Barrels. This reef lay east to west right across the path of the FORTITUDE. To the west of Ramsey Island you had rocks called the Bishops and his Clerks which were described by George Owen in Elizabethan times as "preaching there deadly doctrine to their winters audience." Then 20 miles off the coast you had a group of rocks called 'Smalls.' Fortunately, there was a light house on the Smalls, built in 1776 by Mr. Henry Whiteside.   His light warned you of the Smalls Rocks. All any ships master had to do was to keep a good lookout for this light, then, keeping well 'west' of the light, the crew, vessel and cargo would be safe from all the dangers that lay off the Pembrokeshire coast. It's as simple as that, what could possibly go wrong?

Arriving off the Scilly Isles she became wind-bound, [no wind]. "It's the middle of winter and would you believe it, there's is no wind!" Not till eight o'clock on the morning of the Tuesday 29th, the wind sprung up; at last she sailed from the Scilly Isles. By evening a gale blew up with heavy seas and bitingly cold south westerly winds, with no cloud, so visibility was not that bad for night time. Master Owens put a man at the bow to let him know once he had spotted the Smalls Light.

[Smalls Light; this is what the FORTITUDE lookout should have seen on that fateful night]

About one o'clock in the morning Wednesday 30th December 1812 with the wind still blowing hard, the brig was handling these seas without any problem. All Captain John Owens needed was to see the Smalls Light. Thankfully still with no clouds, the Smalls Light would stand out easily. Master Owens shouted a number of times to the lookout man at the bows "Any light yet" and the same answer came back each time "No light as yet Captain" then Owens always added "then keep a sharp look out." It's almost two o'clock and still no light, by Captain Owens calculations he should have seen the light fifteen minutes ago to the starboard [to the right]. Suddenly the lookout man at the bows came running to the helm where the captain was, he was not shouting; but screaming "BREAKERS AHEAD! BREAKERS AHEAD!" Straight in front waves were breaking upon rocks. She struck, and instantly waves came over the ship.

Amidst darkness and with it blowing hard, with the white foam of waves and surf breaking. All around them now displayed the horrors of their situation. As they were getting out the long boats, looking up they could see above them the dark shape of a tower, it was the 'Smalls Lighthouse', they had shipwrecked right under the Smalls Light, and 'there was no light showing!'

Master Owens shouted orders to abandon ship. Into one the longboats went the Master and nine of the crew went on the port side [left side] including the invalided seaman; in the mean time the other six took to the other long boat, which hung over the stern. They succeeded in getting clear of the FORTITUDE and the stern long boat with six men in began to pull away from the white frothing breakers and surf. On the other side of the vessel, which was now breaking up, was the master and nine crewmen. Amid the noise of breaking waves, winds, and the ships wood against rocks came loud cries from the Masters long boat, as the vessel FORTITUDE fell over onto her port side [left side] on top of the long boat. The cries stopped, all they could hear was the surf and the howling of the gale, for they all had perished, Captain and nine men.

The six crew left alive succeeded in getting away from the rocks, and after struggling with the sea till eleven o'clock next morning, they were picked-up by the DILIGENCE the Milford Customs Cutter, under the command of Captain Dobbin. There were six survivors out of 16 crew. Some of them nearly naked, having rushed from their bunks at the moment of impact and not even having time to put their clothes on.

Captain Dobbin relieved their wants with that kindness and humanity which so eminently distinguishes his conduct. In the afternoon he landed them at Milford, where he has provided for their necessities and locally a subscription for money was raised to the relief of those distressed seamen.

Names of those who perished:	Names of those saved by DILIGENCE
John Owen, Master	Samuel Lovejoy seaman
Humphrey Lewis, Mate	Richard Hess "
John Shettleworth seaman	William Williams "
Hugh Williams "	Owen Pritchard "
Solomon Jones "	Michael Hughes "
William Davies "	Thomas Taylor "
Richard Thomas "	
Lewis Jones "	
Michael M'Cann "	
Invalid seaman, name unknown.	

Why was there no light showing from the Smalls Light-house; the Lantern had been broken on 18 October 1812 in the worst gales in living memory. The light was not working again till June 1813.

[Smalls Lighthouse, with no light showing]

The long boat belonging to the FORTITUDE of London, lost on the Smalls, was on Sunday 3rd January 1813 driven on shore near Solva, bottom upwards. This was the long boat used by the Master and crew who tried and escape from the wrecked vessel.

Late on Saturday evening, 9th January 1813 the five men that survived (being of part of the crew of the brig FORTITUDE of Liverpool, lost a few days ago on the Smalls), arrived in Caernarvon, almost destitute of clothes and money, when several respectable inhabitants open a subscription for the unfortunate suffers, and in a short time collected a sufficient sum to enable them to procure necessaries, and to proceed, on their journey.

[Painting dated 1825 by someone who has been to the Smalls Lighthouse. The ladder coming down from the lighthouse to the rock, was really a 50 foot long rope ladder which opened by a trap door right in the middle of the living quarters. The living quarters, food stores: three bunks, kitchen stove to cook and to warm the room, also had a table and chairs, this room was 13 feet by 13 feet; then after 1801 three men were tendering the light and still in a room 13 feet by 13 feet for a month's duty. You can see the lamp room above with its iron railing walkway around, this was intended for the lighthouse men to walk around and clean the window panes. The door on the north east side, which had a pulley block above to hoist supplies up. Small Lighthouse stood for 85 years, 1776 – 1861 before Trinity House knocked it down]

MOVING FORWARD TO 22ND JULY 1990. Diver & Shipwreck Researcher James Hedley Phillips went looking for the wreck of the FORTITUDE. Having done my research, I thought it had struck almost right next the Smalls Quay, I honestly did not expect to locate her -- after all she's been underwater for 178 years. Putting on my diving gear aboard SPIRIT; my Avon Searider, with its 50 hp outboard; the conditions could not have been more different – a flat calm sea, with not even a breath of wind, very unlike the night when the FORTITUDE was wrecked here in 1812. Looking at the boats Echo Sounder the depth below was 6 metres. Over the side I went, the seabed was covered in seaweed, moving the weed to one side, "there was the wreck." "Just Like that," it had taken less than two minutes.

I wish all the shipwrecks were as easy as this to find. I had found the ships anchors and chains, even the ships bronze pintle [this is what the ships rudder hangs on, same thing as a door hinge, so the rudder can swing back and forth to steer the ship] so after all these years the wreck of the FORTITUDE has been located.

Because the Smalls is 20 miles from Porth Clias, it takes just about an hour to get there by fast boat. Diving on the Smalls needs good forward planning, I had got together a team of divers, who would' happily dive and search for wrecks.' I only planned one diving season's of Search and Locating shipwrecks on the Smalls. Well, that went by the board; one season went on for a further two seasons. In all, over twelve shipwrecks were located around the Smalls. Two known wrecks were located and ten more were discovered. To find shipwrecks, its takes 40% of good research and 60% of sheer luck.

[I remember one day on the Smalls, after working out where the steamer had hit the rocks, then as she went astern [reversed] I had worked out exactly where she had gone down, in about 20 metres of water. I asked Diver Greg Evans to pop over and to search and locate this shipwreck, as he was just about to go over the side; I said to him "Now Diver Greg Evans, I have calculated exactly the position of this wreck, you have only ten minutes to find it!" Well you can imagine Greg did take longer than ten minutes to locate this 100 year old forgotten shipwreck, he took twelve minutes! On the wreck site, one of the gullies was full of sand, about a month later I was showing Shipwreck Researcher Tom Bennett the wreck site and the gully which was full of sand, well, it had all gone, the sand that is and Tom happily came up with four portholes]

I've dived all over the world, and I'm always being asked which the best place I have ever dived. My answer is always the same "The Smalls Rocks." For colourful Marine life, playful Seals (pulling your fins), shipwrecks by the score. The best underwater visibility I have ever seen in UK waters, just over 35m that about 115 feet. But, I have dived there straight after a gale, when you were lucky to see one metre underwater (3 feet).

IN JULY 1813; Captain R. Lewin, one of the Elder Brethren of the Trinity Board, and Mr. Alexander, Surveyor to that corporation, had arrived at Milford, for the purpose of proceeding to the Smalls Rock, to survey the same and the present Light-house, with a view of ascertaining the practicability of erecting a more solid structure thereon.

THE END OF AN ERA
Monday 5th July 1824; Mr. Henry Whiteside passed away; at the aged of 78 years (1746 - 1824) he is buried at Whitchurch, Solva. You will find his and his wife's grave Martha, behind the church. [Personally, I feel this is an end of an era]
INCOME FROM THE SMALLS LIGHT

Collecting revenues from the Smalls Light House was well organized. In all large ports you would find a collector of Smalls Light House dues. At Swansea Port was 68 year old Mr. William Watkins, who, as the Receiver of the Smalls Light for upwards of 25 years he had collected the dues. He died suddenly on Friday 26 May 1826.

As the smaller ports got busier, not to miss out, the Smalls, started to employ more dues collectors, even in Llanelly. Carmarthen Journal of 25 February 1831 reports: W. D. Davies Esq., of his Majesty's Customs for the port of Llanelly, has been appointed collector of the Smalls Light-house dues, for this district.

What was the income from this one Light; here I have the income from the House of Commons Records: Smalls Light-House Income. [We are talking big bucks, here].

Financial turnover of the Smalls Light-House for the year 1832:

Total income collected 1832:	£14,433
Cost of Collection 1832:	£ 2,200
Cost of maintenance 1832:	£ 1,100
Surplus income for 1832	£10,253

Yes, that's £10,253 profit. Plus, the good news is this will increase year by year; as more ships pass by. Even better news, ships are getting much larger, this means larger payment in dues.

This article appeared in the local Newspaper Cambrian, on Saturday 21 April 1832.
The Corporation of Trinity House having recommended to the Lessees of the Smalls Light that a Chinese Gong should be placed at that Light House, to be sounded at intervals in foggy weather, the Lessees immediately ordered the recommendation to be carried into effect, and a Gong to be provided for that useful purpose.
[Just imagine on foggy nights, instead of the fog signal giving that HOOOOT sound; you would hear a Chinese "GONG!" Well, you've got to laugh, I did. Best joke I've heard for a while. GONG! GONG! I'm pleased to tell you that they did not go ahead with this Chinese Gong idea]

1832; SMALLS LEASE BOUGHT BY TRINITY HOUSE.
Trinity House, the lighthouse authority for England and Wales, bought the lease in 1832 for £170,468.

There was a bad gale in March 1833, the Smalls Light; - Although it has received a trifling damage in the late gales, it has regularly continued to be lighted from sunset to sunrise, and there is no foundation whatever (in rumors) for a report that a vessel had passed it one morning at four o'clock, when the light was not in.

Then in October 1833, Mr. Roberts, shipbuilder, at Milford, knocked off his stocks at half-past eight yesterday morning, a very elegantly modeled well-built smack, of the measurement of 54 tons, for the proprietors of the Smalls Light. Lieut. Mott R. N. their resident agent attended from Solva, to be given the name "ELIZA".

She took the water in great style, under a salute of Cannon from Nelson's ship, this brass gun, which were fired in front of that Nelson Hotel, Milford Haven, at which place a dinner was served up in Mr. Pritchard's usual manor, for Mr. Mott, the shipbuilder, and their friends, and they enjoyed themselves very harmoniously and pleasantly on the occasion.

In October 1835; five of the Elder Brethren of the Trinity House have lately been on tour of inspection of the Lights, in their splendid new steamer yacht, VESTAL, 160 steam horse power. On the 7th inst., they landed on the Smalls, and made a perfect and minute examination of the light-house; thence proceeded to the northward, to examine the Welsh coast, preparatory to deciding on the erection of a light-house on one of the Bishops, off St. David's Head, as well as to examine the other light houses on the coast.
[In 1835, they were thinking of building a light house on the South Bishops or maybe on the North Bishops Rocks? These South and North Bishop Rocks are five miles off St. David's Head. With the increase of trade the merchant ships going past Bishops Rocks kept being wrecked at an alarming rate, so it was decided to build another Light house on one of these rocks, but which one, they finally decided to build it on the South Bishops Rock].

BIRTHS
SHANNON. – Thursday 23rd September 1909, at 5, North Gate, Haverfordwest town, the wife of Mr. John Archibald Shannon, Light-keeper, Smalls Lighthouse, of a daughter.

MARRIAGES
On Thursday last 7 January 1846, Capt. Lewis, late commander of the Smalls' tender, Solva to Miss Sophia Bowen, of that place.

DEATHS
On the Sunday 5th November 1853, at Milford, the infant son of Light Keeper Mr. James Smith, of the Smalls Light-house.

On the Monday 27th September 1886, at Pembroke Dock, William Smith Spicer, age 75 years, formerly for many years principle keeper at the Smalls and Castle Head Lighthouses; much respected.

On Monday 25th June 1888, at Honeyborough, Neyland, Roseni, youngest daughter of Mr. H. Weymouth, Smalls Lighthouse, aged 8 years died.

On Monday 25th June 1888, at Honeyborough, Neyland, William Horatio, youngest son of Mr. H. Weymouth, Smalls Lighthouse, aged 6 years died.

SMALLS LIGHTHOUSE

[The wooden 1776 and 1861 towers as seen side by side for comparison. The New lighthouse is twice the height (40 metres, 120 feet). My thanks to Trinity House for the use of photos and drawings]

What is known is that the lighthouse remained in the private ownership until 1836, when an Act of Parliament handed responsibility of all remaining privately-owned lighthouses in England and Wales to Trinity House. The lighthouse was purchased from the Reverend A. Buchannan (John Phillips' grandson) and Thomas P Clarke, for the colossal sum of £170,468.

Work on constructing the new tower began in 1858 and was completed in 1861; it is noted as being one of the finest achievements of the famed lighthouse engineer James Walker, and the tallest of the Welsh lighthouses.

[Smalls Lighthouse as it appears in 2014, surrounded by rocks and hidden underwater reefs]

Dates Pembrokeshire Lighthouses were built:
St. Ann's Lighthouse	(1st. 1714)	1841
Smalls Lighthouse	(1st. 1776)	1861
Caldey Island Lighthouse		1829
South Bishops Lighthouse		1839
Skokholm Island Lighthouse		1916

SMALLS, ITS TIME IS UP;
Now We Come To June 1856; the Smalls Light has stood now for over 80 years. It's time is now up, it's becoming year by year more unsafe. The pillars where they enter the rock are moving about, it's said you could put your hand in the gaps between the pillars and the lead in some places.

You notice that there are quite a number of angled wooden posts have been added over the years to stop the swaying.

The whole structure sways, even in calm weather. The erection of a new Lighthouse building was to be of stone and iron work. The work would have to take place on shore at Solva, and then when completed will be removed to its destination, and permanently placed in its proper position.

THE BUILDING OF THE NEW SMALLS LIGHTHOUSE

December 1856. The plan for the new light on the Smalls was as follows: a stone lighthouse would be built next to the wooden one, with a bridge going across for workmen to use. Once finished, the wooden lighthouse would be pulled down. Vessels for the purpose of conveying the requisite stone and materials from Solva to the Smalls are now being built building at Milford.

SOLVA. – On Tuesday morning 24th February 1857, the sloop TWO BROTHERS, of Portmadoc, laden with planks for the Trinity works, in connection with the Smalls Lighthouse, struck on a reef of rocks near the entrance of Solva harbour, and sustained considerable damage. She was, however, soon got off, and was able to make the harbour, where she is now lying to discharge her cargo and repair the damages received.

SMALLS LIGHTHOUSE, SOLVA, Thursday 7th May 1857 — the works at Solva for this lighthouse are progressing favourably. About forty masons and labourers have been landed on the rock this week (being the first landed there this year), to prepare a base of forty two feet in diameter, for the first course, which is expected will be laid down early in the following summer. A daily steamer was employed to convey the masons and labourers to and from the rock, and also to tow the barges, which will carry the prepared stones, cement, etc., out there whenever the weather will permit them to land and carry on the work.

LAUNCH. – The two barges intended to be employed in carrying the materials for the erection of the new light house on the Smalls, were launched from the building yard of Messrs. J. D. Roberts & Co., Milford, on Friday evening 8 May 1857.

SOLVA, BARGES ARRIVE

SMALLS LIGHT HOUSE. – The steamer for the purpose of towing the barges, carrying the materials for this light-house from Solva wharf to the Smalls Rock, arrived here at Solva, on Monday 11th May 1857, towing two barges around with her. She was built expressly for the purpose to which she is applied, and is apparently a strong boat with very powerful engines, and named 'SS SOLVA,' after the place.

She towed the tender, with the stone masons on board, out on Tuesday morning, and accomplished the distance with moderate pressure under three hours, but the tender was forced to return at night owing to the weather proving too squally for her to remain at her moorings out there.

50 MEN CAUGHT OUT WHILE BUILDING THE SMALLS LIGHT

SOLVA ON FRIDAY 17TH SEPTEMBER 1858; this gale came up suddenly; several trees were blown down in the neighbourhood and roofs damaged. The shipping in Solva harbour was perfectly safe, but, great fears were entertained for the safety of the 50 employed men on the Smalls Rock. There only means of escaping the rock was aboard the moored Yacht – the Trinity sailing tender, she is at her moorings on the west side of the rock, near, but, not that near.

The worries at Solva were whether the men had managed to get off the rock in time, and onboard their tender, in a gale that has came up suddenly, as this one had. They would not find safety in the old wooden lighthouse that already stands; no way could it accommodate 50 men, in a room 13 ft x 13 ft, plus the weight of 50 men.

At Solva Cliffs: many wives and families had now gone up onto the cliffs and just kept looking towards the Smalls, all night. Despite the gale force winds, with heavy rain, they refused to leave. They kept looking for that glimmer of light from a ships lamp. It was felt that if they left this vigil, then that would be the end of hope for their men. They have stood there all night, not one daring to mention what happened in 1812 and Tusker Rock, when 20 men were caught in similar circumstances with the gale coming on suddenly; they were washed off and drowned. At last it was dawn, and thankfully; the winds had dropped and changed direction to a south westerly. With dawn came more crowds onto the Solva cliffs, some with spy glasses, for all eyes were directed towards the south-west towards the Smalls. Time is getting on, with more wives and families arriving the scene was one of desperation, with highs and lows, white sails sighted, but just another ship, on its way, again and again this kept happening, nerves were now at breaking points, with children, wives, families crying, many now feared the worst, but, it's never mentioned, it never said, but, it is thought.

Midday, St. Bride's Bay and far off out to sea there were white sails everywhere – but it's just normal merchant shipping about their business. Now and again some white sails looked as if they were coming towards them, hopes were raised only to be disappointingly dashed, as the ship tacked or changed course. With every white sail sighted, would came bitter disappointment, now it's well passed noon one white sail could be seen coming for them way off to the north of the Smalls, that's the wrong direction, with telescopes now trained on this vessel, she had white sails but, the wrong shape, another disappointment. But, still on it came. It's well into the afternoon and telescopes were now trained on her, you could hear loud voices saying "your eyes are younger than mine, use my spyglass is it her?" "Yes, it is; No it's not, wrong sails, they are white but wrong shape, but she does look like the Smalls tender, but it's the wrong white sails." The sails were white, but, the wrong shape. Still on she came, she was now well south of Ramsey Island. With even more spy glasses on her. When she was just south of Porth Clias, suddenly shouts went up: "IT IS HER!

IT IS HER! IT IS HER!"   It is the Smalls tender, and they could see men onboard, lots of men.

After what the families had seen all night, storm force winds, giant waves hitting the cliffs, and the driving rain beating down relentlessly. Late in the afternoon, she came around the headland sailing into Solva harbour. Now anxious wives, families were desperate to know if their man were missing. They were following the vessel around the cliffs, towards Solva, this was now a scene of desperation, the cliff path is narrow, with hundreds of people rushing along this path following the vessel as she sailed for Solva, some falling over, wives', children, families, shouting, shouting at the top of their voices "ANY MEN MISSING!" Then the whole ships company shouting back with one voice "NO ONE IS MISSING!"   Then with the biggest cheer from all onboard!

All on shore started madly cheering, crying, giving thanks, some women could not take anymore, and just collapsed in shock; disbelief, joy.   Loud cheers from the assembled spectators, families and friends, who lined the shores of the harbour, and many a hearty prayer was breathed for their safety.
50 families had seen the storm blowing with 30 foot waves crashing against the Solva cliffs; they had waited, knowing full well no one could survive on that rock. And they had suffered together, with dawn came high and lows, the strain of it all, emotions were now at breaking point, finally that shout from the whole 50 men, just brought so much relief. Women shouting; "ANY MEN MISSING" then the men shouted back "NO ONE IS MISSING!"

This is There Story:
While digging the foundations for the Smalls light-house, we were all busy working in the early afternoon. Suddenly without warning the gale came up from the south, very fast, waves started to cover the rock, this had all happened before they could get onboard the tender, which was on her moorings off the rock on the west side. Rowing back and forth in the one small tender's rowing boat, taking off as many men each time as they could carry on each trip, bailing all the time as water kept coming over the sides. [They did a lot of bailing over the next 12 hours] a number of times the little rowing boat was filled with water, it was a near thing! Not one man was left behind.
Once all aboard they slipped her cable and luckily taken with the wind pushing them north, she did not touch any rocks. At first they started to make for Solva, and then the wind changed direction, now taking them out to sea, towards Ireland.   But owing to the violence of the wind they had to 'lie to,' [just go with it] and drift with the gale towards the Irish coast, with waves coming over the side continuously everyone was bailing all day and most of the night.
Well before dawn the wind eased and changed direction, taking them to St. Bride's Bay, at last they were able to get up sail and make their way towards Solva. The reason for the white sail being the wrong shape; it had been ripped by the gale force

winds, they had done the best they could, in stitching them back together; but the shape was different.

As one of the wives' said after, *"For the last 24 hours I have lived a lifetime of disappointments, a lifetime of suffering, please God, never again."*

BY 1859: Contractors Reports Wednesday 17TH August 1859; the Smalls are progressing favourably; the new tower on the rock is upwards of sixty feet above the level of the sea.

LOSS OF LIFE AT THE SMALLS LIGHTHOUSE. – A fatal accident occurred at the Smalls Rock, on Thursday 17th May 1860.
Mr. John Croot, mason, while he was crossing by foot from the old Lighthouse to the New Tower, was overwhelmed by a sea that rose suddenly and washed him off the rock, which took him out of sight immediately.
The sea was running to high [rough] at the time that assistance could not possibly be rendered him. Although the place is well supplied with lifebuoys, and throwing safety lines, which Mr. Douglas building manager, takes care to have their ready at hand in case of accidents. Perceiving the wise precautions that have been taken by the gentleman. They still hope that the works would have been entirely completed without the occurrence of so serious an accident.
They are now looking for the body; this is the description that was put out of the missing man:
The deceased, who has left a wife and child to deplore his loss, was about five feet nine inches in height, dark complexion, black hair and whiskers, rather stout, full face with prominent cheek bones; he had on at the time a white duck frock, fustian trousers and waistcoat, white, and heavy nailed laced boots." [His body was never found].

JUST THREE YEARS LATER: – Just three years later, in June, 1857 the first stone of the new tower on the Smalls Rock was put in place, and on Tuesday, the 10th July 1860, the last one was set, by Captain Clarke, R.N., from Bath, amid the cheers of the workmen on the rock. No other light-house of the size has been erected before in so short a period as this one. They are really pleased with this speed, and added 'may state that had it been for the indefatigable zeal of the overlooking engineer this would not have been completed so soon.'

[You have to take you hat off to them, when you take into consideration its great distance from the land, the very rapid tides, currents which surround the rock, plus, the boisterous and the not very nice weather which has sometimes prevailed for many months, and last, but not the least of all, its height, 120 feet high. But they have a few things Mr. Whiteside did not have -- to start with, money. Trinity House is a very rich corporation, Whiteside did not have this plus, which made it all even faster steam

power. Mr. Whiteside only had sail or oars to power his 20 foot boat. [Power Boat Skippers have a saying: The wind is free, but it never blows in the right direction].
Now, all that remains to be done is the placing of the Lantern – the stairs – and the setting of the Smalls Quay for vessels to tie up to if there are calm seas, which would be done in a few months at furthest. It is supposed that during the next winter the Trinity Corporation will cause a light to be exhibited from it.

Wrecked on the Smalls on the rocks to the N.N.E. on Friday 9th July 1858, the Spanish brig MANUEL of Bilbao, struck there. The crew saved their lives by jumping onto the rock. They were hospitably received by the light housekeepers and lighthouse builders, who seldom have the chance to receiving visitors.

ANOTHER ACCIDENT ON THE SMALLS. – A severe accident occurred at the Smalls Lighthouse, on the Tuesday 11th September 1860 to a man in the employ of Mr. Douglas, the contractor. It appears that the injured man was standing beneath a stone which was being lifted up by a crane, when the crane broke and the stepping backwards to avoid being struck by the falling stone, he stumbled over the rock, and sustained such severe injuries internally, that little hope was entertained of his recovery. He was conveyed to Solva in the evening, and was attended to by Dr. Brown, who was sent for from Haverfordwest. He died that night.

THE NEW LIGHTHOUSE AT THE SMALLS. – Friday 23rd November 1860, the new lighthouse on the Smalls is complete as far as the exterior is concerned, the lantern having been placed on the tower, and the workmen being now engaged in finishing the interior.
A landing wharf is being erected to the south-east, to be formed of huge blocks of granite bolted together in the strongest manner to resist the heavy seas. The first stone of the new tower was laid on the 26th of June 1857, so that little more than three years have been occupied in its erection. The Trinity Board will exhibit a light during the winter.

WEDNESDAY 31ST JULY 1861: SMALLS LIGHTHOUSE SWITCHED ON: –
On the first instant the light was exhibited for the first time from the above Lighthouse, and will continue so from this time out, appearing as a star of the first magnitude. The old lighthouse, which is a wooden structure, will be shortly cut down, and be reckoned among the things of the past, although it has for nearly a century stood [85 years 1776 – 1861] in spite of the raging of the waves and the bellowing of the winds, a standing monument of the indefatigable ingenuity, zeal, energy, and cleverness of the late Mr. Whiteside, a music instrument maker from Liverpool.
The light was exhibited from it for the last time on the 31st July. The new one, which is built of granite, will, we hope, warn the seamen of danger until the end of time, and be looked at by the curious and thoughtful as a great boon to all men. We may state that the new lighthouse has been built under the superintendence of J. N. Douglas,

Esq., C. E., in a very short time, without any serious accidents. [Apart from the two deaths; this fact must have slipped the Trinity House Publicity Departments minds]. We wish him the same success he's off to erect another Light house on Wolf Rock, near Cornwall, and wheresoever's he may hereafter be engaged.

[Smalls Rocks, this is just rough sea conditions, not a gale]

WHO'S THAT KNOCKING AT THE DOOR?

The master and crew (seven in all) of the brigantine CARADOC, of Waterford, which was lost by fire some miles off the Pembrokeshire coast, were landed at Pembroke Dock from the Smalls Lighthouse Wednesday 18th March 1886. After abandoning their ship, they succeeded in reaching the lighthouse in the ships boat, and 'one of the crewmen had to climb the lighthouse ladder, and knock at the door,' which they received the greatest kindness from the lighthouse keepers.

The Trinity yacht SIREN had made several attempts to take the men off but failed, owing to the boisterous weather. Finally, the men were taken off and forwarded to Waterford on Monday by Mr. J. H. Teasdale, the hon. agent for the Shipwrecked Mariners' Society at Pembroke Dock.

SMALLS LIGHTHOUSE KEEPER 1893: In 1893 the Smalls Lighthouse man Mr. W. G. Graham said, "He always knew when a gale was coming up, because the seals deserted the rocks".

SIGNALS OF DISTRESS FLYING FROM THE SMALLS LIGHTHOUSE.
The captain of the Great Western passenger steamer which arrived at Milford from Waterford on Tuesday 9th January 1894 in the morning reported that signals of distress were made from the Smalls Lighthouse as he passed by it two hours earlier. The local Trinity superintendent, therefore despatched a tender from Pembroke Dock, but she returned in the evening having been unable to affect a landing in consequence of the heavy sea which prevailed. It was, however, ascertained by signals, that there was sickness at the lighthouse. It appears that the principle lighthouse-keeper is seriously ill, and requires medical attention.

[You can see the strength of the tide, plus the rocks and those hidden underwater reefs that surround the Smalls Lighthouse. My estimate is there are well over 400 wrecks on the Smalls. *Thanks to Trinity House for use of Photograph*]

The Smalls Lighthouse is situated nineteen miles north-west of St. Ann's Head, and is one of the most exposed positions in the whole of the British Isles, being open to the full fury of the Atlantic Ocean. This lonely and desolate rock is only accessible, for the purposes of relief, in favourable weather. It was not until Tuesday evening 23 January 1894 that the trinity yacht SIREN, under Captain Emerson, succeeded in having communication with the lighthouse keepers for the past three weeks, notwithstanding the continuous and persistent efforts that have made to that end, as signals had been made that one of the keepers was ill.

The man, who proved to be the chief light-keeper Mr. Sibert, was taken off the rock with considerable difficulty on Tuesday; and conveyed to Pembroke Dock, under the supervision of Dr. E. A. Saunders, medical officer to the Trinity Board, where he lies in a weak condition.
The unfortunate man had only been on the lighthouse some two days, when he was attacked with inflammation of the bowels, for which he has suffered for nearly three weeks without being able to obtain any assistance, beyond that of his two comrades on the rock, until rescued on Tuesday.

BUOY ADRIFT.
When the trinity steamer SS SIREN was about ten miles south of the Smalls Lighthouse on Wednesday 25th January 1899 Captain Emerson discovered drifting a large whistling buoy, which was thought to have come from the American coasts.

[Aerial view of the Smalls and its rocks and underwater reefs]

NEWPORT VESSEL BADLY DAMAGED ON "THE SMALLS."
On Saturday evening 24th March 1906; a local trader "SS REVEAL" registered at London, arrived in Milford Docks in a damaged condition. The steamer was bound to

Waterford, Ireland with coal from Newport, South Wales and on Friday morning 23rd March; struck one of the rocks near the Smalls Lighthouse. The crew, observing her perilous position, with the ship upon the rock, they took to the ships lifeboats but then the vessel strangely came off the rocks and floated away with the current and winds. The crew now had to chase after her, rowing hard to catch up with the steamer. After a good chase they managed to catch her, with the crew now in an exhausted state after some hard rowing, they succeeded in safely navigating her to Milford Haven.

The steamer is now in Milford dry dock undergoing examination. Only the watertight bulkheads prevented her from becoming a total wreck.

The steamer SS REVEAL, that went on the rocks near the Smalls, discharged her cargo of coals at Milford (after inspection in dry dock), and proceeded to Swansea for repairs last Sunday week. Captain Bevis was found dead in his bunk aboard the ship on Friday 5th April 1906. He had been suffering from chest complaint for some time, his crew reported that he was "very much upset" about the accident and the subsequent chase to his vessel.

SOUTH STACK KEEPER'S DEBTS Friday 20 July 1906

William Henry Fenn, a lighthouse keeper at the South Stack Lighthouse, Holyhead, appeared to explain how he came into a financial position with gross liabilities amounting to £74 and deficiency of £56.

He accounted for his position by saying it was due to the extravagance of his wife. He added that he did not know he was in debt till his wife's death last March.

The Official Receiver said the bankrupt was 38 years old, and been engaged as lighthouse keeper for two years. Before coming to Holyhead he had been engaged at the Smalls Lighthouse, where his family lived at Pembroke Dock. The debtor stated that when he left Pembroke Dock for South Stack he directed his wife to dispose of his furniture in order to pay off all the debts, then due, and he alleged that he thought that had been done. As a matter of fact, the furniture was sold under an execution. On his wife's death, he alleged that he found himself much in debt, whereas he had been under the impression that he only owed a few pounds, which he could easily have paid out of his wages. His wages are 3s 6d a day with an allowance from Trinity Board of Furniture and house rent free. The bankrupt was insured by Trinity for £192, but the policy was vested in the Elder Brethren, and was not available for the creditors. The examination was closed.

SMALLS; ON THE ROCK, THEN OFF THE ROCK!

Lloyd's Flushing agent telegraphed on Monday 12th October 1908 that the Dutch mail steamer SS PRINS HENDRIK, from Queenborogh for Flushing, went ashore on the Smalls, Captain Nieuwesluis.

A tug was sent for to take the passengers and mails off; these were landed later at Milford. The SS PRINS HENDRIK now still lies on the rock, it was decided that the Captain and crew should get aboard the tug and leave the wrecked steamer. But, before they left her, they had to extinguish the boiler fires, leaving the ship without any steam.   Then, while below getting their clothes and personal things ready to abandon the steamer, without warning, without further ado, she slid off the rocks into the sea and floated north with the currents, missing any rocks, off into deep waters. 'The startled Captain and crew realized she is not sinking.' Captain ordered 'please relight the boiler fires', once steam was got up, she calmly preceded on her voyage.

A CLOSE SHAVE: SMALLS.
With the fog prevailing thickly on Sunday 6th February 1910; the Light House men could hear a steamer getting louder and louder. The steamer was coming from the west side, and it was heading straight for the Light house. Then, out of the fog she came, a very large steamer, and she's aiming straight at the Light-house. In the nick of time the steamers crew had seen the danger she was in. With engines now in full reversed she had stopped, she had stopped only 20 feet from the rock. Luckily she was on the deep water side of the Smalls Rock. This would have been a terrible crash on the rocks, with her being so close to the lighthouse, the keepers and crew waved to each other as they parted. Reversing she disappeared back into the fog.

Henry Whiteside of Solva Takes on the French:

HENRY WHITESIDE was a native of Liverpool. He appears to have occupied his time when quite young in fiddle-making, but became an engineer by profession, although when he arrived at Solva, Pembrokeshire, in 1775 then aged 29 he was still the maker of musical instruments. He spent the rest of his life at Solva, having married one of the daughters of William Bevan, [Martha Bevan] who kept the old Ship Inn at Solva. Both Henry and Martha are buried in Whitchurch, Solva. Tradition tells us that he was a man of commanding personality, and that at the landing of the French in Pembrokeshire he led a party of volunteers to oppose them. It is also said that he often went out on the cliffs during a storm and tuned his fiddle to the wail of the wind. At one time nearly every farm-house in the neighbourhood of Solva and St. David's possessed a violin, or harpsichord, made by Henry Whiteside.

MR. HENRY WHITESIDE TAKES ON THE FRENCH
Mr. Henry Whiteside builder of the Smalls Light; takes on the French army that just landed near Fishguard. The account of the invasion by French troops, at Fishguard 22nd February 1797.   The last time the United Kingdom was invaded by representatives of a foreign land.

FIGHT BETWEEN SOLVA & ST. DAVID'S MEN AND FRENCH SOLDIERS
On 23rd February 1797, after the raising of the alarm, "The French have invaded Fishguard" Henry Whiteside (aged 51) called a public meeting for volunteers to fight the French – a grand army of sailors and farm labours took to the flag, along with a

horse [Whiteside had borrowed Mr. Barzy's £60 guinea horse, on the promise he would look after it]. Marching undeterred to Fishguard, they eventually encountered a group of Frenchmen looting a farmhouse. Whiteside's Solva men, who had now been joined by men from St. David's [the St. David's men had really upset the Dean of St. David's Cathedral by melting the cathedral's lead-roof to make lead musket balls], they lined up and fired a ragged volley, killing one French soldier and wounding two more. Pursuing the French hard on their heels, the Volunteers ran straight into a full French company of professional soldiers, who opened fire, scattering Whiteside's men. The volunteers ran, Whiteside wrote afterwards that he let Mr. Barzy's £60 guinea horse run free, as he deemed it unseemly to outrun his men!

[Henry Whiteside leads his Solva volunteers into battle on Mr. Barzy's £60 guinea horse]

One of the brave Solva sailors, Capt. Thomas Beynon, was wounded in this skirmish in the foot, for which he received a pension for life. General Tate (in charge of the French army) was, at this time, in full view of this battle: [this really was not a battle, but, a very small, skirmish] Tate stood upon the Garnwnda rock and used it as his advanced post.

The field where this skirmish took place is now called the French Park. [As far as I can tell, the French soldier killed by Whiteside musket volley is still buried somewhere in this field].

[This is another version I came across, of the 1797 Battle between the Solva men and the French]

FISHGUARD: INVASION BY FRENCH TROOPS 1797

Once the news had reached Solva that the French had landed at Carrig Gwasted Point, near Fishguard several masters of vessels, seamen headed from the port of Solva, to meet the French; these volunteers were led by Mr. Henry Whiteside, who was the contractor for building the wooden Smalls Lighthouse, and had made Solva his temporary residence. A skirmish took place in the early afternoon, between Mr. Whiteside's volunteers and the French; the French were beaten back in confusion, having lost three of their men in the encounter.

This skirmish with the French was witnessed by the French Commander, General Tate, who, with some of his staff, was at the French outpost on the top of Garnwnda.

HENRY WHITESIDE HAS PASSED AWAY

Mr. Henry Whiteside passed away on Monday 5th July 1824 aged 78, b. 1746 – d. 1824. He and his wife are buried next to each other at Whitchurch, Solva. You can see Henrys and Martha's grave; it's directly behind the church. The end of an era.

What a character was our Henry Whiteside; I will always remember what he said after the 1797 battle with the French near Fishguard. Whiteside said *"That he let Mr. Barzy's £60 guinea horse run free, as he deemed it unseemly to outrun his men!"*

This is what is written on their tomb stone:
SECRED
TO THE MEMORY OF
HENRY WHITESIDE ESQ.,
ERECTOR OF AND LATE AGENT FOR THE
SMALLS LIGHTHOUSE, HE RESIGNED HIS SOUL TO HIS
ALMIGHTY CREATOR JULY 5th 1824
IN THE 78TH YEAR OF HIS AGE.

SACRED
To the Memory of Martha
Relict of Henry Whiteside Esq.,
of Solva who departed this life on
the 11th day of July 1832 in the 75 year
of her age.

Martha Whiteside (nee Bevan) died on Wednesday 11 July 1832 aged 75 (1757 - 1832)

Henry Whiteside met the future Mrs. Whiteside; Martha Bevan at the Ship Inn, Main Street, Solva; her father William Bevan was the landlord of the Inn.

[Photograph of Henry's and Martha's grave at Whitchurch, Solva. The grave lies directly behind the church]

The Swansea Cambrian Newspaper, Saturday 8 September 1832 reports:

DIED

Lately at Solva, Pembrokeshire, the widow of the late Mr. Henry Whiteside, the ingenious constructor of the Smalls Light-House, age 75. Also, Aug. 24 1832, Mrs. Oakley, [sister of Martha Whiteside] of St. David's, sister to the above, aged 76.

EVEN AFTER 23 YEARS SINCE THE DEATH of Henry Whiteside he is still remembered, in Solva. This advertisement appeared in the local Pembrokeshire paper dated Saturday 22nd January 1847, announcing an Auction, it reads:

PEMBROKESHIRE.

TO BE SOLD BY AUCTION.

By Mr. Henry Phillips,

At the Ship Inn, Solva, on Wednesday, 27th January, 1847, at two o'clock in the afternoon, subject to the conditions that will be then produced,

THE FREEHOLD DWELLING-HOUSE, offices,

Yard, and garden attached thereto, situate at the upper
End of the village of Lower Solva, formerly the residence of
Henry Whiteside, Esq., deceased, but now of William Miller
Williams, Esq., containing two parlors, kitchen, five bed-
Rooms, and a loft extending the entire length of the house
&c., &c.
Also, a piece of garden-ground, very eligibly situate for
Building sites, containing 11 ½ acres, or thereabouts, at
Lower Solva aforesaid, in the occupation of the said William
Miller Williams.
The above premises were formally let at the yearly rent of
£16, since at £12, but now at the inadequate rent of £8
(subject to all repairs), and are in good repair.
For further particulars, apply to Thomas Pritchard, Esq.,
The proprietor; Mr. Henry Phillips, the auctioneer; or to
Mr. George Parry, solicitor; all of Haverfordwest.

ANTIOPE Troop Transport &Musselwick Bay:

TRANSPORT SHIP: ANTIOPE

PORTSMOUTH DOCKS; what a place to be on a cold winter's day, blowing a bitter wind straight off the sea with heavy snow and hail stones. On Wednesday 16th December, 1807, 250 frozen Officers and men of the 90th Regiment were lined up waiting to board the transport ship ANTIOPE. The soldiers were from the poor backgrounds, and the choice they faced was either work in drudgery for 12 hour day, six days a week, for low wages, or take the 'Kings shilling' and become a soldier, become a Red Coat; with a life of adventure and excitement. Most had never been further than their town or village boundaries, well this was 1807; and to escape poverty or being wanted by the law, they had taken the 'Kings Shilling.' Now, there adventures were about to begin. As they waited to board the ANTIOPE, they might be having second thoughts. I can say that most of these men had never been to sea before. They would have been excited and I expect a little apprehensive too.

For they were bound for Ireland, where the regiment was stationed, because the 'Monster' (Napoleon Bonaparte) was lose in Europe. The British Government worried that Ireland would join the 'Monster' and get independence from English rule, so the English government had stationed thousands of soldiers over in Ireland, to keep them from getting 'Home Rule'.

Because of a gale the ANTIOPE Transport Ship stayed at Portsmouth Docks from Wednesday 16th to Sunday 20[th]No soldiers were allowed up on deck or ashore, they were kept below decks in cramped conditions. You can guess the reason for keeping them aboard ship -- if ashore 'that would be the last we'd see of them', and they'd be saying 'You know what the King can do with his shilling.'

Late on Sunday night, at last, they set sail for Cork. At first, the wind was fair, but after passing the Scilly Isles, they were becalmed for two days [no wind]. Then, on Christmas Eve, it began to blow very hard, and then it increased to a gale, then it increased to a hurricane. The sea rose to such prodigious heights as to alarm 'even the most experienced sailor on board'. Their situation was rendered still more dangerous by a fog so thick, that you could not see the other end of the vessel.

Down below was a scene from hell, 250 seasick Officers and soldiers, [you can imagine the smell and the noise of 250 soldiers, being seasick] this was after all their first time at sea, and to say the least they were now terrified as well having been kept below in these conditions for ten days now.

If you have never been seasick, then how can I describe seasickness to you? Best description I have ever seen is by Mark Twain (1835 – 1910) this is what he said about seasickness: "At first you are so sick you are afraid you will die, and then you are so sick you are afraid you won't die."

With great quantities of water dashing over the decks, and rushing down the hatchways, all hands were wet to the skin, and perishing with cold, 'now all we need is the pumps to choke up.' Well, they did! With sails tearing and ropes snapping, it was with extreme hard work that Captain Mallanty and his crew kept the ANTIOPE afloat.

With the pumps blocked up, and too much water in the bilges, the ship now became hard to steer. The Captain give the orders "that every available man to the buckets and start bailing." Soldiers and sailors formed chains to pass up the buckets, and with this simple method they started to win against the sea. Many of the soldiers, had been seasick for over ten days, they were completely useless. To be honest, they didn't care if they died; quite a number had become unconscious. You're now getting the idea the state these poor men were in by being kept below, and the ship, well she was just about holding its own against this gale -- can it get any worse?

At last, with the morning light, they could see the Irish coast, but, which part of the Irish coast was it? Then the winds changed direction, preventing them making to 'any harbour' on that coast. They passed all that night at the mercy of the winds, in the morning they could see land again, about two leagues from them, [less than a mile] but dare not approach, with huge seas. The Captain could see high cliffs. The Captain had to make a decision, he decided as he did not know his exact position, the safest course of action would be to stay well out to sea. By this method he would save his ship and the lives of the crew and soldiers.

The crew having experienced the most dreadful seas, without change of clothing and starving with hunger. Not being able to serve out provisions was bad enough. Yet, this was trifling compared to what they experienced afterwards. The ship was now left to the mercy of the waves, sailors started falling on their knees, praying for deliverance from their dreadful situation. This was the 14th day at sea and all this time the soldiers had been kept below decks, in cramped conditions. Some soldiers had gone completely out of their minds, with the thoughts that the ship will sink any minute, just think of these young soldiers, seeing experienced sailors falling on their knees and praying "desperately

The ANTIOPE was now being blown towards the Pembrokeshire coast, blown into the south side of St. Bride's Bay, just a mile east of Martin's Haven, into Musselwick Bay. On Tuesday 29th December 1807, surrounded by almost inaccessible cliffs, she was dashed on a large rock, but just as quickly carried off. Now, leaking badly; the situation here was the most alarming that can be imagined. Because of the gale there was not a boat could venture to their relief and all the ships rowing boats had been smashed to pieces. Hundreds of people from Marloes village were viewing them from the tops of the cliffs, without any possible means of affording them assistance. Then the main-mast fell overboard with a dreadful crash, ropes snapped two poor fellows were swept away. Four soldiers attempted to swim ashore, but drowned while the sailors and soldiers left aboard watched. No-one else tried swimming to shore through this huge surf. The ship now hit the sands of Musselwick beach, and became stuck fast. For hours the seas swept over the ship, but, the ship was holding together. Eventually, the seas began to calm down. The storm had changed direction it was now coming from the south and all was suddenly calm in the bay. "They had survived all that had been thrown at them by the worst storm in living memory!" [I bet a great number onboard were thinking, "this soldiers life is not all it's cracked up to be, and just maybe that job working in a shop for 12 hours a day, six days a week, and a weekly wage of 2s didn't sound so bad after all."]

During that evening local boats started arriving, the soldiers were being landed on Musselwick beach, and some of the soldiers once ashore were seen kissing the ground. They had nothing but what they were wearing, apart from a few of the men that saved their knapsacks. The officers had lost all their baggage. After all the soldiers and sailors had quite the wreck, some hardened wretches got on board, and robbed the vessel.

Once ashore the officers quickly restored order in the ranks and then next morning marched the 90th regiment and ANTIOPE sailors to Haverfordwest. Once reaching the town they were quartered and given hot meals. [This is the first hot meal they had for over 20 days, and happily now, they would be able to could keep it down; if you get what I mean].

"In the midst of all these shocking scenes, a soldier's wife was delivered of a very fine boy, and both are doing well."

For months afterwards what could be salvaged from the wreck of the ANTIOPE was, and then she was abandoned to the seas. The wreck site in Musselwick Bay is now lost.

Pembrokeshire Body Snatchers:

BODY SNATCHERS AT WORK IN PEMBROKESHIRE:
Around the early 1800's the Customs Men stopped a small sloop off the Pembrokeshire coast on suspicion of smuggling. Once boarded, the sloops Captain said 'we have no cargo and we are sailing from Pembrokeshire to Bristol', but the crew was acting very suspiciously. The Customs men went below to search the hold to look for the usual smuggled goods such as Brandy, gin, tobacco, salt, tea, the first thing they noticed down below was an overpowering smell, pulling back some tarpaulin to their horror there were five or six dead bodies, recently dug up from coastal churches, some had been dead for a month or so, others only weeks. The Customs men had caught body snatchers taking the bodies to Bristol where the Members of the Medical Profession paid £8 to £10 for dead bodies.

BODY OF A PAUPER: The inhabitants of Haverfordwest were on Monday 2nd of June 1823, thrown into great consternation, with reports that several dead bodies had been dug up from the town's church-yards. On investigation the matter, it was ascertained that the body of a pauper recently interred had been removed. The friends of the deceased, having obtained a search warrant, began searching the houses of those on whom the slightest suspicion rested, they found the body in the house of one in the Medical Profession. The culprit immediately absconded, to avoid the summary punishment of the irritated relations and friends of the mangled body found in the house.

During excavations in Whalley Parish Church, near Aberystwyth in August 1909, which was undergoing restoration, a vault was opened and found to contain a partially decayed coffin filled with earth. The search failed to reveal any bones and it is thought that the corpse must have been stolen by body snatchers just after the burial in 1830's.

[Drawing of body snatchers at work, they usually worked in two's, but sometimes a whole gang of ten men would work an area, then be off out before authorities could catch them]

Surprisingly in the early 1800 century it was not illegal to take a dead body. But it was illegal to take the gold rings, or jewellery, or clothing. Even taking the shroud off the body could put you in prison for up to 10 years or more. But, if you were caught by the relatives of the deceased, then you were in for a good beating or worst. Body Snatchers were quite common throughout the whole country, and Pembrokeshire had its fair share of body snatchers. They were also known as 'Resurrections'. If they were known to be in the county, family members sometimes stayed on guard at the churchyard. The body snatchers would come into the county, look around church-yards in daylight with bunches of flowers in hand, once finding a freshly dug grave, call back at night, digging with a wooden spade, which made no noise, metal spades being too noisy. When they reached the head end of the coffin, it was broken open; a rope was tied under the arms and around the corpse, and then dragged out. All clothes and jewellery were taken off and left at the grave side while the body was placed onto a waiting cart, and away. Night time there was no witnesses to call out an alarm. Working the area for one night, then off out of the county, before they could be caught.

THE DEAD ARE ALIVE. – By 1823, the resurrection men had adopted a new plan to prevent detection, to dress the bodies which they had just raised in clothing. Then place the body in the carriage or on the cart, made to look as if in a deep sleep. Two of them coming from the country, stopped at a public-house about four miles from Haverfordwest town, with the body of a man, whom, after violating the grave, they had dressed in the uniform of a soldier.

While in the public-house, 'taking refreshment', a soldier, who was also taking refreshment at the Inn, went to the door to smoke his pipe, and curiosity having induced him to look into the cart. He saw a soldier, as he supposed, asleep, and thought he might be a deserter, and hailed him with "Halloo, comrade, where to?" Not receiving an answer, he attempted to wake the soldier, exclaiming, "Come, my boy, let us have a drink." With no answer being made, it dawned on him that he was not only dead but had been dead for weeks. Aware of reports of body snatchers working the county, he called the Landlord, and together they examined the body. They both expressed their suspicions that the two fellows, who were in the Inn drinking, were "body-snatchers," what they came up with is this, they placed the dead body in the back of the stables, and the soldier who was in uniform took the dead bodies place. Once our two body snatchers left the Inn, the landlord would follow on horse with flint lock pistols at the ready to assist the soldier in case of need.

This was accordingly done, and the snatchers having refreshed themselves drove off with the horse and cart. They had not proceeded a hundred yards before they found the supposed dead man tumble about and stopped to remedy the inconvenience. On taking hold of him, one of the fellows observed, "I'll be cursed if this one here isn't warm" – the other having felt him, said, "Dam un, but he's hot." Suddenly the dead body sat up and said "And so would you be, if you had come from hell, where I have been." [Can you imagine the faces of the body snatchers?] They were so petrified that they just stood there. They had gone as white as sheets, and were 'terrified to death.' As soon as they recovered they set off, leaving the horse and cart in the possession of the soldier and landlord. The body of the dead man was reburied back in the grave two days later.

Strangely, the two body snatchers never returned for their horse and cart. Sometime later the landlord and soldier sold the horse with livery and cart, splitting the money between them.

Tsunamis, earthquakes and strange weather!:

WALES TSUNAMI OF 1014; this event is mentioned in Welsh bardic chronicles. And in the Anglo-Saxon Chronicle a wide spread flood was said to have occurred on the western side of Britain, from the coast of Cambria, west and south side of Wales all the way to Kent, on 28 September 1014. William of Malmesbury stated that "A tidal wave... grew to an astonishing size such as the memory of man cannot parallel, so as to submerge villages many miles inland and overwhelm and drown their inhabitants."

THE MILFORD HAVEN & BRISTOL CHANNEL FLOODS, which occurred on 30 January 1607, resulted in the drowning of a large number of people (some reports say over 2,000 died in the Bristol Channel alone) and the destruction of a large amount of

Farm land and livestock, especially in the Bristol Channel. A wave about ten feet high came into Milford Haven and carried on up the River Cleddau. Recent research has suggested that the cause may have been a tsunami from deep in the North Atlantic.

IN 1755, a magnitude 9.0 earthquake (the same as the Asian earthquake of 26 December 2004) occurred under the seabed off Portugal. It sent a 15 m (49ft) high tsunami that struck Lisbon, probably killing around 60,000 people. The tsunami or big wave, even reached the Caribbean islands some 3,500 miles away. It also affected southwest Britain. In Pembrokeshire, around nine in the morning, a wave arrived about ten feet high which came into Milford Haven and carried on up the River Cleddau.

STRANGE TIDES AT MILFORD. A remarkable sight was seen at Milford on Wednesday morning 13th July 1824. It was high water in the harbour about 8 o'clock in the morning, the tide started to go out then three hours later while still falling and with just three hours still to go before it reached low tide, it stopped going out and just came back in again and flowed to the high water mark! A circumstance which have been seen before. [Tides going out when half way out, coming back in, my research with local Dale folk, say that about 1990's they last seen this happen. Apart from the 1607 tsunami, oh yes, and the 1755 Lisbon, Portugal earth quake.]

EARTHQUAKE AT ST. ISHMAEL'S

An Earthquake. – The effects of this awful visitation, were severely felt, about ten o'clock Monday night 2nd June 1828, by the inhabitants of St. Ishmael parish, which lies about three miles west of Milford. On part of Skerryback farm, occupied by Mr. Wm. Whitton, (b. 1778 aged 50) and on the estate of Rev. D. B. Allen. It commenced with a rumbling noise like distant thunder, and continued incessantly for about 20 minutes. A solid body of grey rock, adjacent to Sandy Haven shore, and parallel to the sea opposite Stack Rock in Milford Harbour, the shock wave caused an explosion which blew the rock into a thousand pieces, throwing large masses of it a considerable distance. The adjacent rocks and part of the hill, on which there was a thriving plantation of timber over-hanging, were separated from the main land by this dreadful convulsion of nature, and several of the trees split and were torn up by the roots. The noise was terrific, and heard for many miles around. A continued cracking noise is still heard in the rocks as of the breaking of dry sticks. [Maybe this was an underground gas explosion, like you get in coal mines.]

WHIRLWIND – miraculous preservation. Between 7 and 8 o'clock on the morning of Saturday 21 June 1828, as the Hazlebeach ferry-boat was crossing from thence to

Pembroke Dock, under sail with two passengers, it was overtaken by a tremendous whirlwind and which was observed by the boatman before it reached him to draw up the water to a height of between 30 and 40 feet.

Before he could lower his foresail it was shivered to pieces, the boat whirled around and sunk, the water falling upon them as of a water-spout, the two men sized a oar each, a spirited woman held part of the mast with one hand, having her basket firmly held in the other, they thus buoyed themselves up for 15 minutes, when they were relieved from their perilous situation by a boat that had on discovering the accident shoved off from His Majesty's Dock yard, the two men were first seen and picked-up when immediately afterwards the woman was observed. As the boat crew were going to lay hold of her, she begged them first to secure her basket, in which were her green purse with money in as she was going to market, she then suffered herself to be manhandled in.

Too much praise cannot be given to Mr. West, and the boats crew for their humane exertions in saving the lives of these people. The whirlwind passed on in a north-easterly direction damaging the roof of Llanstadwell Church immediately opposite the dock-yard, and finally expanded at Llangwm, after un-roofing some cottages, and rooting up such trees as it came in contact within its progress over land.

PEMBROKESHIRE CHRISTMAS EARTHQUAKES
Friday 11.30 p.m., 28th December 1833 an earthquake was felt all over Pembrokeshire even as far north as Llandovery and east as far as Swansea. Doors rattled and windows, but no damaged caused.

Next night Saturday at 7.30 p.m., a worst shock was felt from deep underground, roof slates came down onto the streets, some damage to buildings.

And again, this time the next morning Sunday 30th December 1833 at 8.30 a.m., one big shock felt over the whole of South Wales, at Haverfordwest, Fishguard, Newport and Tenby chimneys came down, slates came off the roofs, people ran out of their houses. This shock was the worst felt in living memory. This shock was reported as far south as Exeter, in Devon. The following day one of the worst gales to hit Pembrokeshire arrived.

CIRCLE ROUND THE SUN.—On Saturday 16 June 1860, about mid-day, an immense circle was observed round the sun at Tenby, and afforded numerous conjectures amongst the spectators as to its import. We hear that a similar phenomenon in the East is attended by severe thunder and lightning storms, followed by intensely hot weather. Thunder was heard in the neighbourhood of Llanelly, and a few claps in Tenby – whether the degree of heat will be great remains to be proven.

DALE WATER SPOUT. On Saturday 26 November 1870, considerable alarm was created in the neighbourhood of Dale, by the appearance of a large water-spout which was observed to pass over the locality. It eventually burst with such force as to cause the water to flow in a huge volume over Mullock Bridge [this bridge is about mile and a half before you reach Dale village]. Beyond rendering the road impassable for a short time we believe it was the cause of no further mischief.

[Having spoken to a number of Dale villagers, they tell me that they have seen water spouts, quit frequently, but these water spouts normally only last a minute or two].

1863: **EARTHQUAKE** in Pembrokeshire October 1863. People came running out of their houses.

1868: **EARTHQUAKE FELT IN EVERY PART OF THE GLOBE**: San Francisco, Salt Lake City, USA; Peru; New Zealand; Egypt; Belgium; Mallow in Cork, Ireland; Somerset; The Rhondda Valleys; Aberystwyth and it was even felt at our own local Pembrokeshire town of Tenby! A few minutes before the occurrence there was a strange calm prevalent over the town of Tenby, the sea went quiet and flat, no wind, some Tenby folk said they felt something was going to happen. Then at 10.30 p.m. Friday 30 October 1868 an Earthquake followed by a rumbling noise deep within the ground. The people in bed at the time said, the beds seemed to lift under them, doors started shaking and windows rattling, the pictures frames hanging on the walls started to rattling and move, some roof slates fell off houses, farmers nearby said that the horses and cattle in the fields were running and jumping around, people ran out of their houses, it must have been alarming; because they even ran out of the Tenby pubs, the rumbling noise lasted less than 30 seconds, then all was quite again, all those who had run out of the Tenby pubs, ran back in. It was noted that not one cat, dog or canary, give any sort of warning, which it's believed they are supposed to be sensitive to the earth's vibrations?

AURORA BOREALIS
1870: Aurora Borealis lit up the skies on Monday night 22 October and Saturday 29 October, seen all over Pembrokeshire, Wales as far east as London, England.
1871: Wednesday 15th November: Once again, Aurora Borealis has lit up the skies, all over Pembrokeshire, Wales.
1905: Wednesday 15th November: Aurora Borealis Lit up the skies of Pembrokeshire.
1907: Friday 15th February: Aurora Borealis lit up the skies all over Pembrokeshire.

SS COUNT D'ASPREMONT sinks in Ramsey Sound:

SS COUNT D'ASPREMONT of Swansea, under Captain J. Wood, sank Ramsey Sound on Wednesday 9th December 1903.

The ship had been steaming from Dublin, Ireland for Newport, South Wales.

The story goes' like this: Around 10 p.m., the SS COUNT D'ASPREMONT had taken a short cut through Ramsey Sound, because of a gale force 8 blowing from the South – West. The crew needed to have a break from those heavy seas which were rolling the steamer about. She struck Horse Rock, which lies in the centre of Ramsey Sound. With her engine in reverse she managed to get off and turned north with the intention beaching herself at Whitesands. As she was turning, just a short distance north of Horse Rock, she started to sink, and she went down in two minutes. The Captain and crew only had just stepped into the long-boat, and she sank right under their feet. They safely rowed the short distance and arrived at St. Justinian's Lifeboat station.

She had sunk in 30 metres deep of water about 400 metres N. N.E. of Horse Rock. On the sea bed she lies with her bow to the east with her stern to the west. She had been built by Coulson, Cooke & Co., Newcastle on Tyne, in 1874. Steamer of 452 tons.163 feet long. Owners Anglo-American Co., Ltd., of Swansea. Cargo: in ballast [no cargo].

She was once named the SS OTHELLO.

[Photograph courtesy of Diver Greg Evans. SS COUNT D'ASPREMONT leaving Swansea c1900]

For 76 years the SS COUNT D'ASPREMONT lay on the seabed and forgotten. Until 1978, when James Hedley Phillips, Diver & Shipwreck Researcher, having done his research and had worked out roughly where she lay, was ready to begin the Search and Locate Operations in Ramsey Sound for this shipwreck. Getting a team together, and telling them of these "tranquil quiet waters, where nothing stirs, and how easy it's going to be to find this wreck. The Divers: Margaret Senior from Wakefield, England, Clive Llewellyn from Milford Haven, Bruce Jones from Mathry, and myself.

All we had to do was to Search & Locate this 'easy to find' shipwreck -- what's could be the problem with that? Oh yes, by the way it's in the centre of Ramsey Sound. [I said that bit quietly]. So they were all quite happy to dive in a place that looked a lot like Ramsey Sound. The search method was quite simple: a permanent marker buoy was placed just 10 metres north of Horse Rock, about 10 minutes before slack water (with the tide still going north). Divers spread 5 metres apart, and drifted for 20 minutes maximum if not found then up. Drifting in a tranquil sea the current which should take them straight onto the wreck -- what can be simpler than that? If not located on that dive, then the next dive we would move over to the east by 10 metres and the same again if not located.

If I remember correctly it was on the fourth or was it the fifth drift search that we located the wreck. Now instead of going in10 minutes before slack with the current taking you north, we had got quite use to it, and to be honest it's quite exciting just going with the current. You want to go with the current even "FASTER!" Now we were going in 20 minutes before slack! Ahead you see a rock, the current just takes you right over, fantastic feeling, just like flying.

This was in 1978 – we lost it again until 1980. Drifting with the current northwards, Divers kept in a line with Jim on the west side Margaret Senior was in the centre and to the east, of Margaret was Diver Bruce Jones. I could just see Diver Margaret Senior to my right. We went along in a line with the current, and then ahead of me was a very large rock. As I was being taken over this large rock with the current, I noticed what this large rock was in fact the ships upside down hull, the ship's keel. It was the wreck, lying upside down. Margaret and Bruce also had found the wreck and we all met up at the propeller, just as I was recovering a nice silver teaspoon, ½ d coin and a live shell. [These are the exploding type live shells! Live Shells were quite often dumped in Ramsey Sound after the World War two; which has nothing to do with this wreck].

"Having tied my line with a floating buoy at the surface to the wreck, now the wreck was marked. Then after a quick look around, we all went up, to our waiting boat cover. Once in the boat, I asked the boatman to take us to the marker buoy. His replied was this "What marker buoy?" It had gone underwater straight away because of the current was so strong. We could not find our newly discovered wreck till slack water; we had to wait one hour! But there was no marker buoy floating, the line must have cut on the wreckage. I remember at the time saying "How Fearful!"

While on this dive, I had found on the wreck site one of the WW2 live shells, one of the exploding types! When I picked it up, it didn't look like a live shell to me at the time, just a bit of brass. At the surface, Bruce pointed out they had a tendency over years to become unstable and go BANG! Big Time!   So I threw it over the side. I may have been influenced by the bubbling and hissing sounds coming from inside the shell that swayed me quite a lot to listen to Bruce, especially as I was the one holding it. [Don't tell the others, but I kept reminding them for a while afterwards, how they made a big fuss over a little WW2 shell which I was sure was quite safe, apart from the hissing and bubbling, but, I never mentioned that].
We didn't locate the wreck again till 1980, in between these dates. I was very busy with other projects and salvage operations.
In1984, I raised the anchor, from the COUNT D'ASPREMONT, which can be admire it in all its glory outside the Harbour Inn Pub, at Solva.

A few years later, when it was slack water and the underwater visibility was really fantastic, we popped down to one of the deepest parts of Ramsey Sound. Diver Cindy Pearce and I, went down to about 55 metres depth, all we found at that depth on the seabed was lots and lots of boulders about one foot across. The bottom of Ramsey Sound was littered with them, and some sand, disappointingly, no wreckage.
A few days later while on another Search & Location in Ramsey Sound, Diver Greg Evans located a cargo of mill stones, left by an 'unknown wreck', that had sank in Ramsey Sound, but no wreckage at all, nothing, not even an anchor. Mill stones weight ¾ of a ton and were each one foot thick by five foot across. Diver Greg Evans filmed the mill stones and shortly after I used this film at a talk I give to the Wind Mill Society at the Museum of Welsh Life, St. Fagons, Cardiff.   The mill stone experts told me they had been quarried on Anglesey. Two of these beautiful mill stones, salvaged from Ramsey Sound, may be viewed at:
The Gower Heritage Centre, Parkmill, Gower, Swansea, South Wales.

Thanks to Diver Greg Evans for providing the GPS position of the steamer COUNT D'ASPREMONT of Swansea: N51 52.395 W5 19.140

LOCH SHIEL at Thorn Island:

LOCH SHIEL of Glasgow

[Photograph taken before 1894; she's a beauty, wonderful clean lines. You can see she was built to sail around the world]

Sitting in his Llanelly office Mr. T. E. Fielding was not a happy man. He had suddenly come under a lot of pressure from Pembrokeshire magistrates and his superiors. Questions were being asked: what was he doing about what was happening in the Milford Haven area, West Wales?

Mr. Fielding had a nice, cozy job as the areas Collector of Customs and he did not intend to lose it. Although based at Llanelly, South Wales, his district consist of Cardiganshire, Pembrokeshire and Carmarthenshire, which covered about 120 miles of coastline.

His problem was that the previous week there had been a [Tuesday 30th January 1894] shipwreck at Milford Haven, and, strangely, a large part of the cargo had disappeared. Local magistrates had complained to his superiors that within a day of the wrecking men were not turning up for work, at coal mines, farms, fishermen, quarries, limekilns, docks. Even shop assistants in Haverfordwest did not turn up for work.

Labourers were not laboring, fishermen were not fishing, children were not attending schools, and people were not spending in the shops or pubs. In the Milford area the whole fabric of commerce, law and order was breaking down and the authorities wanted action taken.

Even the Temperance Members, Chapels, Churches, businesses, large land owners, Coal mine owners, Shops and even Local Inns and Pubs were complaining.
[I bet that's the first time ever they all found something in common to complain about]

The whole fabric of society had collapsed, but, strangely only in the Milford Haven area. Now what could have caused this, had war started, had there been an earthquake? No, the source of the problem was the shipwreck on Thorn Island, a very small island, just off West Angle.
Mr. T. E. Fielding decided to 'spring into action,' for he had been handed a telegram informing him that some of the shipwreck cargo was being openly displayed at a small fishing village. Mr. Fielding was ready to make an 'example of them.' At 10 o'clock the following morning six of his officers arrived by horse and carriage at the small fishing village of Gelliswick, on the northern shore of the Haven, and in the neighbourhood of Sandy Haven, near Milford Haven. There is only one road in and out of Gelliswick. To get to the village you must go through Milford Haven then Hubberston village, down a hill, and as you get to the bottom of the hill turn right and the village is in front of you, on your left is the sea, or should I say the Haven.

As the officers got near the bottom of the hill they stopped the horse, got down off the carriage, and walked towards the village. About 50 yards ahead they could see a man trying to get up off the road, getting up then falling down, then getting up and then falling down. Coming closer they could see he could not stand for trying. He did speak, but he just mumbled and they could not understand a single word. Then, he just gives up and collapsed in a heap. That was their introduction to the problem that was upsetting the local magistrates, Temperance Members, Chapels, Churches, businesses, shops and even local Inns and Pubs.

The officers dragged him onto the verge and carried on walking to the bottom of the hill. They were finding even more people in this strange state, either unconscious or barely conscious, some had been vomiting in the road or on the sides of the road, or all over themselves.

Then the officers stopped and just stared; walking towards them came two men, or rather one walking while holding up the other, who was completely out of it.   They were staggering all over the road, one side of the road then the other, then backwards, then forwards. When they were no more than four yards from the officers, the slightly more sober man looked up, and doing his best to focus his eyes, while still swaying and still holding up the unconscious friend, he said these words; "There's no whisky

here boy's," then added after a pause "Well; help yourself to a whisky, we've got plenty."
Once he had said his piece he then slowly dropped to the ground, and there they lay the two of them in a heap; in the middle of the road; in total unconsciousness.

Moving them to one side the six Customs men and the horse walked on to the village. As they got closer they could hear what's best described as a 'wild party,' but it was 10.15 in the morning a wild party at this time of the day? The sight that greeted them at Gelliswick village was a crowd of about 40 or 50 people; drunk, singing, shouting, dancing, arguing, laying out cold, or unable to get up. And standing proudly in the centre of the village was a large wooden barrel, a wooden barrel that had held 36 gallons of the finest SCOTTISH WHISKY, which they all were or had been drinking freely from. Some had tea cups, some jugs, really it was help yourself, but, bring your own cup. [Now let's put this into prospective, a wooden barrel of 36 gallons of whisky is equivalent to: 288 pint bottles or 164 litre bottles]. These fine Pembrokeshire fishing and country folk, would hardly ever have tasted whisky, for they would have only have drunk 'warm Welsh bitter beer,' not this spirit of the finest Scottish Whisky, so the effects were so much worst. In 1894 a bottle of Whisky cost around 3 to 4 shillings a bottle, the average wage in 1894 was around 4 shilling a week, today that's about 20p per week.

The barrel had been recovered from the sea just a few days ago, while the tide was flooding. Some of the children had seen the barrel floating by, so the whole village helped in its recovery. It took four rowing boats to tow against tide and wind then once ashore the whole village had to use ropes to pull and roll it 'gently' up to the middle of the village. It's must have been so heartwarming to see a local fishing village with such a community [Spirit] all working together with a common goal, not thinking of themselves but of the common good of this small Gelliswick village. And they did it so enthusiastically, with joy in their hearts. They all pulled together, mind you, after that it was all downhill, no work was done, the village and area just stopped functioning.

Word had got about faster than you could say "I'll pay for the next round." That you can drink as much as you like, just bring your own cup! Within hours of the barrel being found people were coming from afar away as Angle, Sandy Haven, Hakin, Milford even Dale -- how Dale folk found out so fast is still a mystery to this day. Would you believe they had drunk the barrel almost dry, apart from pouring some into jugs to be hidden, in case anyone caught a cold, and we all know that whisky is good for a cold remedy!

Customs Report states that day: "Further investigations proved that the spirits had been willfully destroyed [drunk] to avoid detection, and a 36-gallon cask was ascertained to have been claimed and appropriated by the entire village. The inhabitants paraded the place incapably drunk, and proudly boasted: "We having an abundant supply of liquor at their command."

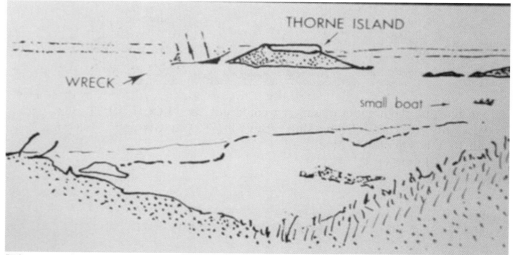

[Photograph and drawing: Thanks to: Tom Bennett Shipwreck Researcher and Diver. The photograph was taken a few days after the wrecking; you can see the ship with its stern underwater, Tom's drawing explains all]

On the right is a small rowing boat, returning from the wreck, having been out to check that all the crew has been taken off safely. Cough! You'll notice that the rowing boat is low at the stern, they must have accidently picked up a few cases of Whisky, which of course they will hand over to the Customs. When they get the chance.   Wink!

Now what was the cause of these happy events: why a shipwreck, oh; yes; I forgot to mention, just part of her cargo was "8,000 cases" of the FINEST SCOTTISH WHISKY! These bottles could be found on the beaches, floating up and down the Haven. Simply put, it was look and find! Then just forget to hand them over to the authorities.

[Photo taken about 1890, what a beautiful ship, lovely lines and look at those masts you can imagine the amount of sail she could put out. LOCH SHIEL of Glasgow. She was full-rigged iron sailing ship. Built in 1877 at Glasgow. Length 225 ft. Breadth 36 ft. Depth of hold 21 ft.
This was a 1,218 ton vessel.
Owners; Glasgow Shipping Co., Mr. James Lilburn being managing owner, 80 Buchanan Street, Glasgow, Scotland. With a crew of 27 and six passengers under the command of Captain Thomas Davies. Her planned voyage was from Glasgow, Scotland for Australia calling at Adelaide, then onto Melbourne]

LOCH SHIEL Cargo manifest: 50 tons of Fire bricks; 100 tons of iron bars, plates and sheets; 150 tons of pig iron; ironmongery; oil; white lead; linen; fire stoves; paints; gun powder; iron sinks; linoleum and some 8,000 cases of beer, plus, some 8,000 cases of SCOTTISH WHISKY. Let's just stick with the whisky, you can keep the beer. Let's add this up: whisky 8,000 cases x 12 bottles a case = 96,000 bottle of Scottish Whisky. WOW!! Yes, 96,000 bottle of Scottish Whisky, WOW! Again, plus whisky in different size wooden barrels from one gallons up to 36 gallons, oh, yes, and we must not forgot a few thousand Jars of 'Pickles', they certainly liked their Pickles in Australia, you can keep the pickles, I'll stick with the whisky!

In total we have a general cargo of 1,600 tons; in 1894 this cargo was valued at £60,000. [Let's put this £60,000 value into context, in the year 1894 an average fisherman's cottage week's rent was about 1s a week that's about 5 pence in today's money, what would the cost to rent today be?]

[Photograph of whisky glass flask, plus one broken top of one of the whisky bottle, recovered from the wreck site by Jim]

The LOCH SHEIL left Glasgow on Friday 12 January 1894 bound for Australia stopping off with cargo and passengers at Adelaide and then onto Melbourne. The vessel was in good seaworthy condition, and properly equipped for such a long voyage. She was well stocked with food and water. She had four compasses onboard, she had four boats, and two were lifeboats. She had five life-rafts, 40 life-jackets, and flares all of which were kept in a place accessible to the crew. In fact under maritime law at that time, legally, she was correctly equipped for such a long voyage.

She was towed out of Glasgow by a steam tug, then let go, and her voyage started. Well, hardly, for nothing happened for six days. She was wind bound [no wind blowing] until Thursday 18 January, when a strong south-westerly gale blew up. Once under sail Captain Davies had to put into Belfast Loch, and remained there at anchor for a further three days, because of the strength of the gale. When the weather had moderated, he put to sea again, on the 23rd January, but winds increased to gales, with heavy seas and waves up to 10 metres high
By the afternoon of Tuesday 30 January 1894, the LOCH SHIEL was 20 miles south-west of the Smalls Light House. She had been battered by south westerly gales for seven days now. With the vessel rolling side to side, and going up and down, a big

problem arose down below in the cargo hold; some of the cargo had shifted. It simply was not safe for crewmen to work down in the holds, with cargo falling about, and a more serious problem was that if enough of the cargo shifted too much to one side the vessel would be in danger of capsizing. The LOCH SHIEL had a problem and it needed to be sorted out fast for the safety of the vessel and all 33 souls aboard.

Captain Thomas Davies decided his best option was to sail for Milford, which would keep the seas and wind blowing from his stern [stern is the back of the vessel] and sailed her to the safety of the port.

All went well at first, with some adjustments to the sails, and if they managed to keep her on course they would make Milford. About 5 p.m. and on a January day in winter it was pitch dark by then -- they sighted St. Anne's Light, and, getting closer, they could make out Castle Head Lights which would guide them into Milford Haven safely. All they had to do was keep the Castle Head Lights lined up.

The sails were shortened and the vessel passed St. Anne's lighthouse to her port [left]. All was going well.

Then about 7.40 p.m., they were hit by a sudden squall [squall means very strong winds which comes up suddenly] accompanied by heavy rain, hail stones, snow. In the darkness they lost sight of St. Anne's Light and Castle Head Light.

There they were just entering Milford Haven, when suddenly visibility went down to less than hundred yards. Then a cry went out "hard-a-starboard" [turn right, very fast] came from the forward lookout. The helm was put to starboard, and in seconds she struck upon what proved to be the south side of Thorn Island, then she started to sink by the stern, the order went out to get the boats out, but before this could be accomplished, the waves began to run completely over her, and, breaking anything in their path, in seconds all the long boats were in pieces.

Flares were sent up, and then with waves breaking and running over her, the order went out to take to the rigging. The Captain and six crewmen took shelter in the stern rigging, while the remainder had taken shelter in the forecastle-head [near the bow].

For an hour in they were stranded in this position, still with heavy seas breaking over the vessel, heavy rains, hail stones, snow and gale force winds. All in the pitch dark and in the middle of winter with a wind temperature of minus 20c as cold as a deep freezer. What a terrible situation to be in.

They were soon suffering from exposure and shivering badly. Flares had been sent up just after they had struck and the crew at the bow soaked a mattress in paraffin and set light to it. Just over one hour after the LOCH SHIEL hit Thorn Island, the Angle Lifeboat arrived -- the HENRY MARTIN HARVEY -- this is not a motor driven lifeboat, but, rowed by 12 men, with Coxswain [That's the title the RNLI like to call their Captains by] John Watkins. They rescued the Captain and six of the crew from the rigging, in sea conditions that would best be described as very dangerous with huge waves coming in. The passengers and crew at the bow were all still alive. It was time for fast action. They too were suffering badly from the cold. Then three of the Life boatmen arrived at the bow section, having climbed around Thorn Island from the north side of the island to reach the stranded crew and passengers on the south side. [Because of the surf coming in onto the wreck, it was impossible to get the Lifeboat into the bow section; the coxswain had made the decision to take the lifeboat to the north side of the island, and to bring the survivors around to the north side, to the lifeboat.]   The mast and rigging had now fallen over the bow, onto the rocks, by this means the passengers and crew were able to climb along the mast to waiting three Angle Lifeboat men. They were frozen and shivering badly, but 'they were alive,' and now they had to get around the island from the south side to the north side where the Angle Life Boat awaited them. The weather never slackened one bit, but somehow they found the strength and clung to the cliff face and slowly they made their way around to the waiting Angle Lifeboat.

It took three trips to get them off Thorn Island and back to Angle Lifeboat station, not forgetting these lifeboat men had been out rowing for a considerable time, and were now suffering from cold themselves, but, they would not go ashore till the last survivor was landed at Angle lifeboat station. There waiting at the station were local Angle village people who had gathered at the lifeboat station ready to take the survivors into their homes. Waiting for them were warm fires, dry clothes, hot meals and warm beds.   These Angle villagers were not wealthy people, but what little they had they shared with the survivors. This is Pembrokeshire folk at their best.
[During my research I have been heartened by the generosity of the Pembrokeshire people who would take in half dead survivors and feed and clothe them bring them back to health. They would share what they had which was very little, knowing that this seaman could never reward them with money, not that they would have accepted a penny anyway]

The following day the wreck started to break up. A large quantity of the cargo was floating about Milford Haven.   News spread fast that the wreck had a cargo of "WHISKY."
Customs men turned up a few days later, but in the meantime the 'enterprising locals' were helping themselves to the cargo. Carts were leaving Angle Beach full of crates of whisky.   Once the Customs men arrived, all this free enterprise stopped, but interestingly the customs men were not paid overtime, so from 5 o'clock at night till 8 in the morning there were no guards at all, no customs men.
Because of the lack of overtime pay, evenings and Sundays were a free for all, and some day's customs men never turn up at all. [That was kind of them]
From as far away as Haverfordwest shop assistants were coming down to the Haven by rowing boats and all you had to do was look around to find floating a crates of whisky or, if you're lucky enough a barrel of whisky.

On Thursday afternoon the 8th February, a father and son, named Buckley, living at Angle, were drowned. The unfortunate men were in a small boat. It is understood, they had a cask of whisky in tow from the wreck when the boat overturned, and the two men were drowned. A third man swam ashore.

It is thought the acquired liquid, is supposed to have in some degree been responsible for the deaths of three more. One was a young man, named William Taylor, of Herbrandston. He found the whisky on the shore, and, in company with his brother, drank so much that he fell asleep in a field. His brother managed made it home, and a few days later they went in search for the missing brother, only to find him in the field but he was dead.

Testing the walls to try and find a recess.

[The Customs man looking for recesses in wall in the fishermen's cottages]

Four and half months later, on Saturday 16 June 1894 at Pembroke County Police Court Mr. and Mrs. William and Ann Phillips of Angle were summoned by the Customs authorities for harbouring non paid customs spirits. Mr. T. E. Fielding Collector of Customs for Llanelly and District, prosecuted, and stated that the whisky in question was discovered by the Customs men concealed in a secret recess in the wall of the kitchen, which was papered over, and a picture hanged immediately over the recess. While the customs men were looking at the picture Mrs. Phillips said "There is nothing there; don't break that picture." The officers tore away at the paper and found a recess full of bottles of whisky, 28 in all. They were still labeled and sealed. They further searched the house and garden but found nothing more. Mrs. Phillips was asked by the customs men if she would pay treble duty of £12, and she replied that she had not 12 pence.

The court was full that day, as there were a lot of local Pembrokeshire folk following this case. The case against Mr. Phillips was withdrawn, but the magistrates said the case against Ann Phillips was clearly proved, and they had decided to convict; but, at the same time they said; that there was great temptation offered to persons to take these things, as they were left unprotected and scattered about the shore for some time. However they had no right to take them. Mrs. Ann Phillips was a poor person the bench decided to deal with her very leniently with her. She would have to pay 20s (£1) and costs of 19s 4d. (About 97p). Mrs. Phillips paid the fine within a week

After the sinking of the LOCH SHEIL a bottle of whisky could be bought in Angle for 1s (5p). Gardens were suddenly dug, even fields were ploughed and you would see the customs men with log rods poking gardens and fields.

It became known to the Customs men that large quantities of whisky had been hidden at Sandy Haven. The very first house they called at was the home of a fisherman. His wife came to the door and handed over a gallon jar of the spirits, vowing that that was the only whisky in the house.

They searched the house, but found nothing more. The men noticed that the back garden had been recently dug and, using rods they quickly discovered buried in the soil another jug holding two gallons of whisky. That day, they found a lot of cottages with freshly dug gardens. All these were searched and dug up, but nothing was discovered. The villagers, hearing that the customs men were checking gardens, removed the items buried, and then covered up the holes and concealed the 'items' in better places.

At Sandy Haven, sadly the customs men found 16 bottles of whisky on the edge of the cliff; the gulls had pulled back the grass covering them. The Gulls had exposed 16 bottles of whisky. [For years after that incident, no Gulls would dare go near Sandy Haven]

Customs Officers probing the ground with "tucksticks."

[Customs men with long rods, poking gardens and fields]

On Tuesday 27 February 1894 Angle Lifeboat men Mr. Mirehouse, Mr. Edward Ball and Mr. Thomas Rees were presented with Silver medals and certificates of the National Lifeboat Institution in recognition of their bravery by the saving of life off the wreck LOCH SHIEL, at Thorn Island, Milford Haven.

On the same day as RNLI medals were being handed out to these brave Angle lifeboat men, at Glasgow, Scotland; the Board of Trade Inquiry was handing out its verdict on Captain Thomas Davies. It read: The wrecking was caused by the neglect of the Captain to verify his position in Milford Haven, and believing the ship had rounded Thorn Island, the Captain alone is in default. But, in respect of his high character during the long period of service, his Masters Certificate is suspended for three months only.

An article appeared in the local Pembrokeshire paper on Friday 29 May 1894, saying Mr. T. E. Fielding customs collector is to be congratulated upon vigorous and zealous way in which he has prosecuted and followed up such successful raids and recovered whisky from the wreck, stolen by plunderers.

My research suggests out of 8,000 cases of whisky that had been on board at the time of the wrecking; only 2,000 cases were ever recovered from the wreck site or by customs men's finds.   Some 6,000 cases were still missing? Some bottles of whisky may have accidently fallen into holes in the ground, and then accidently covered over. Others might have been hidden under the floors, under slate slabs in fishermen's cottages. But where did the 6,000 cases go to?   It has been 'proved that the strong currents which run around Thorn Island, must have taken them bottles and barrels out to sea never to be seen again. Well, that's the story that the locals stuck too, and I for one believe them. And one more thing, for years afterwards it was possible to buy a bottle of whisky named 'Special Angle - for a shilling a bottle'.
I don't think it's anything to do with the LOCH SHIEL, do you? Cheers!

This advertisement appeared in the local papers October 1894

SALVAGE *ex* " LOCH SHIEL." WRECKED
     NEAR MILFORD HAVEN.
   BY   ORDER   OF   THE   GLASGOW
        SALVAGE   ASSOCIATION.
MESSRS. ROBERT LYON & Co. will SELL
    by PUBLIC AUCTION at MILFORD
HAVEN, on THURSDAY NEXT, NOVEMBER 1st,
1894, 55 tons Iron Bars, Sheets and Plates, 8 tons
Pig Iron ; also Paints, Oil, Stoves, Iron Sinks,
Pickles, and other goods.
   Catalogues of J. Phillips, Esq., Milford Haven,
and Robert Lyon and Co., 79½, Gracechurch-
street, London.   [6704

Moving forward to the summer of 1999, a team of divers turned their attention to the LOCH SHIEL wreck site. We went in search of bottles. There had been gales and strong winds I always say it's worth a quick look; you never know what will turn up. I once, sadly, recovered an empty bottle of whisky. Anyway, I wanted some fire bricks. While under-water there among the wreckage the sand had moved and showing were a number of bottles of beer. They were still full, and still corked, because they had been buried in silt, the corks were still in place and not rotted away. Once at the surface one of the corks started to come out, I tried and tried, but I couldn't push back the cork. There's only one thing to do with an uncorked bottle of beer, and that was 'to drink it, so I did.' This appeared in all the national papers, over the TV news, internet saying "Diver drinks a bottle of beer and finds out its worth £1,000."   That's the most expensive bottle of beer I have ever had. What happened to Captain Thomas Davies of the LOCH SHIEL, when his sea days were over? He retired to Mariners Terrace, New Quay, in Cardigan Bay, West Wales to one of the houses overlooking the harbour, overlooking the sea.

[Captain Thomas Davies' house in Mariners Terrace, New Quay, West Wales]

New Quay was the place for Sea Captains to retire too, they would meet up and tell stories and relive old times of their days at sea. All the retired sea captains had a tradition in New Quay; to name their houses after their favorite ship; you'll easily find the house that Captain Thomas Davies retired too, just look above the front door and you'll see the words "LOCH SHIEL."

[The name above the door to Captain Thomas Davies House]

Shipwrecks off the Smalls:

The barque MONTEZUMA, of Falmouth, while carrying a cargo of coal, was seen by the crew of the Royal Mail steamship SS COURIER to be in trouble one mile north east of the Smalls at 3.20 p.m., on Friday 2 March 1866.

Captain James Aylward, of the SS COURIER, saw an ensign flying from the main, a recognized appeal for help.

On arriving at Milford Captain Aylward told the following story: "During a southerly force gale, when one mile North East of the Smalls, we sighted the MONTEZUMA, a barque, belonging to Falmouth, with ensign flying at the main. When first seen the barque was apparently unmanageable. She was under close reef, fore and main sail and the seas were making clean breeches over her.

There was a heavy sea running at the time, and, having got under the lee [lee of the ship means to use the other ship to shelter from the wind or waves] of the barque, we hailed the master and asked him what help he required. The Master replied, "We have 15 hands aboard, the ship is leaking badly, we must abandon ship."

Captain Aylward then asked if he could get his boats out, but the reply was that their boats had been washed away in the gale. Captain Aylward ordered his crew to lower their lifeboat, and brought his steamer round to come again under the stern of the barque, but before he had time to do so the MONTEZUMA went down by the bow, and all on board with her.

Captain Aylward said later, "In all my years at sea, I have never witnessed a ship sink so fast." The Captain and crew of the SS COURIER could not believe their eyes, and just stared at where the ship had been. It was as if the sea had suddenly swallowed her up. The Captain started shouting orders to "search for survivors." But, there were none, not one person in the water swimming; they had all gone down with the ship. Captain Aylward stood by for some time in the hope of saving life, but none of the crew was seen to rise after the vessel sank.

The 462 ton MONTEZUMA had been built in Quebec in 1846 and was owned by Messrs. H. Pellard, E. Hancock, J. Trethrowan, J. E. Downing and J. Phillips, of Falmouth. P. Nicholls, the Master, lived at Gerrans. The Mate, John Lenty was from Falmouth and the carpenter was a resident of Flushing. The MONTEZUMA was bound from Cardiff calling at Swansea, then onto Alicante.

PROOF THAT SMOKING CAN KILL YOU

The barque IDA of Caernarvon, 179 tons, sank off the Smalls on Friday 8th August 1890, taking with her a cargo of phosphates in calm conditions. She was on voyage from Newport, South Wales, for Liverpool, England. She was captained by Master Owner H. Williams, of Portmadoc. The crew of 6 was saved. She had been built in 1877 by David Jones shipbuilders of Borth y Gest, near Portmadoc, Mid Wales.

A few years earlier she had taken a load of gunpowder, from Hamburg, Germany to Alexandria, and then on her return voyage to Hamburg, she loaded up with blocks of stones.

At Hamburg, two German merchants entered the hold to inspect the stones, with a view to buying them. They were smoking cigars and apparently some of the gunpowder had been left lose amongst the blocks of stones, with the result that a heavy explosion took place, killing the two German businessmen on the spot.

The ship's Mate, Mr. Griffith Edwards, was imprisoned for nine months for negligence.

ELLEN OWEN and who's that Knocking at the door:

KNOCK, KNOCK; WHO'S THERE!

James Pape, master of the brig ALPHA, of Workington, arrived at Briton Ferry, near Swansea Town, on Friday 28th April 1876 and reported that the day before, Thursday 27th, at 4 p.m., while passing west of the Smalls Lighthouse, he saw a brigantine sunk on S.W. Rocks, on the Smalls, with topsails, jib and top gallant sail set; fore top-gallant yard on the lifts, and bowsprit above water.

The vessel reported on the Smalls proved to be the ELLEN OWEN, of New Quay, West Wales under Master Thomas, from Workington, England for Swansea, Wales with a cargo: pig iron. Wrecked at 3 a.m. Thursday 27th April in dense fog. It appears that during dense fog, the vessel struck on the 'South West Rock' near the Smalls Lighthouse.

How did this wrecking happen, let's look at the Board of Trade Inquiry:
Board of Trade Inquiry was opened at the Lord Nelson Hotel, Milford Haven, on Tuesday 23 May 1876 in reference to the standing of the brigantine ELLEN OWEN,

which occurred on the 27th of April last, when on voyage from Workington to Swansea. At three a.m., during the dense fog, the vessel struck on the south-west rocks near the Smalls Lighthouse.

Thomas Davies' Evidence: I was an able-bodied seaman on board the ELLEN OWEN. She belonged to Aberystwyth; her registered tonnage was 131 tons, and she belonged to Captain Thomas and others. He lives at New Quay, Cardigan, West Wales. She was a brigantine, and built of wood at Runcorn, near Liverpool being classed A1 at Lloyd's.

The crew consisted of six hands. She sailed from Workington on the 22nd of April last, about nine a.m., it being high water. The weather was fine, but there was a nice breeze from the eastward.

We had two boats on board, in proper order, light and staunch. The ship was bound to Swansea. About midnight on the 24th the weather was thick, and clearing up now and again; that was the character of the weather all Sunday; the wind then was light.

All was going well, then after that we tacked the ship a number of times we had no wind to speak of, off St. David's Head, we tacked the ship again, about seven or eight o'clock, out to seaward. Continued on that tack till 11 p.m., again we became calmed; there was no steerage way of the vessel. The weather was fine and clear. We were drifting to and fro with the tide, and saw no land. The Bishops Rocks were sight the first watch. We were becalmed during two tides. We fell in with the Bishops on the 26th, at 12 noon; and we worked down between Skokholm and Grassholm. Here was a light breeze. We were on the port tack towards Grassholm at seven p.m., and going about one and half knots. We sailed N.W.

Later weather became thicker; we lost sight of Grassholm and everything. About midnight we could hear sea roaring on the weather bow – I mean breakers, about S.E., of us. The vessel at the time was heading south; weather thick with light wind. We saw no light, and were going about one knot.   Nothing Particular happened until 3 a.m., when I saw something like a star. We could see nothing but the star in the north. It was on our lee bow. The ship then went on the rocks. Immediately she struck we put the jolly boat out.

The captain did nothing but walk to and fro on the deck. He afterwards went below, but did not stay long. After we got into the boat, we steered clear of the rocks, and left the vessel.

At daylight we found ourselves among the Smalls rocks, and we could just hear the sound of the bell on the lighthouse.

We afterwards, about five a.m., got on the Smalls Rock. One of the crew climbed the ladder to the Light-house door, using the butt of his knife knocked the door! It was a while before one of the light-house men answered! They fed us well and did all their powers to help us. For five days we stayed at the light-house, then taken from the Smalls lighthouse by the Trinity yacht on the 1st inst., and were landed at Milford about seven a.m., the same day. When the vessel struck the rock, we were very short distance from the Small's rocks, about a cable length. All hands were on deck all night keeping a look-out.

Able seaman Evans evidence: We left the vessel to her fate, and did not hang about her. We thought only of saving our lives.

Able seaman Nicolas: I shipped on the voyage as able seaman. The crew consisted of the Captain, three able seamen, and an apprentice. The captain and all hands were on deck. When the light was first seen I was at the wheel – all the hands on look-out. I heard the men sing out that there was a light. I cannot say who first mentioned it. The captain was there at the time.

When the light was visible the ship was going about two or three knots. She might have passed clear of the rock, but I cannot say. We have a hand lead and a line on deck, but did not use it. When we struck we knew where we were, we could see the Light-house N.E., of us. There was nothing to prevent the lead being used. The captain was perfectly sober. She appeared to me to strike somewhere forward. The weather was hazy. Saw the rocks in-shore. There was nothing to prevent the launching of the large boat. The tide was running about four knots; it was about half ebb, running in the south-west. We rowed to get clear of all danger. I do not know whether if the lead had been used we should have realized our danger. Between three to six o'clock we did not sail more than three knots. It was high water about ten o'clock. When we got ashore we saw the masts of the ship.

On Wednesday the court give the following decision: -- "The court is of the opinion that the loss of the ELLEN OWEN, on the Smalls rock, was caused by the master, Enoch Thomas, not having made sufficient allowances for the great strength of tide in the locality. From the evidence as to the courses steered, it appears that (with light and variable winds and the fine weather) the vessel must have been set several miles dead to windward in a few hours. The fog was also so dense that although a good lookout was kept the light on the Smalls was not discerned till close to it, and the vessel was within a few yards of the rocks. After striking the rock the crew appears to have been panic stricken and abandoned the vessel in the greater haste, without waiting to ascertain if she had sustained any damage. The master however, was the last to leave, and did remain long enough to discover that she was rapidly making water. In other respects the navigation of the vessel appears to have been well conducted, and the court does not consider the above nautical error of judgment on the master calls for more than admonishment to be more careful for the future. Under these circumstances the court will request the Board of Trade to renew to Mr. Enoch Thomas his certificate of service.

Let's move forward to 1981.
One day while having a rest and a bite to eat between dives on the main Smalls Rock, I started to look around at the holes of the original light-house pillars, oak stumps in the centre with lead surrounding. Looking to the S.W. with the low tide and it being

slack water, I could easily make out the South West Rock; I asked the other Divers if anyone was up for looking for the wreck ELLEN OWEN.

Off we all went, and I don't know this rock or the underwater area around it. But, I can tell you this, it was one of the most beautiful dives I have ever dived.

How can I describe this dive on the South West Rock, Smalls to do it justice? Above water, it was one of those perfect days, the sea was flat calm, the sky was blue, the wind was very slight and the sun was shining. Once underwater, I was hit straight away by the colors: pink sea anemones, soft sponges of bright orange, sea squirts colours red and orange, reddish brown sea weeds just moving so gently back and forth as if they were made of silk, just waiting for the tide to start up again.

Everywhere there was life, everywhere there was colour. Moving around the rock to the east side, I found something strange: cracks in the rock about one foot wide and 30 feet deep, all the way along. They went all the way down 30 odd feet and stayed one foot wide, I have never seen anything like them before. A bit deeper still on the east side the sea bed was covered in white Dead man's fingers, so many; it reminded me of a snow scene, I actually started to feel cold just looking. Moving back to the west side and still keeping shallow which was more beautiful than the east side, all I could do was just 'look.'

"When I say I've dived many times before -- I'm talking over 3,000 dives -- but this was the first time I just looked and I enjoyed. I'm a Diver, I'm a Shipwreck Diver, I'm a Search & Locate Diver; I have never had time to look at the marine life under the sea. I've been diving for over 40 years now, but, really, I have never looked, I mean really looked at what was there on the seabed before. 10 or 12 minutes later I came upon tons pig iron, this was the cargo of the shipwreck ELLEN OWEN, another shipwreck located, but, this dive has always stuck in my mind, one day I will go back to the ELLEN OWEN and have a look at the wreck or the marine life, I wonder which?"

AMAZONENSE wrecked at St. David's Head:

WHERE DID THIS CLIFF COME FROM?

It's 10 o'clock on Saturday morning, 16th April 1881 and the fog was thick. The SS AMAZONENSE, had not seen land since Holyhead, that was six hours ago.

SS AMAZONENSE of Liverpool was 287 foot long, 1,865 tons steamers she had been built at Southampton 1879. Commanded by Captain Hulgate, with a crew of 35 hands, and one passenger, she should be 30 miles west of where she was. The Captain though he was steaming out into the Atlantic Ocean on her voyage to Portugal, when suddenly there were 200 feet cliff dead ahead. WHAM! BANG! CRASH! STOPPED DEAD! She had hit the cliffs at Gesail-fawr, about a mile to the north of St. David's Head. Let's be clear about this, this steamer should be 30 miles to the west! Not here at Gesail-fawr, St. David's Head.

[The wreck lies at the first Point on the right, with her bows pointing inland]

Her cargo consisted of 1,000 tons of coal and about 1,200 tons of general merchandise, which consisted chiefly of Manchester goods, spirits and beer, she intending to call at Havre and Lisbon, Portugal where she was to take in another 700 tons of cargo then she was bound to Para, Brazil, she also carried the Brazilian Mail. She left Liverpool at 10.30 on Good Friday morning, 15th April 1881.

The Captains Story:

The Captain states he preceded at half-speed at intervals, while he was going at the rate of about 6 knots at the time of the disaster, and nothing occurred to indicate their approach to land until they found themselves stopped by the cliffs, plus, she had driven head-on to the almost perpendicular cliffs, the vessel landing her bows up on the rock several feet above the waterline. The Captain states that after passing Holyhead the ship was kept on the South-Westerly course in the channel and he had calculated she was well clear "off St. David's Head, by 30 miles," steering down channel on a course to keep her well clear for the Smalls by minimum of 5 miles west of or more.

The influence of the ebb tide under the circumstances may, in a great measure, account for the mishap. Had the ship been going at full speed the current would have had little, if any, influence. [This next bit about compasses and fogs is not true, but it was used by many a Captain to explain why they were so far off course] "The compasses, too, might have misled the captain, as it is well known amongst sea-faring men that fogs are prolific sources of magnetic irregularities, and it is impossible to make any calculations as to the extent of the sequential variation of the compass".

[Now I don't buy the fog and compasses, and I don't buy the currents pushing him this far east of his assumed position, "30 miles out" but I do say there was something wrong with the ship's compass.]

Ships Fog Horn:
For two hours before she struck, her fog signals could be heard in St. David's, some distance inland, before she went ashore and those who happened to be in the neighbourhood of the cliffs could distinctly hear her approaching. She struck at a quarter past 10, but her crew remained aboard her for some hours, until there was 14 feet of water in the after compartment, and then they left her in the ships boats, landing on the rocks, the sea being as smooth as a mill pond at the time. The Captain upon landing give charge of the vessel to Capt. Davies, of St. David's, who, with Capt. Oakley, immediately put men to work to save the cargo. Mr. W. Williams, Lloyd's Agent, arrived soon after to whom Capt. Davies delivered up his charge.

When the vessel struck the rocks, a fireman named John Lowe, who was standing on the deck, fell down dead. They think the unfortunate man must have had disease of the heart, and the shock probably caused his death. The poor fellow had only been married for only about six months. His body was taken to the Cathedral, and it was buried on Monday 18th April. After landing, the crew was sent to St. David's, and on Monday morning was forwarded to Liverpool by train from Haverfordwest.

This steamer was only two years old, and owned by Messrs. R. Singlehurst and Co., Liverpool, being one of the Red Cross Line of steamers. Captain Hulgate has been in his Company's employment for about 14 years, and has been master of this ship since she was built.

Upon the rise of the tide on Saturday evening the vessel heeled over on her starboard side, [right side] her stern slipping off the rocks and sinking till the water was up to the ships wheel, on the bridge, and at high-water the sea was just covering the bridge.

The work of discharging the cargo was proceeded with until late on Saturday night, throughout Sunday, and part of Monday morning, the casks, boxes, etc., being transported in the ship's boats and then hauled up over the rocks.

On Monday afternoon a tug arrived from Liverpool having on board pumps and other appliances for getting the vessel off, and strong hopes are entertained, providing the weather holds fine, that the Underwriters will be able to save the ship and cargo. Should the wind, however, come round to the West, and blow heavily, the ship is in such a position that she would be broken up completely in one tide.

Large numbers of people from the surrounding country visited the scene of the wreck on Sunday and Monday last, young and old flocking to see this unusual sight.

[Looking south at the bottom of Ramsey Sound. Shoe Rock is on the bottom left]

Five days later, on Wednesday 21st April 1881, another vessel wrecked off St. David's. On Wednesday the paddle steamer tug BRITISH KING, of Liverpool, Captain Jenkinson, was heading to the wreck SS AMAZONENSE to seek employment. Heading from Milford at the southern entrance of Ramsey Sound she struck the Shoe Rock at 12.30 p.m. She remained on top of Shoe Rock until 3.15 p.m. Then as the tide dropped, she just slid off the rock and sank. The crew managed to save themselves but none of their clothes. She now lies with her mast showing at low water. [Why the Captain hit Shoe Rock is still a mystery. He was well acquainted with this area, having towed upward of 55 vessels through Ramsey Sound].

On Saturday 30th April 1881 this appeared in the Pembrokeshire & Kemes Guardian Newspaper, letters to the Editor section. The paper was printed at Solva.

THE LOSS OF THE STEAM TUG "BRITISH KING."
To the Editor of the Guardian.
Sir, --We beg to publicly thank Mr. and Mrs. Williams, of the City Hotel, St. David's,
for their kindness to ourselves and crew when we were rendered entirely destitute
through the loss of out vessel in Ramsey Sound on the 21ˢᵗ April 1881.
Signed on behalf of the crew –

T. JENKINSON, Master.
J. B. SWINBURN, Engineer.
Liverpool Steam tug "BRITISH KING." April 26, 1881.

While the paddle steamer tug boat BRITISH KING was busy putting herself on Shoe Rock, the Liverpool Salvage Association has gone all out to save this valuable cargo. They had now placed a steam boiler on board to work there water pumps and supply steam to the winches belonging to the ship.   Also three sets of divers are also employed, and the work of discharging was going on most satisfactory. [What they are worried about is the weather: the ship was well exposed to south westerly's or westerly's, which would make it too dangerous to work on the wreck. Also, she might break up, but it was still thought the ship could be saved].   Day and night the goods are put on board steam tenders belonging to the Salvage Association, and conveyed to Solva from where they are shipped to Liverpool. The Divers reported that the hull of the ship was not damaged further back than the bridge, and those who had the matter in hand have every confidence that they will be able to get her off, provided the weather continues to be favourable. In the course of another week, when sufficient of the cargo has been discharged and the ship was lighter, the plan was to tow her off. That would be more than two weeks since she came to St. David's Head, and spring gales were bound to blow up.

Liverpool: On Thursday 19ᵗʰ May 1881, the Board of Trade Court of Enquiry at Liverpool; found that the vessel SS AMAZONENSE was stranded and lost through being steered down channel on a course too much to the southward and at too high a rate of speed in a dense fog. They had no reason to think that the compasses were not in good condition, but they were not compensated, and no table of deviation seemed to have been supplied before leaving port. They were of the opinion that no iron ship should be allowed to go to sea without having the compasses compensated. A proper course appeared to have been steered after leaving the Bar lightship, but the course steered after rounding Holyhead in point of fact put the vessel on shore, which would not have been the case had the master's estimated deviation been correct.   They were also of the opinion that the vessel was navigated at too high a rate of speed, considering the density of the fog; for she had gone an average of about 8 ½ knots throughout the voyage.

They regretted that they were compelled to find the master in default. Under all the circumstances they considered that his suspension of Mr. Holgate's certificate for three months would meet the requirements of the case.

171

FATAL ACCIDENT. – A very horrible accident occurred on Wednesday evening 25th May. [They had been working on the wreck SS AMAZONENSE for the best part of a month now, and the ship was not going to be saved. It was now, all out to get her cargo off, and then take off the ship anything of value]. A sailor named Frank Gustas, a native of Sweden, who was employed on board the steamer "ELAINE," one of the Bristol and Liverpool steamers, which is engaged in taking off the cargo and materials was the victim. The goods were taken from the wrecked vessel by a steam tender, and whilst transferring them to the "ELAINE," a sudden roll caused the crane arm of the tender to strike against the side of the "ELAINE," and on the rebound the unfortunate man was caught across the abdomen, and crushed between the side of the ship and the crane arm. The poor man died within an hour, and before medical aid could be procured.

Auction held at Milford Haven, on Tuesday 31 May 1881. SS AMAZONENCE wreck has been bought by Messrs. Lake & Co., for £230. Her original cost to build was £50,000. Lake & Co, also now owns the shipwreck paddle steamer tug BRITISH KING.

ANOTHER TUG CASUALTY IN RAMSEY SOUND. – The paddle steam tug DIGBY GRAND, of Swansea, engaged in attempting to lift the BRITISH KING, tug, which lies next to Shoe Rock on the south east side of Ramsey Sound. On the 2nd June while the pilot was in charge of her, she hit some rocks, and was at once run into Porthlysgi where her damage was patched. DIGBY GRAND was taken to Milford on the 3rd June; to temporarily repair the damaged plates (five in number) on the starboard bow, prior to returning to her work.
The attempt to lift the BRITISH KING, on the 2nd June was a failure, the chains having broken. Another attempt will be made as soon as she can be again slung.

An attempt was made again on Sunday afternoon 12 June 1881 to raise the "BRITISH KING," paddle steamer tug, of Liverpool, again, which struck the Shoe rock, in Ramsey Sound, some time ago. The wrecked vessel has been purchased by Lake Co., of Milford, and so far their one pervious attempt has been made to raise her, which failed. Three barges have been brought in on this next occasion, the whole being chained down upon the sunken tug at low water, so as the tide flowed in she should be gradually lifted. When the strain became somewhat heavy, some of the balks of timber to which the massive chains were fastened snapped like reeds, and the attempt to raise her was aborted. Another attempt will be made to save the vessel, whilst one of the divers James Mathias, engaged at the work, was underwater on Saturday, the air pipe fouled with some of the iron work, and he had a narrow escape from losing his life. The man at the surface at the life-line end, finding no long receiving rope signals hauled the diver up, and only just saved in time to save his life, as he was black in the face and quit rigid.

With regard to the wrecks of the two steamers on our immediate shores, the "SS AMAZONENCE," and the "BRITISH KING," they remain as they have done for weeks, "underwater." Some people thought that it is possible to raise them both. The local newspapers, wrote, *"And in our opinion is very great pity that more efficient efforts have not been made sooner, as during upwards of 50 years' experience, we have always found that the months of May and June are far the best for operations of this sort. To see a vessel as the "SS AMAZONENCE," mast half above water, a vessel that has cost a great amount of money, lying without an effort to raise her from there, creates feelings in us which are quite the reverse of cheerfulness"*.

RAISING A SUNKEN PADDLE STEAMER. At Last! The paddle steam tug "BRITISH KING," which sunk on the Shoe rock in Ramsey Sound, since 21st April, was successfully raised and beached in Porthlysgi Bay, on Friday evening, the 15th July 1881. By Messrs. Lake & Co., of Milford Haven, had purchased the wreck off the owners for a nominal sum, and placed the arrangements for the recovery of the vessel in the hands of Mr. Frank Jones, ship-builder, who appears to have fully merited the confidence thus placed in him. The vessel lay in an extremely awkward position, and directly in the tide-way, where, upon spring tides, the stream runs at the rate of fully nine miles an hour. The flowing tide set upon the wreck, pressing it down-wards, so that Mr. Jones had to contend against the enormous weight of water in addition to the weight of the vessel. Two large barges were chained down to the wreck at low tide so that when the tide rose they should lift the wreck bodily, and convey her to the beach.

Porthlysgi was the only place near at hand suitable for beaching her, but to reach that place the two barges and the sunken vessel had to be towed against the full weight of the north stream. Two previous attempts to raise her had been made, but owing to mishaps they proved failures.

On these occasions the tug boat in attendance was, FRANK STANLY. A powerful little boat, she proved equal to her work, with the assistance of the winches and ropes to the rocks ahead to start the whole. The vessel now lies in Porthlysgi, where she will probably remain until the next spring tides. The whole work was carried out without a hitch, which speaks well for the foresight and ability of Mr. Jones, and he is to be congratulated upon the successful result of his labours. Messrs. Lake & Co., it is said, will pocket £5,000 – a very respectable sum of money: -- by this transaction. Paid £100 for the wreck.

The tug "BRITISH KING" was moved again, into shallower waters, more onto the beach. She was lifted by two barges, again slung between them on Tuesday 2 August 1881, and carried nearly her own length. But one of the barges to which she was slung sprang a leak and the chains had to be slipped. It has been found that some of the fittings have been washed away since BRITISH KING was beached, but no damage has been done to the hull or machinery.

Now we have come to Tuesday 6[th]September 1881, how much more can this iron paddle steamer tug boat take? She has been lifted dropped, lifted dropped; a few times now!   They once again lifted her, but, the BRITISH KING broke! She broke amidships, and now lies broken in two; a distance from one half to the other half is two feet. The engines are being salvaged, and anything of value taken off, she will then be abandoned. The steam paddle tug BRITISH KING still lies exactly where they left her in Porthlysgi Bay.

You think it's all over don't you! It's not! There's more, would you believe the two barges engaged in the diving operations in connection with the paddle steam tug "BRITISH KING" also have sunk in the gale on the following Monday night in Porthlysgi Bay.
Many articles since her demise have her named as 'paddle steam tug SAINT GEORGE,' I can confirm this paddle steam tug is BRITISH KING, and she lies almost on the Porthlysgi Beach.

All this started on that Saturday morning, 16th April 1881, when the SS AMAZONENSE, arrived uninvited near St. David's Head. What happened to the SS AMAZONENSE wreck? She was sold by Auction on Tuesday 31 May 1881 to Messrs. Lake & Co., for £230. Her original cost to build was £50,000. Over the next following year she was salvaged, when all of value was salvaged, she was abandoned. The paddle steamer BRITISH KING of Liverpool, now owned By Messrs. Lake & Co., which he paid £100 for, when all that could be was taken of her she was also abandoned. Remember those two salvage barges that sunk in Porthlysgi, they were later lifted and taken to Milford.

It's September 1881 [Seven months since the SS AMAZONENCE was wrecked].
Let's look at the tally:
   One steamer SS AMAZONENSE shipwrecked.
   One of the ship's crew died of heart attack.
   One Tug boat paddle steamer BRITISH KING shipwrecked.
   One paddle steamer DIGBY GRAND badly damaged.
   Two barges damaged and both sank later.
   One salvage crewman dead.
   One Diver nearly died.

Thanks to Diver Greg Evans GPS POSITION is: N51 51.842 W5 17.929

SOPHIA at Aberbach:

WELCOME TO ABERBACH BEACH at three in the morning

By three o'clock in the morning of Tuesday 27th of March 1821, a storm had been battering the SOPHIA for a day and night. It was pitch dark, with, hail, snow and temperatures well below freezing, and the ship's Master did not know where she was. The brig of Glasgow, had been on route for Gibraltar with general cargo, but now she was being pushed towards the shore and awaiting them were huge breakers. Master Jas. Gossard, ordered both anchors down, but they held only a minute before both cables snapped!

She was now a doomed ship: taken towards Aberbach Beach, near Abercastle [its two miles north from Abercastle to Aberbach Beach]. She had now touched the sea bed, and waves were sweeping completely over the wreck. On board we have a crew of 10 and one female passenger.

Captain Jas. Gossard explained what had happened in a letter he wrote two months later:

He says;

It is true the brig "SOPHIA", was forced on shore the morning of 27th. March, 1821, through heavy squalls of wind, hail, and snow. The sea being high. [big waves]

With a tremendous surf running onto the beach, the wreck, from its height created a furious re-action of the surf.

The vessel struck, and sunk about low water mark, spring tides; it was half ebb; she fell over and heeled in with her broadside to the beach [bottom of ship towards the oncoming surf] *her position forming a kind of breakwater against the surf; when two of my crew at hazard of their lives, swam on shore with a rope through the surf, by which means we afterwards hauled ourselves on shore. Farm workers, fishermen even the Preventive Boatman* [Coast Guards] *stationed at Abercastle were waiting to help survivors.* [Where did all these people come from? It's three in the morning and blowing a gale!]

At this time, three in the morning Mr. George Harris Esq. of Tregwynt farm, being present, pulled off his coat, and wrapped it about one of the naked sailors, and whom I feel much indebted for his humane exertions and kind attention in this unfortunate affair.

All crew of 10 and one female passenger, had survived; they were taken to the local homes and farms, where there needs were taken care of.

SS GRAFFOE and St. David's Lifeboat:

SS GRAFFOE

As the steamer was passing well off the Pembrokeshire coast, the first mate became very seriously ill, the captain decided to put into Milford Haven. When heading for Milford and west of the South Bishops light with the gale getting worst, Captain Ivor Honeyman did not want to hear this. "Captain, the helms not responding" shouted the helmsman. Now with her steering completely gone he had lost control of his ship the SS GRAFFOE of London, on voyage from Glasgow to Montevideo in South America with a cargo of Coal, plus the fog was coming in thick and fast, heavy seas [big waves] was rolling her, also strong south westerly winds plus the currents pushing the steamer, to wherever the currents and winds wanted to take her. To make the situation even worst the Captain had just taken his ships position and he is not a happy man, he was just west of the South Bishops and Clerks Rocks, which lie west of Ramsey Island. So now he's in thick fog, with heavy seas running, in strong currents, in a gale plus his steering has gone, in addition his ship is close to the Bishops and Clerks rocks.

Some hours later, and being pushed and turned around by the currents, the stern section [rear, where the propeller is] struck rocks at 11 p.m. Sunday night 25 January 1903. They had no idea the rocks they had struck; in fact they had no idea where they were at all.

Directly the vessel struck, distress rockets were fired, but they do not appear to have been heard or seen. As she was sinking one of the lifeboats was got away with fourteen crewmen. Some refused to get in the lifeboat, and chose to stay with the ship. The longboat once away those in the lifeboat tried to shelter under the rocks. However, this longboat was blown out to sea, and at the time it was not known what happened to these fourteen men. Waves started to cover the wreck and one caught the Captain and chief engineer who were swept over the side and drowned. The steamer now settled on the seabed, thankfully her masts were above water. There was only one way the seven crewmen could go and that was up into the rigging, to wait for help to arrive. Their ordeal was to last for 48 hours, clinging to the rigging in the winter cold with waves sweeping over the wreck and to add more danger the masts with every large wave swayed back and forth. The cold was making them fall asleep, and to stop themselves falling into the sea, they lashed themselves to the rigging and sang songs, and just waited.

With no means of signalling their distress, even though St. David's Lifeboat Station was only two miles away for them. On a clear day they would be able to see the lifeboat station and St. David's Lifeboat station would be able to see the wreck, but the fog was just as dense as the night they were wrecked, that was two days ago. They had been wrecked on the South side of Ramsey Island on the east side of Ynys Berry Island, at the entrance to Ramsey Sound.

Two days later a boy herding sheep on the cliffs saw the poor fellows – at last, they had been seen. The St. David's lifeboat GEM under the command of Wm. Nesbitt, second coxswain, The order was given "Launch the Lifeboat" once at the scene of the wreck, the coxswain had to be handled with extreme care owing to the position in which the vessel had gone down, and the rough state of the seas. The survivors insisted upon their dead comrade the first engineer to being first taken, and then one by one they were rescued from their perilous position, the lifeboat had to go in take a man off, back off, then back in, take a man off, back off, then back in. A few seamen in the rigging not forgetting they had been exposed the elements for days, the lifeboat crew did a good job, they handled each seaman with such care, some of the seamen could not move, they were really done in, without hesitation the Lifeboat crewmen went into the rigging, and bodily carried them down to the waiting lifeboat, and all the time the masts were swaying six or nine foot one way and then the other, with huge waves coming from the south. The St. David's folk are very proud of their lifeboat crew, and justly so.

The second coxswain proved himself a worthy successor to the chief coxswain, who had died recently, and whose place has not yet been filled. It was generally admitted that the rescue was smartly affected, and the boatmen were loudly cheered on returning to the boathouse. Beside the six survivors the body of the third engineer was brought ashore.

Alfred Maycock, steward, said he was with the dead man in the rigging from the first until he died between three and four on Tuesday morning. They all huddled together to keep themselves as warm as possible, and he did his best to keep the man awake, taking to him, slapping his face, and rubbing his hands. In the rigging looking across Ramsey Sound they could see people on the mainland working in the fields. But, on the mainland no one could see the wreck.

Dr. Parry, Solva, said he was summoned to the Lifeboat Station. From examination of the body and what had been told him, he came to the conclusion that deceased died from cold and exhaustion consequent upon exposure.

One of the rescued seamen was a Russian Finn, whose appearance at first gave little hope of his survival. He was promptly subjected by the boatmen to "first aid" methods till a medical man arrived. The Finn revived in response to the treatment, and before long had completely recovered. All the survivors were in need of attention, and they were well looked after by those on shore. The names of the men are:

John Jones,	Borth,	Portmadoc.
John Edwards,	Borth,	Portmadoc.
Richard Jones,	Cardiff.	
Arthur Maycock,	London.	
Charles Wiedou,	Sweden.	

The name of the Russian Finn I could not ascertain.

The SS GRAFFOE was a steel screw steamer of 2,996 tons gross, built at Hartlepool in 1892, and owned by Messrs. E. Morgan and Co., of London. She was a total wreck. St. David's Lifeboat Second Coxswain William Nesbitt received the RNLI silver medal.

What had happened to the fourteen seamen in the rowing boat?
The GRAFFOE longboat's with 14 crewmen had disappeared, and most thought they had drowned. But on Tuesday evening the SS GATESGARTH, one of Messrs. Rea's colliers, arrived at Penarth, Cardiff and reported that she had picked up the lifeboat of the SS GRAFFOE, with 14 deck and engine-room hands on board.
The boat had been sighted in the Irish Sea off Holyhead, 80 miles from the wreck site. The men when taken aboard the SS GATESGARTH were in an exhausted state. They, however, soon recovered in response to the kindly attentions of the master and crew of the steamer.
On arrival at Penarth the rescued men were taken in charge by Mr. C. S. Hall, the local superintendent of the Mercantile Mariners and hon. Agent of the shipwreck Mariners Society, who provided them with clothing and substantial tea at the Queen Restaurant. Afterwards they were sent to Glasgow where all except the cook belong. He is a native of London.

The 14 men left Cardiff Train Station for Glasgow at 8 o'clock in the evening. They had little time to wait for the train, and clustered together on the platform, they attracted some attention; for it was clear to the mostly unobservant that they had recently undergone severe hardships. To some inquiries if they were shipwrecked mariners they briefly outlined their experiences, and showed sever scars on their hands received in the endeavour to hold their boat under the lee of the jagged rocks alongside the SS GRAFFOE. Out of 23 crew, three were lost.

The longboat men's story:
The boat had been sighted in the Irish Sea off Holyhead, and the men when taken aboard the SS GATESGARTH were in an exhausted state. Their account of the matter is that the SS GRAFFOE, which left Grimsby on Friday night in fair weather, passed the Tusker Lighthouse [Irish side of the St. Georges Channel] at three o'clock on Monday morning, and then encountered very heavy weather, during which the vessel developed some defect of the steering gear, and would not answer her helm. The result was that she was driven on the Bishops Rock. The boats were ordered out and one was launched. This boat, with fourteen of the crew, in charge of the steward, was ordered to take shelter beneath the rocks, but the heavy seas, made it impossible to remain in the position. The men were obliged to let her go, and the boat was speedily driven out to sea.

All their efforts to return to the ship failed. They, therefore, hoisted an oar, and fastened a sail to it, and kept the boat before the wind. They were frequently in danger of being swamped, but they had to be constantly bailing kept afloat till daybreak, and then found that they had drifted out of sight of the vessel and land. They were beaten about at the mercy of the sea until they were picked up by the SS GATESGARTH at three o'clock on Monday afternoon. Being very light clothed, they had suffered considerably from exposure, and they were famishing for food and drink, which they had not had for over 30 hours. The men speak highly of the kind treatment accorded them by Captain Cooper, of the SS GATESGARTH, and his officers and crew.

SURVIVORS AT ST. DAVID'S DOING WELL
The survivors of the SS GRAFFOE, rescued by the St. David's lifeboat, were cared for by Mr. William Arnold, Lloyd's sub-agent. Food, clothes, comfortable lodgings, and every necessary are provided, which the crew gratefully acknowledge. The deceased man brought off by the St. David's lifeboat, and now lay in the cathedral awaiting an inquest. Depositions were taken on Wednesday by the divisional officer, the chief mate, John Jones, John Edwards, Richard Jones (second engineer), Maycock (steward), and Charles Wheaton giving evidence, Raphael Anderson being not well enough to give evidence. There was much surprise at the wreck not being observed on Monday, as the weather was clear.
Raphael Anderson was four hours regaining consciousness. St. David's inhabitants are doing all possible for the crew.

05° 20' 00" W

Wreck of the GRAFFOE

[Photo taken of the wrecked steamer SS GRAFFOE just days after her wrecking]

After the SS GRAFFOE was salvaged that summer of 1903, she was left and forgotten about, until 1968 when Divers David Evans, Ron Scott and I, went in search of this wreck. Ron, had a photograph of the wreck on the rocks, and they asked me a young 20 year old Diver James Hedley Phillips to come along and help in the search. We arrived off Ynys Bery Island, and using Ron's photograph, tried to find this wreck. David and Ron, would say 'that looks like the spot' and over the side I would go. After looking around and not finding a wreck, we'd try again at another spot, and so on. On the fourth or was it the fifth time over I went. Depth from my memory was about 18 metres, and the underwater visibility was about 8 metres. Half way down "there was the wreck 'just like that'. I could see the ships ribs, but most of all, what sticks in my memory was the whole wreck was covered in Cray fish. They were under every bit of metal. I had a good look around the wreck site, two boilers, and one long propeller shaft! Up I went and reported the find. I thought to myself 'how easy it is to find shipwrecks?'

Later that same year 1968, by accident I located another shipwreck the ketch PORTLAND, driven by 25 hp auxiliary diesel engine. She had sunk 1927, in Porthlysgi Bay. So during my first year of diving, I had located two shipwrecks. Then the following year more proof of my 'how easy it is to find shipwrecks' theory came with finding a big pile of limestone at the entrance to Porthlysgi Bay, on the west side. The wreck had well-rotted away, but, just a big pile of limestone, her cargo was left. It was many years before I managed to find the name of this wreck. She was the sloop PILGRIM, of Solva, which sunk on Tuesday 23rd September 1845. While going through Ramsey Sound she sprung a leak. The master was trying to make for Porthlysgi beach, where he planned to put her on the beach and fix the leak. But as he started to round the headland into Porthlysgi Bay, she sank.
The master and one crewman swam the 60 yards distance to the cliff. From there it was an easy climb up onto the cliff Path, which they followed all the way back to Solva Village. I don't think they were enjoying the coastal views while walking what is now "Pembrokeshire Coastal Path! That's three shipwrecks found in my first 18 months of diving, not a bad start.

Forty years later with more than 30 shipwrecks discovered, I think back to my early days of searching for wrecks and about the innocence of youth!
I honestly did not know it was supposed to be difficult, I just thought you would go over the side and there you are another shipwreck! Just like that!

Thanks to Diver Greg Evans we now have the GPS position:
SS GRAFFOE: N51 51. 022 W5 20.044
PORTLAND: N51 51. 535 W5 18.540
PILGRIM: N51 51. 535 W5 18.540

SS LANGTON GRANGE on North Bishops:

SS LANGTON GRANGE of London

The SS LANGTON GRANGE was big, especially for 1896. She was one of the early electric freezer ships that would make meat affordable to the average British family, and not just once in a while luxury, but meat affordable for the Sunday dinner table. UK farmers could not complete with the arrival of the SS LANGTON GRANGE with 7,000 tons of cheap meat.

[Photograph taken around 1900 SS LANGTON GRANGE of London]

At 420 feet long, 54 feet wide, 30 feet deep, this steamer of 5,852 tons, could carry 7,000 tons and was built with one cargo in mind--meat. Either beef from Argentina or lamb from Australia and New Zealand. She had four boilers to generate steam to turn the propeller but also to run huge electric generators for she was a cold electric freezer ship. Normally, she carried a crew of about 60 officers and men. Built 1896 by Clark Workman of Belfast, for the Houlder Line of Steamers, of London.

THE WRECKING OF THE SS LANGTON GRANGE

Thursday at three in the morning 5th August 1909; the inhabitants of St. David's were awakened by the firing of guns and rockets announcing that a ship was in distress somewhere off the coast. The sea was hidden in a dense summer fog, and it was impossible to be sure where the distress signals were coming from. With great speed the Chief Coastguard, Mr. H. Hunt, and his [L.S.A.] Life Saving Apparatus Company, raced to St. David's Head to search the cliffs.

For some time they searched along the neighbouring coast, but owing to the heavy fog they were unable to determine where the steamer was. Aboard the LANGTON GRANGE even Captain Graves did not know exactly his ship's position. On his starboard side, [right] he could just make out a small island about 200 metres away.

In the meantime the lifeboat authorities had been warned, and the St. David's Lifeboat "GEM," commanded by Coxswain Stephens, left St. Justinian's about 4 a.m. and went in search for this wrecked steamer. Shortly afterwards the fog lifted, and it was seen that a large steamer had gone aground right on top of Bell Rock, North Bishops, about five miles south west of St. David's Head.

After some delay owing to the strong currents the lifeboat reached the vessel, and she was found to be the freezer container ship SS LANGTON GRANGE of London. The ship's crew of 54, and there was also an Australian passenger named Mrs. Fergusson aboard. The LANGTON GRANGE had left Glasgow, Scotland on Wednesday bound for Newport, South Wales, in ballast [no cargo], under the command of Captain F. A. Graves. Captain Graves asked the lifeboat men where his exact position was. They told him that he had perched his steamer right on top of Bell Rock, on the North Bishops, five miles off St. David's Head.

[The North Bishops Rock where the SS LANGTON GRANGE was wrecked on top of Bell Rock. Bell Rock is just in front of the first high bit of the rock on the right side. You could see the wreck easily from St. David's Square]

The Captain and crew remained aboard her, hoping that the tugs that had been sent for could pull her off on the high tide. All that night the crew did not sleep as the hull moaned and creaked as she rocked about on top of Bell Rock.

Next day it was realized that the SS LANGTON GRANGE could not be saved, as the ship's back had now broken, [she had broken in half] and she was starting to slide underwater the bow section to the south side and the stern section to the north side of Bell Rock into deep waters. The crew collected their possessions and abandoned her for good.

This is Captain Graves's story. "Everything went well until approaching the Pembrokeshire coast where a heavy fog set in, and, although every precaution was taken to pass the dangerous rocks of the Bishops and Clerks, she went aground. The rock which she was on top of was studded with sharp rocks, and soon her holds were full of water, while there were several feet of water in the engine-room and in 1, 2, and 3 holds.

Captain Groves at once put off distress signals, and the crew put lifeboats in readiness. Fortunately the sea being calm, the vessel remained high and dry."

Finding there was no immediate danger the captain declined assistance from the lifeboat, and the crew and lady passenger declined to come ashore, deciding instead to await the arrival of the salvage party who were at once communicated with. It is expected that the crew and passenger will be removed from the vessel the next day. On Friday the tugs arrived from Milford Haven. Owing to the extremely awkward position of the ship [middle of the steamer was right on top of Bell Rock] it was decided not to tow her off. But she could be salvaged, and they can cut her up where she lies.

Although there was slight mist, crowds gathered in St. David's square. The wreck was plain to see from St. David's square. She had been on route for Newport, South Wales to collect coal for her voyage, and had been due to sail from there to New Zealand.

On Saturday Captain Graves and the crew finally abandoned her. The following day they caught the afternoon 3.35 express train from Fishguard, the captain destined for London and the men for Birkenhead. The tug VIGILENT had been used to convey the men to and from the scene of the disaster. But the ship's cat refused to leave. A party visiting the wreck on Monday tried to capture it, but without success.

The LANGTON GRANGE had come to grief on August 5 1909. Just six days later the SS MANATON of London, bound from Liverpool to Karachi, ran ashore on the Smalls Rocks, right next to the lighthouse, the Smalls is about 20 miles from Bell Rock.

At the time the when the SS MANATON arrived on the rock, the Smalls light-keepers were right at the top of the lighthouse firing fog signals, as the atmosphere was very thick with fog all that morning. The steamer hit the rock and carried on going. This frightened the living daylights out of the light-house men as the whole lighthouse started the shake, looking over the side of the lighthouse looking down they watched as the steamer stopped with her bow about 5 feet away from the lighthouse door. The lighthouse men went down to the door, on opening it, they were so close that the lighthouse keepers were able to speak to the crew and pass them mugs of tea. The ship's crew walked around the Smalls Rock with mugs of tea in their hands and joined by three light keepers. [That's not a sight you see every day]

As soon as the SS MANATON struck a telegraph message was dispatched to Chief Coastguard Hunt, who at once sent one of his men to St. Justinian, and informed Capt. Burge, Underwriter Director from London, and Capt. Anderson, salvage steamer owner, who had been engaged during the previous few days on the wreck of the SS LANGTON GRANGE.

Capt. Anderson and all the salvage men proceeded in the salvage steamer LADY OF THE ISLE, with pumps and appliances to the Smalls to render assistance. Later, at high water, the SS MANATON got off the rocks under her own steam and steamed south. It was feared she had been badly holed. The crew pumped out her water ballast in the fore compartments, and kept her engines going continually until she slid off at high tide, and headed south.

The 4,025 ton SS MANATON was commanded by Capt. R. J. Work. She carried a crew of 48, and had on board two females. She was built in 1902 at Sunderland by J. Prestman and Co., and was owned by Messrs. Lambert Bros., London. She steamed straight to Mount Stuart Docks, Cardiff, for repairs.

WINSTON CHURCHILL–IS ASKED QUESTIONS IN PARLIAMENT - ST. DAVIDS WRECK, AN UNCHARTED ROCK

Winston Churchill, then President of the Board Of Trade, 1908 – 1910, was called to Parliament to answer questions about the wrecking of the steamer LANGTON GRANGE.

In the House of Commons on Thursday, 26 August 1909 Mr. Jeremiah McVeigh (N., Down, S.), asked him about the recent stranding of the steamship SS LANGTON GRANGE on the North Bishop's Rock, St. David's, and whether he was aware that the disaster might have been averted if the rock had been indicated by a red line on the admiralty chart, and whether the charts would be revised in order that such points might be indicated.

Mr. Churchill replied, "*I have ordered a formal investigation into this casualty, and until I have received the report of the court of inquiry I cannot say what the stranding was due to or whether it might have been averted had the rock been marked on the Admiralty chart by a red line. I understand the Admiralty are of the opinion that to increase the marks on their charts in dangerous places in the manner suggested would render the charts illegal in places where legibility is most required, and would be more likely to confuse mariners than to help them.*"

[Years later they did put red lines on charts to show shipping lanes, but, Captain Graves at the time of the wrecking, he was miles off course].

MASTER OF SS LANGTON GRANGE SEVERELY CENSURED
Judgment was delivered at Liverpool on Monday 20th September 1909, concerning the stranding and subsequent total loss of the SS LANGTON GRANGE. The court found the total loss of the vessel were caused by the master not making sufficient allowance for tides and currents, and steering too fine a course to clear the North Bishop's Rock after sighting Strumble Head in light, but hazy, weather. The court found the master in default, and severely censured him, considering that he placed too much reliance on the approximate distance from Strumble Head light. The vessel evidently experienced a strong southerly inset towards Ramsey Sound, and in consideration of the circumstances the court did not deal with his certificate. [They did not take his Captains certificate off him].

There have been a number of attempts to salvage her over the years, but the slack waters are so short and tides are so strong on Bell Rock, thus prevented anyone from really succeeding.

MOVING FORWARD TO THE SUMMER OF 1982. I was working the LEWIS shipwreck, salvaging her cargo of Welsh slates, just a mile south of Porthlysgi Bay, with Divers Andy Jack from St. David's and Richard Powys.

I was staying at Porth Clais Farm Camp site, owned in those days by Mr. Morgan. One day in early summer 1982, Mr. Morgan said to me that a relative of his who knows of another slate shipwreck in Ramsey Sound and if I was interested I should call around and have a chat with him.

Mr. Morgan said the gentleman lived on the road to St. Justinian's Lifeboat station. It is the last farm painted white, before you go down the hill to the lifeboat station just on the right. Months later, when we had the August gales, which meant no diving operations, I called over to see him. Finding the farm house, I knocked the door, the gentleman answered. I explained that I was Jim, salvaging the slate wreck cargo, and that Mr. Morgan of Porth Clais Farm said to call and see you, as you knew of another slate shipwreck. With that I was invited in, sat down and given 10 cups of tea and 10 slices of his sister's homemade cake!

We chatted for a while, I found him a very relaxed, easy to talk to gentleman, and he was very knowledgeable of shipwrecks and the maritime history around the St. David's area especially the Bishops and Clerks Islands. I must tell you this he had a very sharp memory; he was well into his 80's. As a young boy he had helped his Dad with the fishing and lobstering. He knew how to sail, and he knew 'the stones' [the local St. David's lobstermen called the South Bishops and the North Bishops and all rocks and islands on the west side of Ramsey Island, 'the Stones']

This is the story he told me: His father had told him; about the year 1890 he had seen a sailing ship sink with its cargo of slates. It sank in deep water right in front of the St. Justinian's Lifeboat Station, just off the corner.

[Years later I went in search for this wreck, with divers Greg Evans, from Pontardawe, and Clive Harris, Cindy Pearce and Clive Hayes, from St. David's. We located two big anchors, and lots of slates, some of them broken and some whole. The slates measured 24 inches x 12 inches, but they were not the main cargo. I think the cargo of slates might be under 10 metre deep sand banks next to the anchors]

Then he told me this incredible story as well:
When he was 10 years old in August 1909, he was working in the fields, when his Dad called him saying "They have left the wreck on Bell Rock, and gone to the Smalls, now's our chance." His Dad was a St. Justinian's lobsterman. With the salvage boat gone from the SS LANGTON GRANGE to the Smalls to salvage the SS MANATON, they the local St. David's fishermen could also help in the salvage work, and forget about the Customs men and keep what they helped to salvage.

His Dad's lobster boat was about 18 feet long, with a single mast and one sail; he kept it moored at St. Justinian's. In those days it was a case of sail or row. Sailing around the north side of Ramsey Island, with a wind coming from the south, they could easily see the wreck perched still on top of Bell Rock even from that distance you could see quite clearly she was broken at the middle from miles away. About a mile from the wreck, they make out one of the other St. Justinian's lobstermen's boat coming from the wreck. But the boat did not look right, she did not sail the way she should, "very strange that", his Dad pointed out to him!

As they got within hailing distance, they could see why. One 18 foot sail boat with three St. David's men on board, plus tied to the single mast was an upright piano, yes, an upright piano in an 18 foot boat. As they passed each other, one of the men lifted the lid and banged away at the keys, his dad said "daft buggers, why a piano, they can't even play it." Once they arrived at the wreck, his Dad climbed one of the many ropes hanging over the side, while he kept hold of the rope and waiting for whatever his Dad would lower down. What his Dad went after was -- food. This ship had been stocked up for a long voyage with over 50 mouths to feed daily. She was a floating super market, and it was all free, if they could be quick about it.

Other St. David's fishermen were turning up, saying to the 10 year old boy; 'did you see them daft buggers with a piano.' Then up the ropes they went to help in the lightening of the ship. His father told him afterwards, that once he was on the ship, she was so big; he just could not find the food stores room, where does one start on a ship this size? Then suddenly as he rounded the corner he met one of the St. David's men who showed his Dad where the ships food store room was. But there was a big problem, the flood tide would soon be picking up so speed was of the essence also those salvage people might be back any time and the ship was well broken in half, and every now and again, the whole ship creaked very loudly and she would move, plus all the tin food was in one big mess, at high tide the room had been underwater, shelves had collapsed and the tined food was all over the place. The boy who still held the rope with one hand and the other against the ships side, he did say to me that; you could feel her moving an inch now and again. Back in the food store room which was full of one foot square tinned foods, but his Dad had a big problem, the food inside the tins was perfectly okay, but all the labels had come off! Now he could end up with one foot square tins of powder milk. Not exactly what was wanted!

[Photograph: Can you imagine, arriving on deck, of a steamer this size, then trying to find the ships food store room! Where do you start looking? Luckily his Dad met a St. David's man on board who showed him where the store room was located. Opening the door, what confronted him was a room that had been underwater at high tide, and everything was all over the place, all the shelves had collapsed, tins everywhere, and the libels; well, they had all come off!]

What his Dad did was this, he went by the weight of the tins; all the tins were one foot square. So he sent down different weight tins, this way they got a mixture of food tins: what they ended up with was one foot square tins of: coco, pears, [he remembers he liked the pears best] other tinned fruits, sugar, tea, marmalade, and other jams, corned beef, etc., etc., his father was lowering them down to him in a net, while he stacked them in the 18 foot fishing boat. Also his dad lowered down bacon, now we're not talking about one or two rashers of bacon we're talking about frozen half pigs. Once loaded, well he did say well over loaded, they cast off, problem was, his Dad could not get into a rowing position, their little boat was that full, with the side's only inches above the water. It took them hours of gently sailing her back to St. Justinian's; thank goodness it was a calm day.

Crossing Ramsey Sound, they sailed gently down the mainland side towards St. Justinian's Lifeboat station. He could see his sister waving and shouting it was safe to come into St. Justinian's. No Customs men waiting. In a place like St. David's everyone knows everyone, so strangers would stand out, especially customs men. Rounding the corner they could see there waiting at the bottom of the steps at St. Justinian's lifeboat station was his mother, brothers and sisters, all waving them to come in. His Mam, had borrowed her neighbour's two donkeys [in those days everybody in St. David's seems to own a donkey] and the whole family spent hours unloading and taking up the steps all that they had 'acquired'. Once they finished hiding the 'acquired items,' that evening his Mam cooked the biggest family meal he had ever seen in his 10 years of life, this is the first time he could have not only seconds, or thirds but even fourth's! Next morning he and his mother took the donkeys back, with a whole pig as a reward for the neighbour. That must have pleased their neighbour, for he remembers her saying "You can borrow my donkeys anytime."

For months after, as his mother would bring out a tin, (these are the tins with no labels on), then the whole family would sit around the table and had to guess what food was inside the tin, then she would open the tin. [It's so heartwarming to hear of them old St. David's family parlor games] He did say out of all these tins, only two were powdered milk.

Just a day later the two half's of the wreck slid into deep waters, taking all that good food with it. At least some had not been lost.

[At this point he stopped for I could see his mind had gone back to that time, we both just sat in silence, not saying a word, I let him recover his composure. Then we had another cup of tea, and some more cake. You had to have been there to understand what I mean, he's a very good story teller, very accurate, the atmosphere in his farmhouse sitting room, the clock ticking in the background, his Mam his Dad were alive again, let's not forget he was reliving something that had happened over 70 years ago, but, he was telling it to me as if it had just happened - yesterday]

SEARCH & LOCATE DIVERS

[Photograph: centre of the plates, with the company logo]

On the top of Bell Rock there are a few wrecks, two steamers, and a few sailing ships, I wanted to have a look and see if I could locate the SS LANGTON GRANGE, this was in 1985 and straight away we found the wreck, strangely we kept finding electric light switches, of course the steamer had electricity. At a depth of 40 metres I discovered row upon row of china plates, which had fallen out of the wreck as she had broken up over the years. All of them bearing the company motif the Maltese cross. On the other side of the plates the date of manufacture, 1890, and the stamp of the manufacturer, W. T. COPELAND & Sons, Stoke-on-Trent, England.

[Photograph: selection of different size china plates, with company logo in center. Some of the dinner plates were perfect as the day they were made, others you can see the Patten has gone? Bottom right, the top of a Casserole dish, I think?]

THE MEN IN BLACK FROM SCHWEPPES
Deep inside the wreck we came across full and corked bottles of 1909 Schweppes tonic water. The bottles had been buried deep in silt so the corks were protected; there wasn't any oxygen to rot the corks. A few days later I telephoned the Head Office of Schweppes in England and tried to explain that I had 90 year old bottles of Schweppes tonic water. They did manage to find someone to take my call; he might have been a manager or a director? After I explained that Divers had recovered Schweppes glass bottles from a shipwreck, his response was 'Mr. Phillips thanks, but we have plenty of 1900's Schweppes Tonic bottles in our museum, kind of you to tell us.'

But, I had a punch line ready "But, these 1909 bottles of Schweppes Tonic Water are still full, and corked," a longish but, not to long pause, then he said, "What is your address Mr. Phillips." At nine the next morning four smartly dressed men in black arrived from Schweppes Head Office at my house and bought the lot. As I told the diving team afterwards, "I was quite happy just to get 'a penny back on the bottles', but these four smartly dressed men in black from Schweppes Head Office insisted on giving us this big fat cheque."

[Photograph: recovered by Divers 1909 Schweppes Tonic Water bottle still full and still corked]

In August 1985, one of the diving team, Diver Clive Hayes of St. David's, located the ships Alcohol room, [We called it the booze room] which was full of silt. Under the silt were wooden crates, each crate held 8 bottles. The nails had rusted away, but the wood was almost perfect. All the bottles were still full and corked: white wine, red wine, lime juice and Champagne. The date on the side of the Champagne corks read '1900

[Photo of Jim's inflatable boat, no room for the Divers]

CHARLES HEIDSIEK, OF REIMS'. A company bought them off us, but it was undrinkable. The smell alone would have put anyone off the idea of drinking it.
Interestingly, we never found one bottle of whisky, gin, or brandy [brandy, that's what I was after] I know that they are there, but it's just too dangerous working in the room, once you touch or move anything, the silt, I mean absolute zero visibility, absolute zero, you work from memory and touch, with a lifeline attached to you and a Diver at the other end to lead you back out. I think they might be right at the back of the room.

[Photograph: top left to right, Champagne, Lime juice, red wine, Schweppes Tonic water, red wine, small bottle of red wine. Bottom lying flat left to right, red wine, and Schweppes Tonic water]

THE RED WINE: I took one of the bottles of red wine to Mr. Colin Pressdee, who, in 1985, ran a restaurant in Wind Street, Swansea, which was one of the best in Wales if not the UK. Colin is a wine expert and I wanted his opinion on this salvaged red wine.
Firstly, I wanted to know if it was safe to drink after lying on the seabed for 90 years. This is what happened and not a word was spoken just silence, it was almost like a religious experience. By candle light Colin had a good look at the wine through the bottle, then a good look at the bottle, and then slowly he uncorked it, sniffed the cork, examined the cork, sniffed the top of the bottle, and took a good look at the cork again and then very slowly poured a small amount of wine into a glass. He looked at it some more, swished it around in the glass, sniffed it yet again, held it up to the candle light, swished it around a bit more, lifted it to the light again, 'still not a word was

said, just silence', giving it a really intense look, then before I could say 'Bob's your uncle' he drank it.

As I waited for him to keel over screaming, I was thinking to myself, how am I going to explain this to the police? The police would get a 999 call, in they would burst, and Colin would be on the floor screaming, with a strange terror look on his face. And I would be saying "but officer, I only asked Colin to look at some red wine off a shipwreck that's been on the seabed for 90 years, that's all! I didn't expect him to drink the bloody stuff! Honestly, it wasn't me officer' on my children's lives."

After Colin had finished making some strange sounds swilling a 90 year old red wine around his mouth, he swallowed it. And then after some seconds he actually spoke for the first time saying, 'It's a fine French Claret of the Bordeaux region. It's good, but not their best.' I thought if Colin could drink it so could I. So there we were, sitting in his restaurant drinking a fine 90 year old French wine, from Bordeaux. That's the way I like to spend a Friday afternoons.

A few days later we dived the wreck again. It was about six in the morning, you can only dive this wreck at slack water, and slack water is about two and half to three hours after high or low tide. After the dive and as we were sitting in the boat talking, with a number of bottles of red wine on the floor of the boat, when two of the corks just popped up. Now it's impossible to push these corks back in, once they do this, so there was I with two open bottles of vintage red wine from the region of Bordeaux, France.

What am I to do? Well, I drank one of the bottles, and then the other one. In the meantime, I did offer it around, but, strangely, the others Divers refused to help me out [the big softies]. Well you just can't let a cheeky Bordeaux go to waste, can you! Now, I had not eaten all the day before, or had any breakfast that morning, it was now after seven in the morning and I had just drunk two bottles of 90 year old vintage red wine on an empty stomach from the Bordeaux region, France.

That was a good start to the day! But strangely once back at Porth Clais Harbour I could hardly stand. I can't think why? It could be nothing to do with two bottles of 90 year old vintage wine on an empty stomach, could it? Sitting on Porth Clais harbour floor, holding my head in my hands and swearing never to touch another drop of 90 years old vintage red wine again. Boy, did I have a headache."
The bottles were sold for more than £1,000 each, and as Colin said 'they are not the best year' can you imagine if we had salvaged a really good year? That was the most expensive wine I have ever drunk. I have been asked many times what was it like to drink £2,000 worth of vintage red wine, and my answer has always been, "It was okay, I've tasted better."

PORTLAND and Dai the Mill:

PORTLAND

1968, while diving the BRITISH KING paddle steamer in Porthlysgi Bay, I got bored, so up to the surface I went. Had a quick chat with the boat cover, telling them that I was going to swim due south. So off I went to the south. Nothing but weed and sandy seabed. Then after 10 or 15 minutes, I came onto a big pile of stones. About 100 tons in weight. It was a shipwreck! Looking at the bow section, two anchor chains were going off into the distance, so she was at anchor when she sank! Staying on top of the pile of stones I headed for the stern, passing davits [these are where the ships rowing boat hung from] and other large bits of metal, then onto a very large diesel engine, with shaft, and a two bladed iron propeller. I went to the surface as I was now out of air and told the boat cover I had found a wreck! As one does with every dive. It was the Ketch PORTLAND of Porthgain.   In 1985 Diver Greg Evans came up with the ships Bell, it was just off the wreck; about two yards.

Let's move on to 1986, David Chant of St. David's, was opening up a Marine Life Centre, in St. David's. I have known David Chant for a few years; working with him on the salvaging operations of the wreck COLONIAN on the North Bishops in 1984. My job was then Diver on this project. One night if I remember it correctly, we lifted eight to ten tons of copper and brass. There was a great big barge with crane on. It was a month of great fun.

[Photograph of anchor. As you head out of St. David's towards Haverfordwest, just on the right you'll notice a very large anchor on the right side hand side of the road. Salvaged off the COLONIAN in 1984]

Back to the story of the Marine Life Centre
David Chant asked me did I have any ideas how to get free news coverage on TV about the opening of his Marine Life Centre, at St. David's. [With my background in marketing and publicity.] After some thought, I said "Lifting the anchors off the

PORTLAND would be a nice news item. Then putting them on display at your Marine Wildlife Centre, I think the TV news people will go for that, with plenty of Divers and action bits!"

David asked "What did you say the name of the wreck was?" "PORTLAND it's wrecked in Porthlysgi" I replied? Well would you credit it, David knew a man who had been crewman on that same ship, which had sunk in 1927. It's 'Dai the Mill!' [I must say, it's a small world]. So I met up with 'Dai the Mill' who I had known since the early 70's. First thing I said to him was "Why did you not tell me you were a crewman on the PORTLAND" his reply was fast and deadly "You never asked!" [What can you say to that?]

This is 'Dai the Mills' story [Thank you 'Dai the Mill']: He had worked on the PORTLAND as a young man; she was a ketch with a backup diesel engine, for going in and out of ports, or if no wind, most importantly, to get her out of trouble. The propeller was two bladed, and once the sails were set, you had to make sure the prop was straight up. Reason for this was less drag. He said you could tell this by the chalk mark on the shaft if the prop was correctly set. Dai, was the cook and crewman. He remembers that diesel engine well. Once they were in Porthgain Harbour, the harbour was full of ships, bit of a tight squeeze! Once loaded the master wanted the engine running, to get them out of harbour. To start the engine as it was winter Dai would use a blow lamp to warm up the diesel engine. Light the blow lamp then run over the cylinder parts of the diesel engine for about 10 minutes. Once he had warmed her nicely up, you would always have to give her a really good swing with the starting handle, sometimes, she would blow back, and then the engine would be spinning, in reverse. Instead of the ship going forward; the ship would be going backwards! Dai said "You knew if this was the case, by listening? " "Listening to what" I asked? 'Dai the Mill' giving me one of his cheeky smiles and said: "For the screams of panic from the crew above!" [He got me on that one, like I said he was a good story teller]. "Then he had to try and stop the engine, with all that panic going on deck. With other ships crews shouting abuse, like Dai said, they were in a tight squeeze.

At the time of sinking, Dai was on leave. Dai said the Captain told him the story the following day. She sank because as the wind took her over. Then the mast at the bottom broke clean off, and went and put a hole in her side, off the North Bishops, the Captain then sailed for Porthclais, but the water was gaining on her so fast that he turned for Porthlisky, there she sank in the bay, with her anchors put down.

Cargo 100 tons of Porthgain road stones. Porthgain for Haverfordwest. Sunk Friday 9th December 1927.

['Dai the Mill' told me that this photo is not of the PORTLAND, but, this is what she looked like; a two masted ketch with a diesel engine added]

There she lay till 1968 when I located her. Now it's 1986; we were going to use this wreck and recover those anchors which I had not seen for 18 years. What if they had gone? First of all, I went back to check, David Chant, came diving with me, I showed him the wreck site, and would you believe it, David Chant at the Diesel Engine located the actual blow lamp, used by 'Dai the Mill' all those years ago! David presented it to 'Dai the Mill' as a memento of the PORTLAND. The good thing was the anchors were still at the ends of the anchor chains. We were going ahead to film then being raised by Divers, so the film could be used in the news item.

I pulled in a number of Divers for this Epic Movie Project; on the wreck site PORTLAND; filming all day, above water, underwater, these anchors were lifted half a dozen times, and after each take, down again, then up by buoyancy Bag, then down again. By the end of filming the anchors looked a bit worse for wear! Filming this for the TV news item was Diver & camera man: Phil Landig. Action Divers were: Greg Evans, Cindy Pearce, Clive Harris, Clive Hayes and I.

One of the planned scenes was; we all go over the side and straight down, I told them this scene was going to look really an exciting footage! I told them with the threats of "Hell and Damnation, do not muck up this BIG scene!" So over we went problem was I forgot to turn on my air! Darn! Up I shot! [I was reminded of that for the rest of the days filming]

Next day the TV News people turned up and filmed the interviews with David Chant, and they also interviewed 'Dai the Mill'.   At last, the big day came, all the deep sea Divers film team, were going to be big Hollywood film stars, we watched the TV News, 'this was our ticket to Hollywood!' Big movies offers were going to be falling on our laps! Well, these were our thoughts and they sounded okay to me! So on came some boring bits before our slot: but, then on came the really important bit, our item came up on the TV screen at last; The interviews went well, the shots of the Marine Life Centre looked really good, and our big part, we got less than 10 seconds, all day filming and all we got was less than 10 seconds!!!!

I must tell you this story; around 1985, I had got the team to search for a steamship wreck, west of Ramsey Island. We had searched the area, for a few weeks now, one of the Divers was searching his planned area, when he came onto a big pile of anchor chains, and right on top were two very big anchors! Now I'm talking very big links on this chain; with lots of dead eyes in the area [Dead eye are used instead of knots] anyway, I recovered some pulley blocks with the wording on the brass bits "MASSACHUSETTS USA"   Well it's American and it's big, that had been shipwrecked here! She might be the American clipper "CALIFORNIA; might be?" A few days after locating this wreck, what I wanted was a good old Welsh steamship shipwreck, not an American clipper shipwreck. I was showing David Chant this clipper wreck site, as we were swimming along towards the pile of chains with two big anchors on top. Suddenly David Chant lifts up the ship's Bow Bell, just like that! Just lifted it up in front of me.

PRINCE CADWGAN & Cardigan Town Shipping WAR!

This story started by one of the Porth Clais Lobsterman; In 1969 I was approached by one of the Porth Clais lobster fishermen, who had a problem with his lobster pots; he could lift some, but, not all, they were just south of Garreg-y-Fran also known as Crow Rock. Crow Rock is about a mile west of Porth Clais Harbour. He asked if I would have a look. We met up south of Crow Rock that afternoon, at slack water. Over I went to a depth of about 18 metres that's 6o feet. There was his rope caught up, somehow, the rope had gone around a rock twice. Simple job, undo the rope and up I went. He said "I'll buy you a pint," "Thanks" I said. [To be fair, he did not say when he was going to buy me this pint? But I know it will be any day, soon?] Then he said; this to me: "My father said there was a steamship wrecked on the point of Crow Rock, around 1880's; if that will be of any help with your shipwreck diving?" "Thanks" I said, "I'll have a look."

Photograph of Carreg Fran, on the left side of the island in 1876 the SS PRINCE CADWGAN of Cardigan, was wrecked. In the distance top left is Grassholm Island]

Before I tell you about this steamer wreck, I must tell you about another lobsterpot man story. Again he had got his Lobster pots caught up. This was around 1980. Diver Dickie who lives at Carnhedryn, said me one day, that he had promised on Friday to go with a Solva lobsterman, and recover his pots off the Westside of Skomer Island. But he had damaged his ears, diving the other day, so it was impossible for him to dive for at least a month till it was healed, and as he had promised. Would I do the job for him? "Okay" I said. So Friday Dickie and I turned up at Solva. The lobsterman was waiting for us at Solva Quay; we loaded my diving gear aboard, and steamed out towards Skomer Island. The lobsterman had timed our arrival to be at slack water. He said the pots were caught in about 80 feet depth or less [note the words 80 feet depth or less!]

We arrived, I kitted up, and asked where's the pot buoy and line? This pot buoy with line, I would use to get straight to the pots! He said "It's underwater, but, I'll put you right on where they are." A few minutes later, he said "We're over them!" Over I go to about 80 feet depth, but as you have guessed no pots. I did a big square search, but still no pots, all I found was a large part of iron ship, about the size of a car. But, no lobster pots! Up I went and said "no pots!" Once on board, over we went to another place; I said to the lobsterman from Solva "This is a long way from the marks I just went in on?" "This is the place, we're right over them, and the depth is only 80 feet!" he said. So over I go, down and down I went, and down I'm still going, down, now I thinking to myself, this feels a bit deep! I still could not see the seabed, looking at my depth gauge it read "180 feet", yes you read this correctly, just as I read my depth gauge correctly on that dive "180 feet" and still I could not see the seabed, oh yes, and by the way the underwater visibility was fantastic around 60 feet!!!! Now, when you doing a dive deep, it's easy to go down, but, when you have to swim up, it's not so easy. Once aboard the lobster boat I said to our Solva lobster fisherman: "That's 180 feet down there!" He turned and looked at his depth Sounder and said "No it's not, it's 200 feet." Then he said "I think it could be a bit more over there." I can tell you now; I did not dive again! So back we went to Solva. On the way back he said "I'll buy you a pint." [Once again, another pint; do you know, I'm still waiting for all these lobstermen 'fictitious' pints of beer? I'm owed about ten pints of beer all together now!]

I'm thinking I had better get back to the story of Crow Rock and the steamship wreck! So months later I went and had a look at Crow Rock, right on the point I pop over, the area is just all seaweed. Moving around to the east side of the point, there was the wreck, it's well broken up, and the maximum depth was 15/17 feet, that's about 4/5 metres. So this is my 2nd year of diving and this is my 5th shipwreck found, [I forgot to mention I had found my 4th wreck in Ramsey Sound a month ago] do you remember how once I said; finding shipwrecks was easy. Well, I must be straight with you; I did actually think that at the time. My excuse is quite truthful; I did not know any better, with some shipwreck research, or told by local lobsterman of a shipwreck, then over the side I'd go and there they were, just like that.

My research showed me this wreck on the south east side of Garreg-y-Fran also known as Crow Rock, was the SS PRINCE CADWGAN of Cardigan. Wrecked Saturday 30th September 1876. Steamer of 65 tons, she could carry a cargo of about 70 tons. Built in Lancastershire 1864. Steamship and Schooner rigged. Cargo: Iron, Petroleum, and General Goods.

She did a fortnightly service Cardigan to Bristol, stopping at Fishguard, Solva and New Quay. On her fateful day after leaving Solva Harbour, she was heading for Aberayron, when she struck Half Tide Rock, also known as Stodair Rock, also known

as Porth Clais Rock. This rock is about three quarters of a mile south of Porth Clais
Harbour. The rock show's at low spring tides.   The steamer hit this rock and her
propeller blades all broke off. Now with the steamer out of control, she was taken by
the tide, and wrecked on the Crow Rock Point. [Why did they not lower her anchors?]
She was under the command of Captain Thomas Evans.
She started working this route in July 1869, when they first started, they use to have a
bit of a problem with Solva, if they arrived at low tide, then of course she could not
enter the harbour. To solve this problem in June 1870, moorings were placed just
outside Solva Harbour, then if there was no water to enter the harbour, waiting there
would be a fine little craft. This was used as a barge or stores boat, they placed the
Solva cargo on the craft, and she would sail in at her convenience or the other way
round. It is hoped it will be a source of profit to the company and that they will
henceforth be more liberally patronized.

On Saturday 2 January 1875 a nice little earner came up, Salvage! A vessel was seen
apparently in distress off Caer Bwdy Bay, St. David's, [That's about two miles west of
Solva] she was boarded by Capt. John Rees, Lloyd's Agent, of City Hotel, St. David's.
She proved to be the French brig "ERNEST ET BLANCHE," of St. Malo France for
Swansea, South Wales in ballast, [no cargo].
Captain Rees, after conferring with the master, made for Solva to get assistance to
remove the vessel from her perilous position. When Captain Rees arrived at Solva,
the Bristol trader "SS PRINCE CADWGAN," happened to be in port, she was
immediately taken to the distress vessel, which she towed into Solva harbour.

The Cardigan Rebellion' a number of Cardigan farmers, shop keepers and businesses
were saying, that the SS PRINCE CADWGAN owned by the: Cardigan Steam
Navigation Company, was charging too much for the carrying of goods and services to
and from Bristol!

On Thursday 17th February 1876 a meeting of share owners of the SS PRINCE
CADWGAN; Cardigan Steam Packet Company was held at Cardigan Town Hall, T.
Davies, Esq., of Bank House, was in the chair, there were also present a large number
of shareholders. They were all pleased with the profits, this is their words exactly:
"This successful result he thought was owing to the great efficiency and indefatigable
exertions of Captain Edwards and crew, who had always shown a character of
indomitable courage and firmness". The chair with much pleasure in declaring a
dividend of 25s. per share, together with £95 to the reserve fund. The proceedings
then terminated. [A very happy bunch of share owners I see, don't forget; Rebellion
was afoot!]

Arrived on the scene: "Cardigan 'NEW' Steam Packet Company," to ply between
Cardigan and Bristol weekly, [the only difference between the two companies was the
word "NEW!"] read on about the Cardigan Town shipping WAR!.

Cardigan Port: Arrival of the SS SEA FLOWER. -- Considerable excitement prevailed amongst the inhabitants of Cardigan town at an early hour on Saturday 2nd September 1876, owing to the arrival of the SS SEA FLOWER, from the Clyde. This ship was purchased at Glasgow by Dr. Thomas and Captain Gillespie, on behalf of the "Cardigan 'NEW' Steam Packet Company," to ply between Cardigan and Bristol weekly. [This is direct competition for the: Cardigan Steam Navigation Company and for the steamer SS PRINCE CADWGAN. It's all excitement at Cardigan; now let's see what happens over the following years!]

SS SEA FLOWER; [this is the new companies steamer] she is beautifully built, and most exquisitely fitted up, with the latest improvements, and is adapted to travel at the rate of 10 ½ miles an hour. Near the bow there is a monster tank to contain water as ballast, which self-acts in every way. To prevent considerable amount of manual labour, a donkey engine is attached to her to discharge her cargo [small steam boiler]. It is intended by the shareholders to proceed on a pleasure trip to Aberystwyth in a short time. She sailed on her voyage to Bristol on Monday 4th September 1876. The directors have confirmed the office of commander upon Captain Owen, of Dogmell's, who has not yet arrived home from sea; therefore, that post is at present held by Mr. Thomas Jones, mate.

Competition starts on the 2nd September 1876, and then the SS PRINCE CADWGAN of Cardigan is wrecked on Crow Rock, on Saturday 30th September 1876.

Now let's follow the wrecking story: Wrecked Saturday 30th September 1876. "SS PRINCE CADWGAN," the trader between Bristol and Solva, Fishguard and Aberayron. She left Solva on Saturday morning for Fishguard and in a short time after leaving struck Half-tide Rock, just south of Porth Clais, she drifted and was wrecked on Carreg-y-fran [also known as Crow Rock].

The crew happily saved themselves in their own boat and landed at Porthlysgi, at Lower Treginnis farm where they were hospitably cared for by Mr. and Mrs. Geo. Owen Williams.

Some portion of the cargo was saved on Saturday morning, before she became a total wreck, under the directions of Mr. Samuel Williams, and Capt. D. Hicks, Porthlysgi. The steamer at the time of the disaster was, as usual, under the command of Captain Thomas Evans, one of the most persevering and careful masters on the coast. He had commanded her for the last twelve years and had, for the last seven years, been bringing her into Solva with goods from Bristol without incurring any damage or loss of goods or crew.

Of Captain Thomas Evans, it may be now said, that he has met with a great misfortune, but it is consolation for him to find that unusual sympathy is felt for him, as well as for the Cardigan Steam Navigation Company. The vessel was only insured to the amount of £1,200. The vessel herself was worth from £6,000 to £7,000, so, consequently, the company has sustained a very severe loss.

Steam Navigation Company [old company]. – A new company has been formed Thursday 11th January 1877, for the purpose of carrying on the trade between Bristol and Aberayron, Fishguard, New Quay, and Solva. The company has purchased the "S.S. IANTHE," of Glasgow, which will run in the place of the late "PRINCE CADWGAN." The company consists of the majority of the directors of the late Steam Navigation Company with the addition of some "fresh blood" and prospects are very favorable. The only change of agent is at Aberayron where Mr. J. James has been appointed. The "SS IANTHE" is a very handsome boat, and is fitted with steam winches and other appliances for the diminution of labour. Capt. Evans has been appointed master.

Now we're going to follow that 'NEW' steamer's voyages, that's the one that belongs to the Cardigan 'NEW' Steam Packet Company; SS SEA FLOWER: On Thursday 28 November 1878.
Collision with schooner CHARLOTTE of Belfast, which sank, 8 miles off Mumbles Lighthouse in very light winds. SS SEA FLOWER sinks her first ship! You have read it correctly, [Sinks her first ship].
The first ship she sank was the schooner CHARLOTTE of Belfast she was on voyage from Portaferry, Ireland for Newport, South Wales. Owner H. Brown of Portaferry, Co. Down, Ireland. Vessel of 75 tons. Built 1844. Master T. Reating. Crew of 4. No crewmen injured. Her cargo was 100 tons of potatoes.
Following the collision the schooner at once sunk, but the crew were saved, and brought to Cardigan in the steamer.
At the time; value of the cargo is estimated at £450. The steamer has been detained by the authorities since her arrival at her berth at Cardigan.
Next meeting of the 'NEW' Cardigan share owners were not happy, as a bill had just arrived. The SEA FLOWER was found at fault for the collision, and her bill was for £1,300.

End of February 1879: Another stormy meeting of the shareholders of the 'NEW' Cardigan Company owning the SEA FLOWER vessel. Remember it was the SS SEAFLOWER that ran down the Irish potato schooner in the Bristol Channel, for which nearly £1,300 damages have been demanded. Reminder: she was purchased by Cardigan trades people and others intended as an opposition to its rival, and to bring down costs. They did not the plan for a £1,300 bill! What had happened in the collision; SS SEA FLOWER, while going at full steam, struck the CHARLOTTE, in the beam end [struck her in the backside, and she sank, SS SEA FLOWERS at fault, without question]. Now, there are even more stormier meetings of shareholders, there have been held reports of share owners nearly fighting, [must have something to do with £1,300 bill] then it was decided to wind up the company, Mr. T. Griffiths, auctioneer, being appointed liquidator in the matter.

Now we move forward to July 1887. You can take it as read, that the SS SEA FLOWER is still running, and still owned by the trade's men in Cardigan, and they are not a happy bunch of Cardigan trades people. Company dividends paid out, Nil!

They are now being accused of exorbitant cargo rates, and we have more problems! There competition has cut their cargo rates, so now we have a 'Cardigan shipping price war' as well. You can imagine the Cardigan town was buzzing with what was going to happen next!

Are you ready for this: During the past week, the Cardigan town crier announces another radical reduction by the 'OLD' Company. To carry flour at half the former rate. This announcement is creating considerable talk in Cardigan town. Of course everyone in Cardigan is following this Cardigan shipping fright WAR! No one is backing down! It's is anticipated the other company will now follow suit, which of the two will survive the longest under this new but trying ordeal

The SS SEA FLOWER, steamer, 'New Company' it's just been confirmed, for the last six months or more she's not been insured, or her cargos. But still, we have no sign of anyone backing down! Cardigan town waits!

THEN OUT OF THE BLUE THIS HAPPENED!

While the SS SEA FLOWER was steaming up the Bristol Channel, she sees flares being fired from another steamer. The SS BAKUIN of 1,669 tons, on voyage from Hamburg to Cardiff, on 11th November 1887. She had collided with a steamer and became helpless. This is a big steamer, and the SS SEA FLOWER would not be able to tow her, especially in the Bristol Channel not forgetting those tides. But, she was summoned to help the two other steamers that were already towing her. The first steamer that came along was our very own SEA FLOWER, and now we're talking here salvage money, big time, big bucks! The captain of the SS SEA FLOWER would be getting a percentage of any salvage money!

Saturday 10th February 1888, at the Admiralty Division of the High Court of Justice, London.

SALVAGE CASE & SS SEA FLOWER, JUST £ REWARD

Let's look at the Case: It appears from the evidence that the SS BAKUIN, barque rigged steamer on 1,669 tons, 200 horse power, was in ballast on a voyage from Hamburg to Cardiff to load bunker coals, but whilst proceeding up the Bristol Channel on the 11th of November 1887, when about four or five miles S.W. of the Nash Light, she came into collision with another steamer, the SS DERWENTWATER, which wrought such havoc to the SS BAKUIN as to make her perfectly helpless. Her steam boiler fires were put out; her stern was sinking under water, and her bow sticking out of the water. The Cutters WAVE and MARIAM of Cardiff immediately appeared on the spot in order to render any assistance required by the crew consisting of twenty-one hands.

About 3 a.m., [they had been towing her for about six hours, before 'our' brave SS SEA FLOWER came along] on the 12th a steamer was noticed going up channel, and an order to attract attention was made. Flares were sent up, which brought the steamer to bear down, which proved to be 'our' brave SS SEA FLOWER on her usual trip from Cardigan to Bristol. A tow rope was immediately taken, and the task of towing commenced under great disadvantage owing to the height of the SS BAKUIN'S bows, and the WAVE and MIRIAM pilots each side fearing she would sink.

A direction was taken for Penarth Roads, with the wind being light with a moderately smooth sea, but with the tide flowing ebbing [flowing out] which previous to the SS SEA FLOWERS help they were in danger of all steamers being pushed towards the shore, towards the rocks. Then there was 'our' steamer, 'who saved the day!'

Their share was for two hours work, or two hours steaming, was a nice crisp £300, plus all legal costs!

When the news reached Cardigan town early in the afternoon, just an hour later 'our' brave SS SEA FLOWER was arriving at Cardigan town, [Onboard they did not know the court settlement]   They were greeted with booming of cannon fire, steamers blowing their ships whistles and the crowds cheering all along on the quay side, even the band turned up 'a bit breathless,' as they were practicing on the other side of the town when they heard the news. Now with the band playing, ships whistle's blowing, cannon firing and the town's people cheering, it must have been a grant sight! Cardigan town went wild, and I'm pleased for them all. It all sound as if they had a great time!

SADLY ON SATURDAY 18th February 1888, [Just five days after their triumph in court and their triumphal arrival back at Cardigan Town] Captain John Davies, master of the SS SEAFLOWER, died.

On Tuesday before his death he had attended the funeral of Mr. James, ironmonger of Gwalia House, the former Managing Director of the steamer. He did not on Wednesday feel well enough to undertake the weekly voyage then on Saturday morning he died. Many passengers of the SS SEAFLOWER and others who knew of the kind manner in which they were attended to whilst under his care, as well as many other qualities, will regret to hear of his death at so early an age.

[2nd Salvage]: Shipping Casualty Cardigan Bay.—On Saturday morn 8th February 1889, during the full force of the gale which was then blowing from the North, a vessel was sighted flying distress and fast drifting in Cardigan Bay. The Lifeboat men were immediately summoned, and the boat was soon with the vessel, which by this time had drifted on the Black Stones on the Pembrokeshire side of the bay. The crew were safely taken off and taken to the Webley Arms, Poppit Sands, and well taken care of. The vessel proved to be the HARVEST HOME, of Preston, with a cargo of china clay on a voyage from Fowey for Liverpool.

The gale, having moderated, the vessel was got off on Thursday morn 14th February, by the services of the SS SEA FLOWER, the Bristol trader, another nice salvage reward.

[Sinks her 2nd ship] 2nd Collision by the SS SEAFLOWER. At the trial on Wednesday 23 July 1890 of the action brought by the owners of the barge EVA, of Bristol, against the SS SEA FLOWER Company, of Cardigan, for £200 damages for the loss of the said barge through collision with the SS SEA FLOWER steamer in the Avon about a month since the Court found the SS SEA FLOWER at fault, they had to pay £200 with all legal coasts.

SAD DEATH BY DROWNING. – On New Year night at about 10.30p.m. 31st December 1890, Mr. W. Morgan, the respected agent of the SS SEAFLOWER was drowned in the Cambrian Quay, Cardigan. It seems that shouts for help were heard by the inhabitants living near the Cambrian Quay and even the falling of something into the water was heard by one old woman named Peggy Bowen. These people having given the alarm several people rushed down towards the Cambrian Quay, where the SS SEA FLOWER remained alongside attached to her moorings. Grappling hooks at once took place but in vain. About one a.m., (the grappling party having now given up until daylight) a rumour was circulated that the deceased was missing from his home, viz., Davis House in High-street, and the neighbours again commenced operations in order to find the body which was found in the following afternoon about three p.m., a few yards from the bow of the steamer, and proved to be that of Mr. Morgan, the respected agent of the company.

The deceased it is reported, was in the habit of going down late at night in order to see that all was right, and that evening proceeded as usual in his slippers, informing his wife that he would return in a short time. There was a very large amount of gold, silver, and paper money on his person, when found. On the following day (Saturday) an inquest was held at his residence before J. H. Evans, Esq., coroner, and a jury, when a verdict of accidentally drowned was returned. The affair has cast a gloom over the town as the deceased was a very sober intelligent and respectable member of the society.

[Sinks her 3rd ship] Vessel Lost in St. Bride's Bay: The steamer SS SEA FLOWER, from Cardigan with a general cargo, hit and sunk the ketch GWENDOLINE, of Milford, on Wednesday 16th September 1891, the ketch sunk in two minutes, and one hand went down with the ketch, Morgan Alexander, aged 15. Collision took place just North of Jack Sound, in St. Bride's Bay.

GWENDOLINE was built in 1887 at Milford Haven. Vessel of 32 tons. Owner and master at time of sinking John Davies of Llandysul, Cardiganshire. Her cargo: 59 tons of Roofing Slates. Voyage from Caernarfon for Cardiff.

Ketch not being able to weather Wooltack Point, so as to enter Jack Sound, she went round and heading North West, she was run down by the SS SEA FLOWER, of Cardigan. The Master and crewman saved themselves by jumping aboard SS SEA FLOWER.

Master David Owen of the SS SEA FLOWER was at fault; his certificate was suspended for six months.

Master David Owens of SS SEA FLOWER said at court: At 10 p.m. on the 16th September 1891, the SS SEA FLOWER was crossing St. Bride's Bay. The weather was fine and clear, with moonlight, and the wind moderate from the W.S.W. The master was on the bridge, and Evan Rees, the second mate, was at the wheel, and they were the only persons on deck, no one being stationed on the forecastle head as a lookout, the master himself undertaking that duty from his station on the bridge, which was merely a raised platform on the hurricane deck not extending from side to side the wheelhouse occupying the centre of it. She was going full speed 8 or 8 1/2 knots an hour and steering to go through Jack's Sound. On nearing the Sound a vessel, which proved to be the ketch GWENDOLINE, was seen; according to the master, 80 or 100 yards. He thought at first she was going the same way as him-self, making for Jack's Sound. He declares that she had no lights, but he admitted that he saw the tops of sails only, and not the hull, and he was therefore not in a position to see whether she carried her lights or not. Immediately perceiving that she was approaching him, he ported the helm then hard-a-port and stopped the engines, these; orders following in quick succession. He also ordered the engines to go astern full speed, but countermanded it immediately as the collision happened.

The steamer ran into the ketch on the starboard side amidships, cutting her right through to the main hatch. The mainsail at the same time was torn to pieces. The ketch sunk instantly, and with her one of the crew, who was drowned. Lines were thrown over the bows by order of the master of the steamer, but no life-buoy or belt was used, and no boat was lowered.

Master John Davies of the GWENDOLINE said in court: At 10 p.m. the ketch, not being able to weather Wooltack Point. So as to enter Jack's Sound, went round on the port tack, heading about N.W. Our lights must have been plainly visible during the preceding fifteen minutes. At this time the red and white lights of the steamer were seen broad on the starboard bow, and presently all three lights came in view. When the steamer came within hailing distance, all three men on the ketch shouted loudly to her, receiving no answer. Seeing a collision impending, the master of the ketch put his helm hard down, letting go the jib sheet to make the blow, as he says, a sliding one, and the boy proceeded to cut the gripes of the boat, while the man let go the head-sheet. On being struck by the steamer, the master immediately called to the men to get on board the steamer, and he himself climbed by the rags of the mainsail on to the steamer's bows on the port side. The mate sprang into the fore rigging, and got on the steamer on the starboard side. Nothing was seen of the boy, though the master stated that he heard him cry for help. The master believes that he became entangled in the mainsail. No boat was lowered by the SS SEA FLOWER for the purpose of examining the wreckage, under the possibility of the boy still slinging to it, the master stating that the race in the Sound was so dangerous that he believed that both boat and crew would have been lost if he had attempted it.

As the casualty happened outside the Sound, and under the lee of Skomer Island, there was no ground for such apprehensions. No lifebelt or buoy was thrown over. The steamer remained about a quarter of an hour on the spot amongst the wreckage, cruising about for five minutes of the time. The rescued men were landed at Barry Dock on the 17th September. It should be remarked that no entry of the collision was made in the official log of the SS SEA FLOWER.

The Court, however, is of opinion that a boat ought to have been launched and diligent search made for the missing lad, and so provide for the possibility, although remote, that the lad might, before life was extinct, have been rescued from entanglement with floating wreckage. Hence the Court is of opinion that every possible assistance was not rendered by those on board the SS SEA FLOWER.

THE SS SEA FLOWER. – Great fear was entertained at Cardigan town for the safety of the SS SEA FLOWER which is the trader to Bristol. She had left Milford Haven over a week ago, on a voyage to Cork with a cargo of bricks, but had run for Milford because of the weather, where she remained; the Captain without giving any notice, Quit! The Directors having now appointed Capt. Davies, of the Royal Oak, in command, he proceeded to take charge, and on the following Friday evening 11th December 1891, left Milford Haven for Cork.

No news for a week, it's believed she has sunk in the gale. Then at last a telegraph arrives reported their arrival at Waterford after experiencing fearful gale. Great anxiety prevailed in the town, till the telegraph arrived.

On 13 December 1895, the Aberayron Steam Packet Company sold the SS IANTH to Mr. Thomas Steele of Ayr, Scotland.

[Only damages this ship; this time!] The SS SPRIGHTLY, bound into Swansea, was anchored in the Mumbles Roads on Friday 7th April 1899, when about noon the small steamer SS SEA FLOWER, of Cardigan, moored close by, then parted her cables in the gale and bore down upon her, damaging three of her iron plates. The SS SPRIGHTLY subsequently put into Swansea with the afternoon's tide, and when entering the harbour she was blown against a barge, but sustained no further injury. On Saturday she entered the Albion Dry Dock, Swansea.

What did the Vikings ever do for us in Pembrokeshire?:

"What did the Vikings ever give us?" Well, for one thing they left behind Viking names (Or should I say Scandinavian names?) all over Pembrokeshire. Names like: Hastiholm (Cardigan Island), Dinas Head, Fishguard, Goodwick, Strumble Head, Ramsey Island, Bitches Reef, Emsger (South Bishops Rock), Green Scar, Elvis, Goultrop Roads, Musselwick, Stack, Tusker Rock, Jack Sound, Midland Island, Skomer, Wick, Grassholm, Gateholm, Skokholm, Milford Haven, Dale,
Angle, Skerryback, Stack Rock, Gelliswick, Hubberston, Haverfordwest, Hasguard, Freystrop, Haroldston, Derby, Colby, Pen y holt Stack, Stack Rocks, Stackpole, Lydstep, Caldey, Tenby, Amroth, Steynton, to name but a few.